IMAGES
of America

HOUGHTON LAKE

On the Cover: The Pines Theatre was the new attraction at Houghton Lake in 1941. In this photograph, two enthusiastic movie fans stop by to check out the coming attractions before the Pines opened. (Courtesy of the Pines Theatre.)

IMAGES
of America

HOUGHTON LAKE

Deborah I. Gouin

ARCADIA
PUBLISHING

ISBN 978-1-4671-1052-5

Published by Arcadia Publishing
Charleston, South Carolina

Printed in the United States of America

Library of Congress Control Number: 2013933842

For all general information, please contact Arcadia Publishing:
Telephone 843-853-2070
Fax 843-853-0044
E-mail sales@arcadiapublishing.com
For customer service and orders:
Toll-Free 1-888-313-2665

Visit us on the Internet at www.arcadiapublishing.com

For my husband, Wilbert M. Hines III, with love; and in memory of the courageous people who made a community out of the wilderness

Contents

ACKNOWLEDGMENTS

I would like to thank the Houghton Lake Area Historical Society (HLAHS) for preserving the history of Houghton Lake. The society was founded in 1972 and opened a historical village, preserving the first schoolhouse from Prudenville. In 2001, it bought the Houghton Lake Playhouse from the chamber of commerce for $1. The society thus saved one of the few historical buildings at Prudenville.

HLAHS has been dedicated to preserving both paper and three-dimensional artifacts since its beginning. Without their collecting, this book would not have been possible. All photographs in this book, unless otherwise noted, were graciously lent by the HLAHS.

I owe a debt of gratitude to Violet Ester (Fowler) Gonzales, the past president of the HLAHS, for all her help. I would ask for images, and she would somehow find them for me. Her assistance was invaluable.

I would also like to thank Dr. Jim Sullivan for assisting me with all things Prudenville. He opened his personal archive to me and shared his extensive research. Additionally, he shared his photograph collection. Dr. Sullivan's wealth of knowledge lightened my load and greatly enhanced my knowledge of Prudenville.

Vera (Randall) Parsons graciously shared her knowledge of Roscommon Township and her family history and photographs. I thank her for her help. I also thank Sheryl Tusssey, Markey Township clerk, who provided me with township information. I also want to thank Mark Barnhart Sr. and Clark Harder for sharing their love and knowledge of the Music Box with me.

There are too many people who talked to me and who shared their knowledge and photographs with me to mention in this short space, but I thank every one of you. Your help has added to this book and made this an enjoyable adventure. Finally, I would like to thank my husband, Wilbert M. Hines III, for his help and support and love during this project. He assisted me in scanning images and he lightened my load, and I am always grateful for his love and support.

SOURCES

Carman, Beulah. *Looking Back: A Centennial History of Houghton Lake*. Houghton Lake, MI: Bankov Printing, 1979.

———. *Capsules of Time: A Saga of Houghton Lake*. Houghton Lake, MI: Bankov Printing, 1987.

Houghton Lake Resorter, Houghton Lake, Michigan.

INTRODUCTION

The federal government acquired the territory in which Houghton Lake lies through the 1836 Treaty of Washington. The following year, Michigan received statehood. All the territory north of Midland became part of Midland County. It would be years before white settlers came to the Houghton Lake area, then known as Red Lake. In 1852, the State of Michigan bestowed upon it the name Houghton Lake, in memory of Douglas Houghton, the state's first geologist.

The first white settler was Augustus Emery, who settled in the area in 1869. He and his family traveled the Saginaw Trail by foot and ended up in the area that is now Houghton Lake. They had brought all their worldly possessions with them, intending to make a permanent homestead, which they did upon reaching the area of Emery Road, just south of Prudenville. They had to timber the land to build their log cabin. Others followed after the Emerys.

Albert Wickham was not far behind. Having served in the Civil War, he received a land grant from the government. A month after Augustus Emery arrived, the Wickhams settled just north of Five Corners. Streets still bear the names of these adventurous pioneers.

The trail that pioneers took to the area determined where they settled. More families came to the area in the next few years, and Lawton Knapp and his kin settled in the area that became Roscommon Township. As the 1870s progressed, more families came to settle the area, and lumber barons arrived, seeking their fortune in timber.

Fortunes were made timbering the land to build the Midwest. The cork pine was highly sought after, and it was easy to float down the river. Houghton Lake was an ideal place to timber, as it was at the mouth of the Muskegon River. A railroad trestle was located in Prudenville. It connected to the train that brought timber from Meredith and dumped it in Houghton Lake for the drive southwest. Muskegon was a large lumber town at the end of the river. The timber that was not processed at Nels Michelson's mill made its way to Muskegon. Once the timber was cut, another wave of businessmen arrived: land developers seeking their fortunes.

By 1874, there were enough residents to form a county. The name Roscommon was chosen in honor of County Roscommon in Ireland by the male residents of the new county. The meeting was held at the Hall farm, in the Heights, because it was centrally located. Roscommon County initially had three townships: Roscommon, Denton, and Higgins. For the next four years, the courthouse was at the Hall farm, in the Heights on Houghton Lake.

The men voted in 1878 to relocate the courthouse to the village of Roscommon, in Higgins Township. Houghton Lake occupies about 22,000 acres of water, so travel accessibility was an issue. Train service was very limited in the Houghton Lake area, because laying track was difficult around the lake. Roscommon, however, had direct train service from Bay City. Locating the courthouse in Roscommon would allow traveling judges easier access.

Soon after the lumber era, Houghton Lake gained a reputation as the best fishing lake in Michigan. People traveled by train and then traversed rugged trails to reach the shore of Houghton Lake to catch fish. At the beginning of the 20th century, the lake was teeming with fish. Pan fish and northern pike were the favorites of fishermen. The pan fish was great eating, and the pike was fun to catch. As the first decades of the 20th century wore on, more hotels and resorts were built to accommodate all the visitors to the lake. This was the birth of the tourism industry, the mainstay of Houghton Lake.

By the mid-20th century, Houghton Lake was at its peak as a resort town. There were resorts with cabins everywhere. With the advent of the unions, the common laborer now had leisure time, and Houghton Lake was an ideal place to spend that time. For many autoworkers, cottages at Houghton Lake were affordable, and many took advantage and bought second homes in the area. No cottage was complete without a speedboat.

This period was ideal for the youth. No longer were they looked upon as another worker. Teens had leisure time, also. Houghton Lake offered entertainment for this age group. Many young people fished, swam, and waterskied during the day. At night, there was a range of activities, including movies at the Pines Theatre, go-carting, and miniature golf. For those 16 and older, the Music Box offered a night of dancing and romance under the stars. These were the times that shaped the next generation, and Houghton Lake has held fast in the memories of those who experienced its wonders.

The 1950s and 1960s were the zenith of Houghton Lake's tourist industry. Families from the adjacent states of Ohio and Indiana, as well as those from lower Michigan, made annual trips to the area, many to the same resorts each year. Others rented private cottages or had family members with cottages. Many resort workers knew their guests as "our people," because they spent a part of each summer vacationing with them. Summer visitors enlivened and enriched the community. It was their support that made it possible for many businesses to survive the long winter months. They became as much a part of the community as the locals were.

This book looks at the development of Houghton Lake as a resort community, focusing on those businesses that were the lifeblood of the community. I will visit the ones that have survived and remember the ones that are gone but that live on in memory. Houghton Lake and its relaxed atmosphere continues to draw visitors today. Many of Houghton Lake's summer people found the area a friendly place to retire. I hope you will enjoy this look back at Houghton Lake's past.

One

Roscommon and Lake Townships

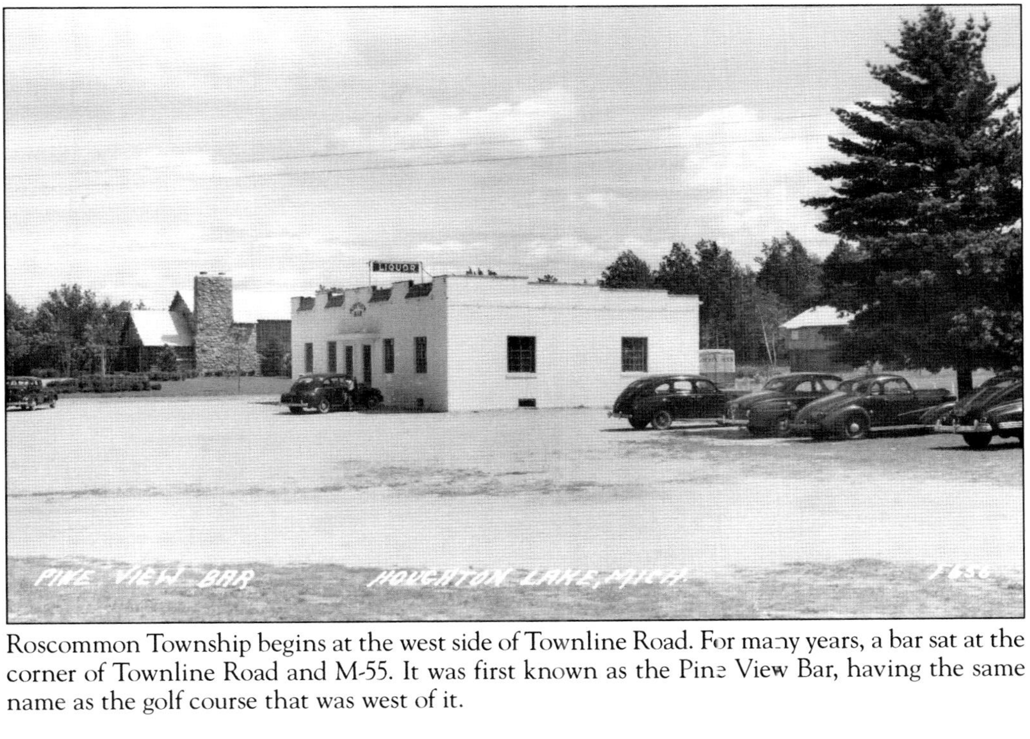

Roscommon Township begins at the west side of Townline Road. For many years, a bar sat at the corner of Townline Road and M-55. It was first known as the Pine View Bar, having the same name as the golf course that was west of it.

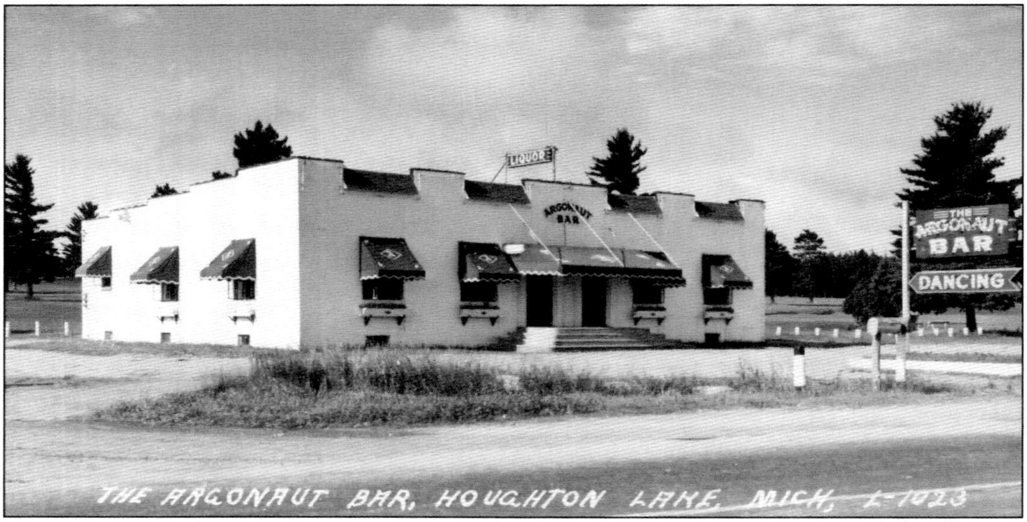

At some point, the Pine View Bar was renamed the Argonaut Bar. For many years, the Argonaut was one of the most popular nighttime entertainment spots. It was known for great live bands in the 1960s and early 1970s and as a gathering place for golfers after a round on the links. It was owned by Al Hill. In the mid-1970s, Gerald Fitzgerald of West Branch bought the Argonaut and renamed it Jerry's Junction. He and his two partners, Michael Husby and Thomas Fitzgerald, operated the bar for several years. On November 26, 1980, the bar was set ablaze and destroyed. Investigators concluded that it was arson. The Pine View Golf Course now has a parking lot where the bar stood.

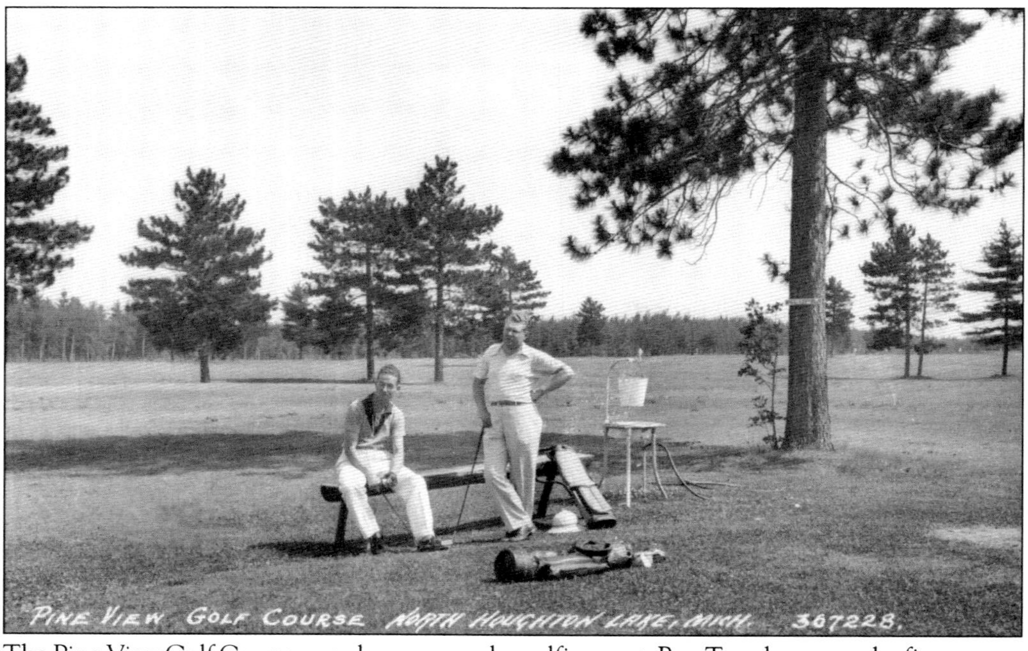

The Pine View Golf Course was always a popular golfing spot. Roy Treachout was the first owner. It opened in 1932 as a nine-hole course and was expanded in the 1970s. It is the only original golf course remaining on the south shore. The other course, the Heights Public Golf Course, was closed when M-55 was straightened and ran through the course.

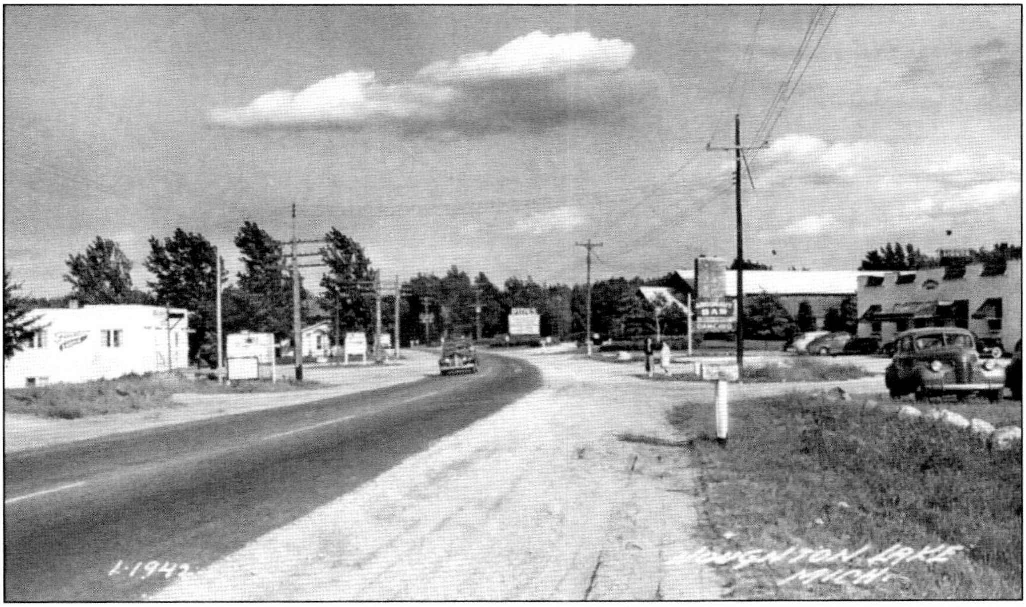

The main road around Houghton Lake is Michigan Highway 55 (M-55). It developed from a trail to a two-lane road to, finally, a four-lane highway. Most of the businesses are on M-55. This photograph was taken before the road was expanded. The Fountain Diner (left) was across from the Argonaut Bar and Pine View Golf Course. Not much is known about this building. Today, Bunkers Restaurant is located approximately where the diner was.

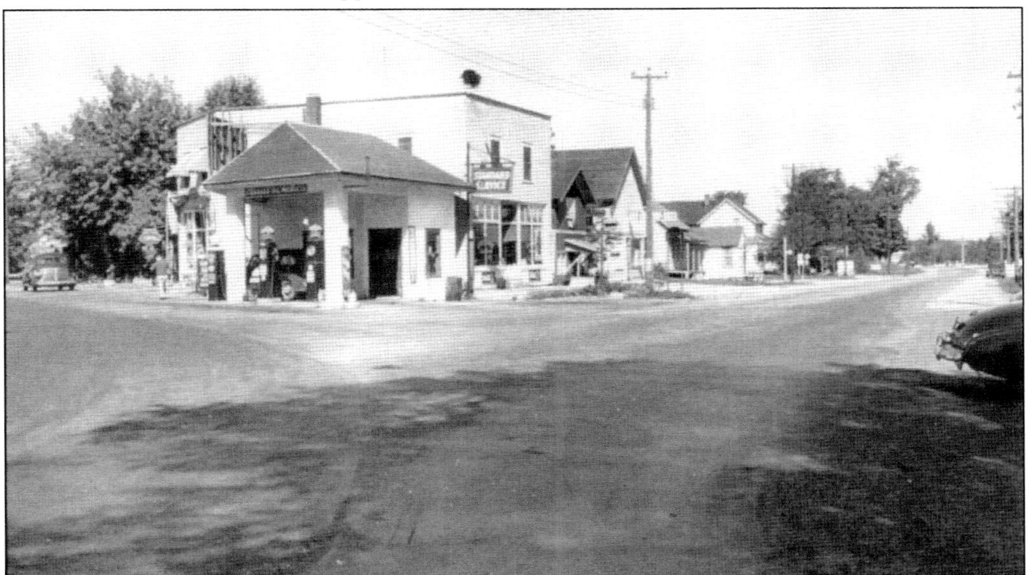

In the early 20th century, US 27 joined M-55 at the Houghton Lake village. US 27 was the main road coming into the area from the south. As such, this crossroads was a good area to build a business. A Standard Service station stood on the corner. This business also served as the Greyhound bus depot. Travelers could find lodging and a meal in this area. This building remains at the corner today, on what is now Federal Avenue.

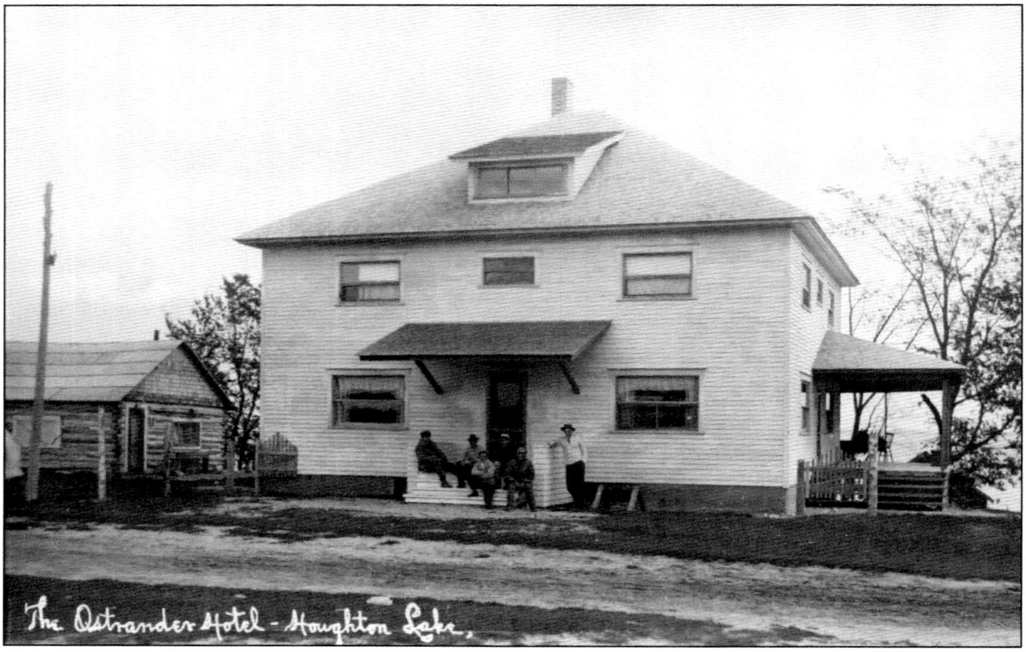

The Osterander Hotel (above), built by Dr. Day and Jim Osterander, was the first to occupy the location directly across from US 27 (Federal Avenue) in 1916. It was a modest hotel located on the lakeside. In 1922, the hotel was added on to, doubling its capacity. Eventually, it was sold to Tommy Heard and named the Houghton Lake Tavern (below). Ownership of the hotel changed over the years. It was last operated as the South Shore Inn, in the late 1970s. At that time, only the dining room and bar were in operation. The South Shore Inn was destroyed by fire in 1981.

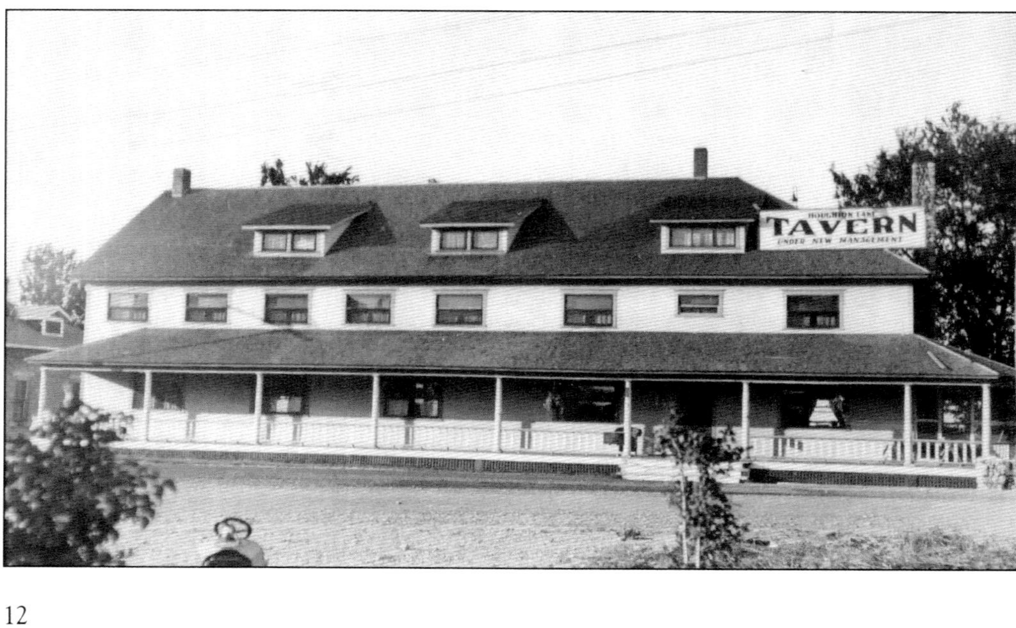

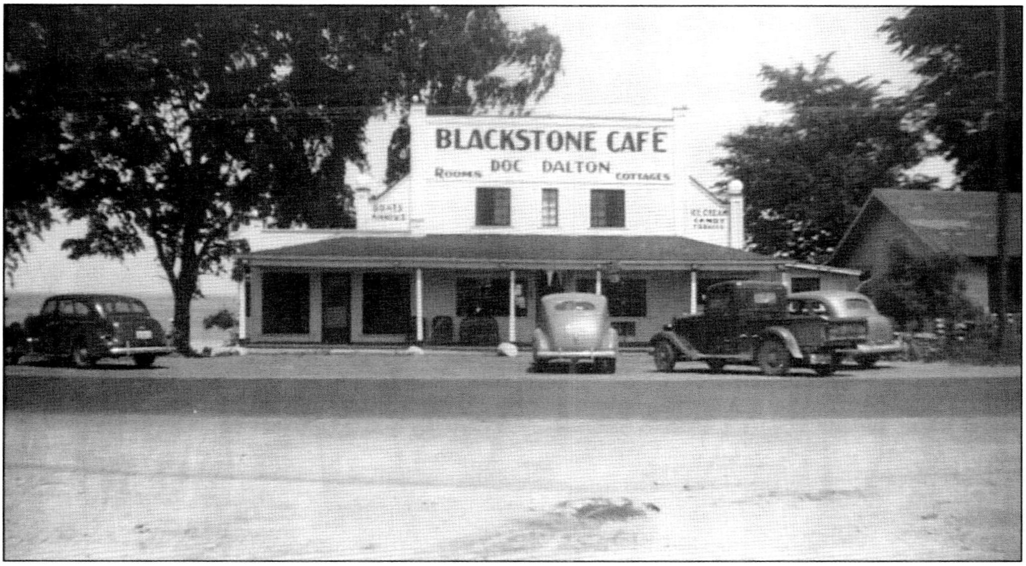

The Blackstone Café was also located at the corner in the village. A café and hotel, it also had cabins available for rent. Visitors could also rent boats for fishing from the café. At one time, it was known as Doc Dalton Blackstone (above). By 1943, Tommy Heard was operating the café (below). In the late 1940s, it was Young's Cafe. (Above, photograph by Doc Dalton; courtesy of Christler Funeral Home.)

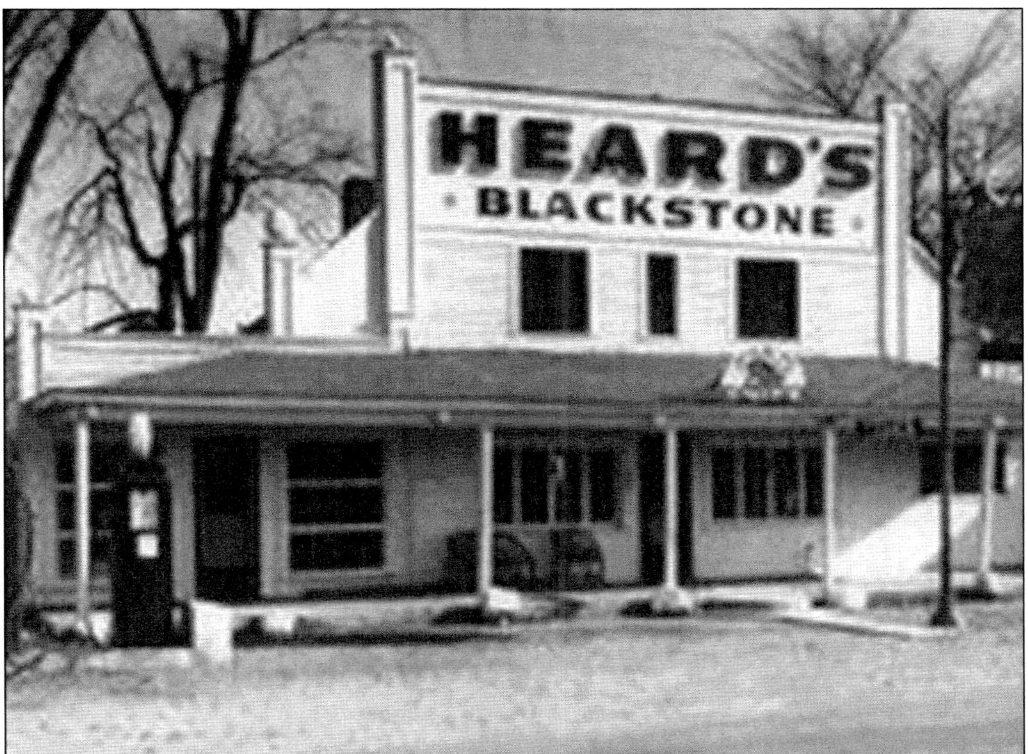

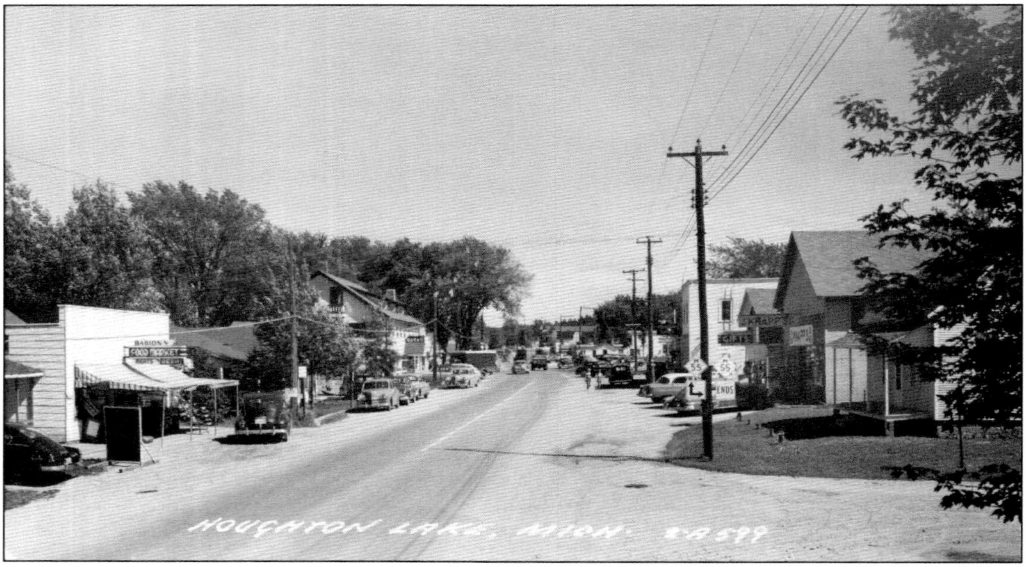

As the 20th century progressed, more businesses were established in the village. Babion's Food Market (left) was on the lakeside on M-55. Knapp's Five and Dime Store and Cloutier's Gifts were on the south (right) side of the street. Gift shops were popular all around the lake because they carried a large selection of Houghton Lake souvenirs. Knapp's carried a wide variety of items, from small toys to sewing notions. It also had a candy counter, selling bulk candy and nuts. In the late 1950s, the road was expanded to four lanes. Babion's and Cloutier's are gone today, but the Knapp's building still stands and is now a cosmetology school.

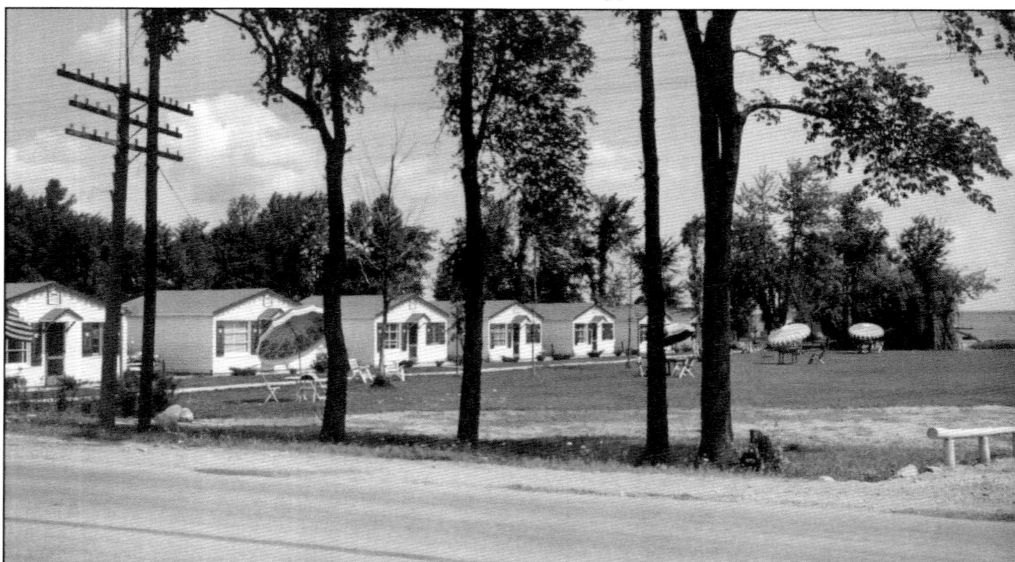

Wismeg's Dreamland Cottages was a popular resort on Houghton Lake. It was located on M-55 just west of the village. The economy of Houghton Lake was based on tourism, and the area was very popular for fishing and water sports. Resorts were necessary to accommodate the many visitors that came each summer. Until snowmobiling became a popular winter sport, most of the resorts were only open in the summer. These cabins still stand today, near Lyman's on the Lake.

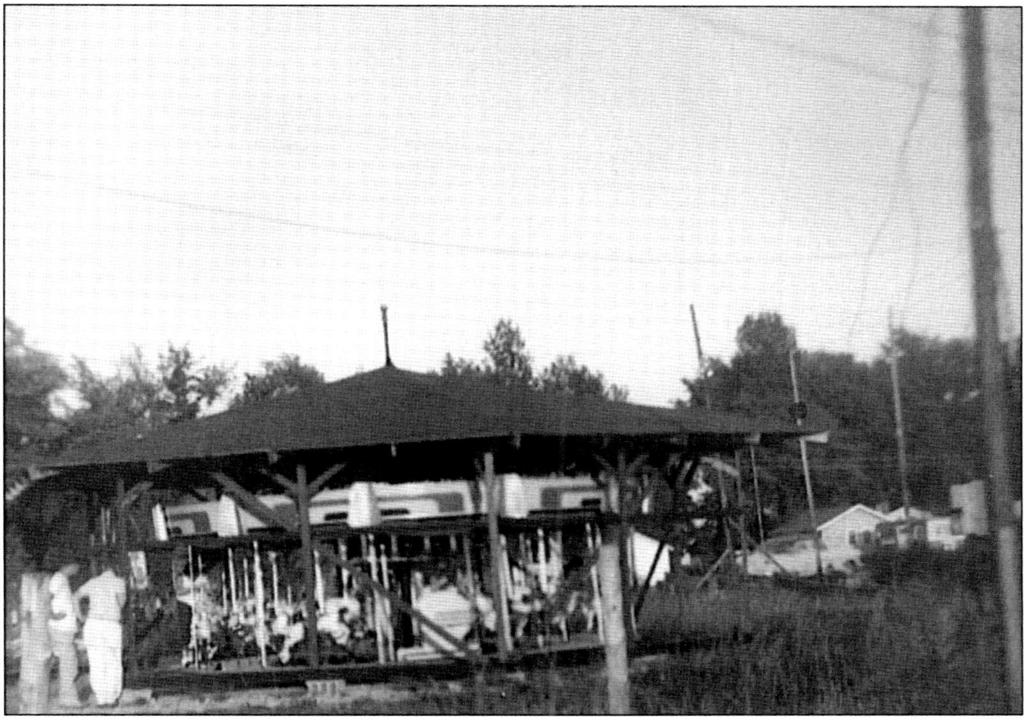

Just west of Houghton Lake village was a child's delight, a carousel (above). For many years, there were two other rides along with the carousel: a scrambler and an airplane ride. The original rides still remain at the site, along with a few additional rides. The first miniature golf course in the area was located here. In the photograph at right, Ralph Humley tests his skill on the course in 1956. For many years, the site was owned by Lynn and Robert Sohn and was named Fun Land. They expanded it and added go-cart rides, an arcade, and a waterslide. It is now owned by Gary Daniels. The carousel still thrills children. (Both courtesy of Fun Land Amusement Park.)

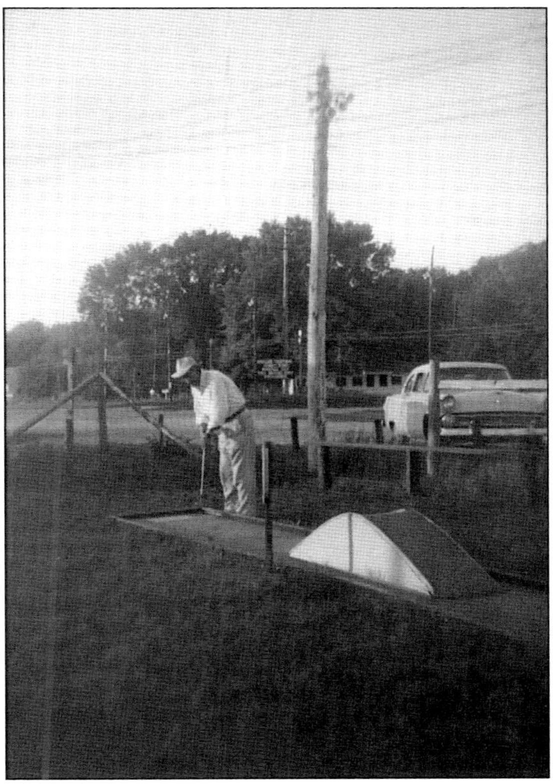

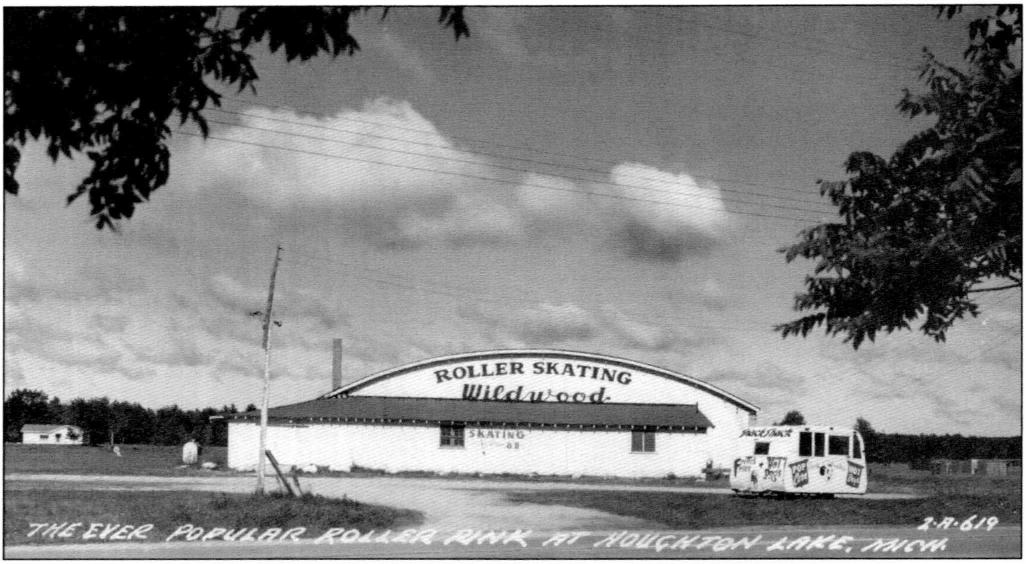

One of the most popular places at Houghton Lake was the Wildwood skating rink. In the 1940s, after World War II, the rink was used for the Hunter's Ball each November during deer season. The rink was open from 8:00 p.m. to 11:00 p.m. year-round. In the 1960s, it also had Sunday afternoon skating. The Wildwood was destroyed by fire in the fall of 1966.

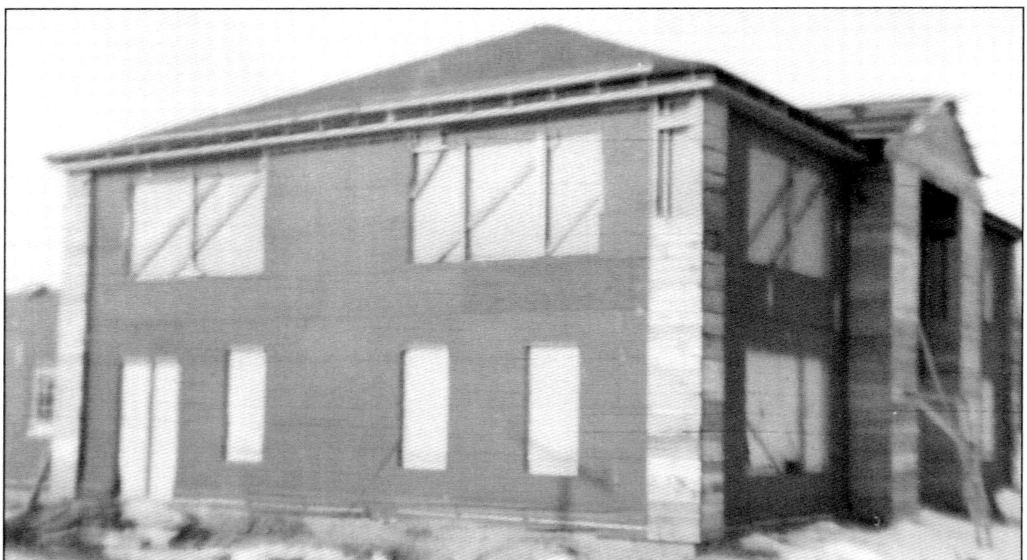

In 1945, a funeral home owned by Charlie Madison was established at the Heights. It was sold to Jim Barger in 1949, and a new building was erected on M-55. Hazen Randall was the contractor. It operated under the name Barger Funeral Home. In 1960, Ron Smith bought into the business, and it was called Barger Smith Funeral Home until 1965, when Smith took over. Until the late 1960s, it was the only funeral home serving the Houghton Lake area. In the late 1970s, it was called McWilliams and owned by Brad McWilliams. Stan Christler bought it in 1982. Through the years, an addition was built and the interior was remodeled. This photograph was taken while the building was under construction. (Courtesy of Christler Funeral Home.)

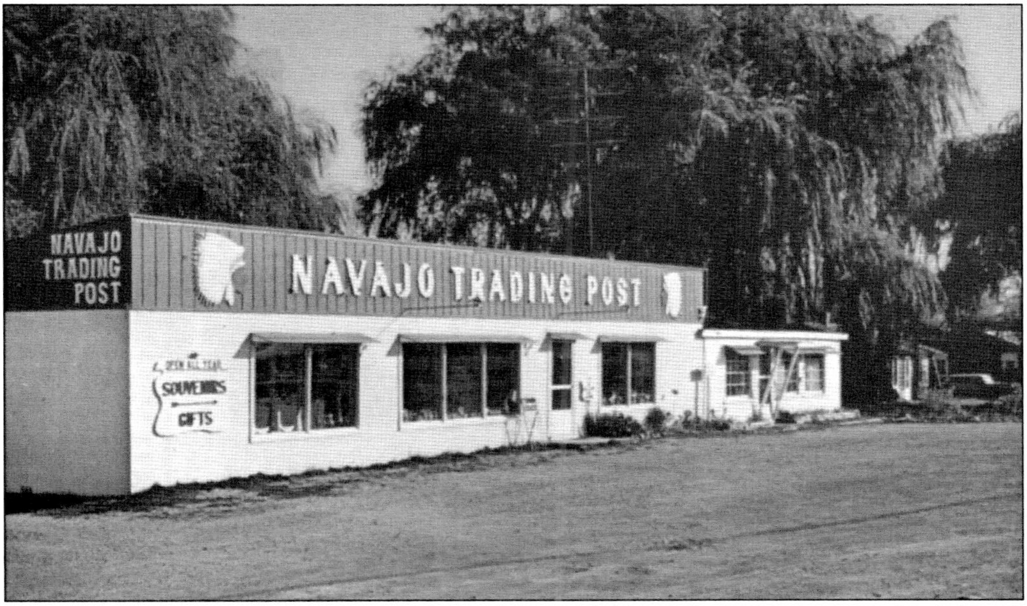

The Navajo Trading Post, owned by Eldon "El" Greenfield, was built sometime in the 1950s. El Greenfield was a justice of the peace, and the trading post served as his office for official business. Misdemeanor offenses were handled at this store. This was before 1958, when the district court was created by the state legislature. For most visitors, the store was a great place to shop for moccasins and turquoise jewelry. The Navajo Trading post is still in business and still sells those items.

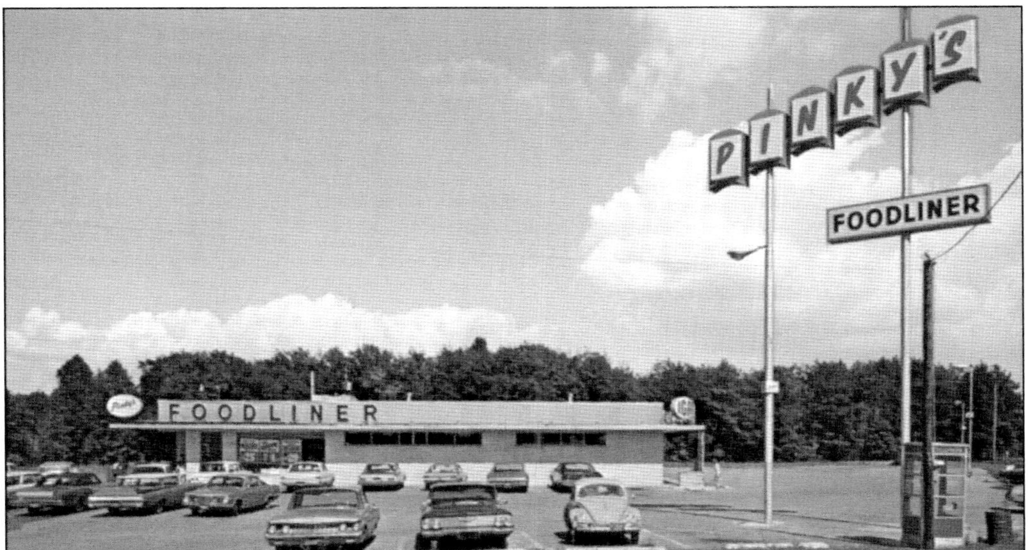

Pinky's IGA was the first modern supermarket in Roscommon Township. Murl "Pinky" Randall had been in the grocery business for seven years when he built and opened this store in 1961. Pinky's was an IGA (Independent Grocer Alliance) store. Randall sold the store in 1974 to Carter's, an employee-owned grocery chain with 30 stores throughout Michigan. Carter's built a bigger store in 1993 in the K-Mart plaza. In 2006, Carter's went bankrupt and closed its stores. The new Carter's store remains shuttered. The Pinky's IGA building is now a Save-A-Lot grocery store.

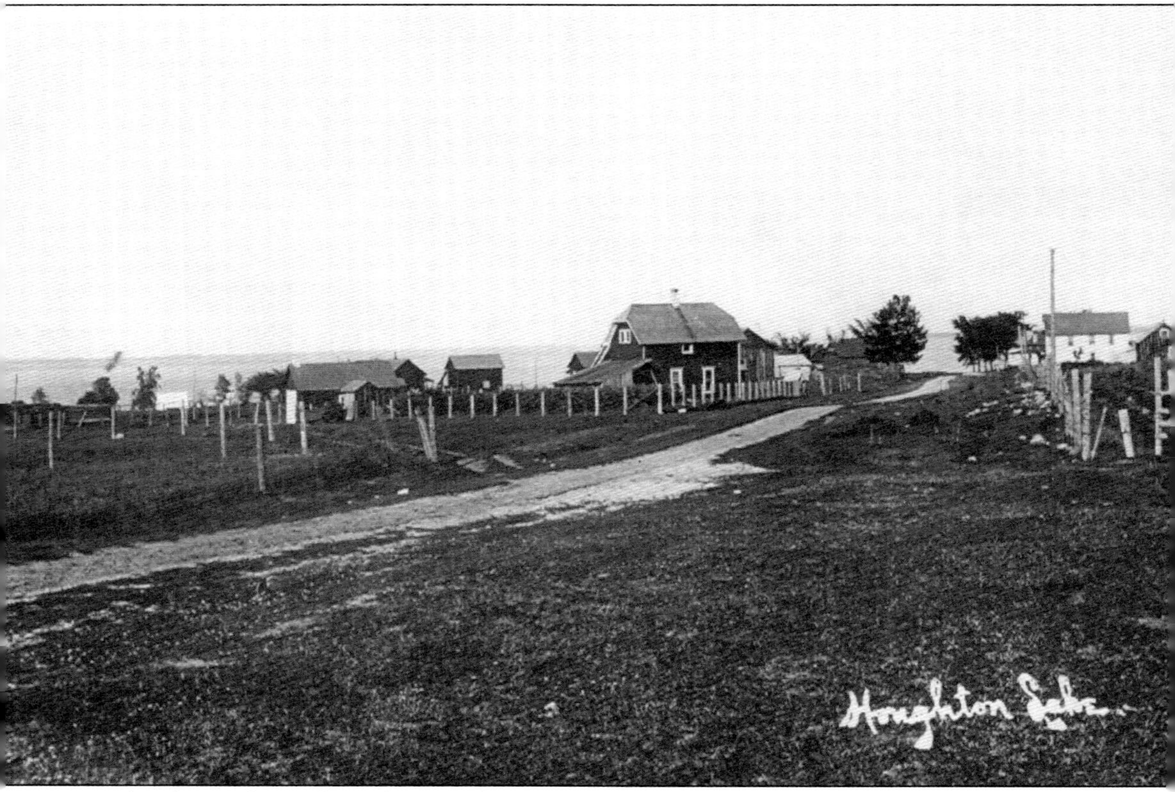

This farm is located on what was then US-27, coming into Houghton Lake. It was very near to what was then called the Village. While it was part of Roscommon Township, it was never as well developed as the Heights. The Heights was originally the main business district of the township. Much of the Heights was farmland for many years, as was much of the township. However, the first courthouse was in the Heights at the Hall farm. The courthouse was in the Heights for four years until the county residents voted to move it to Roscommon Village, some thirty miles away. Roscommon had train service at that time. (Courtesy of Vera Parsons.)

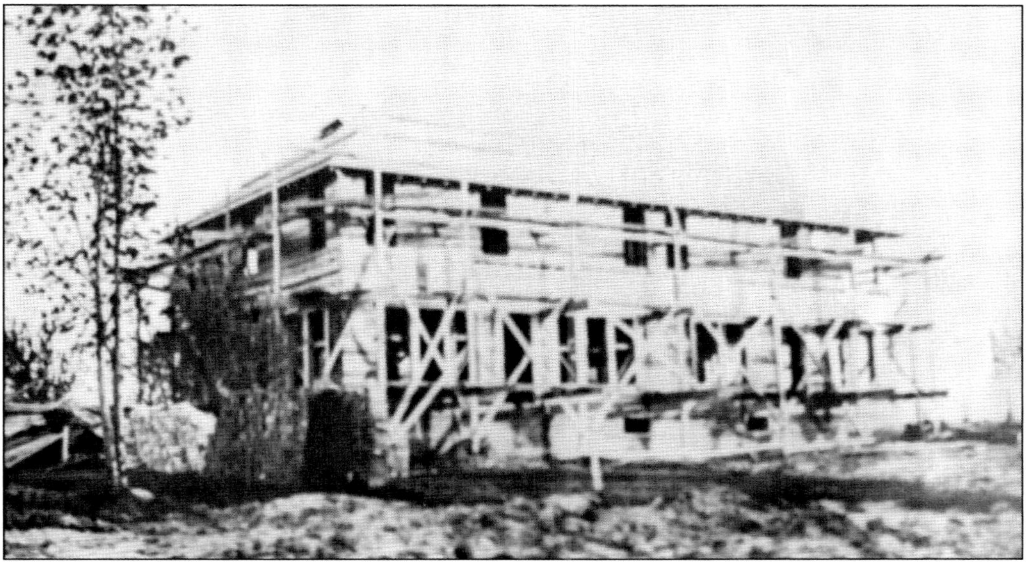

The Smith Hotel was built in 1915. The wood frame hotel was large for its day in Houghton Lake, but William Smith, who built it, had an eye for the future. It is located very near the water in the Heights.

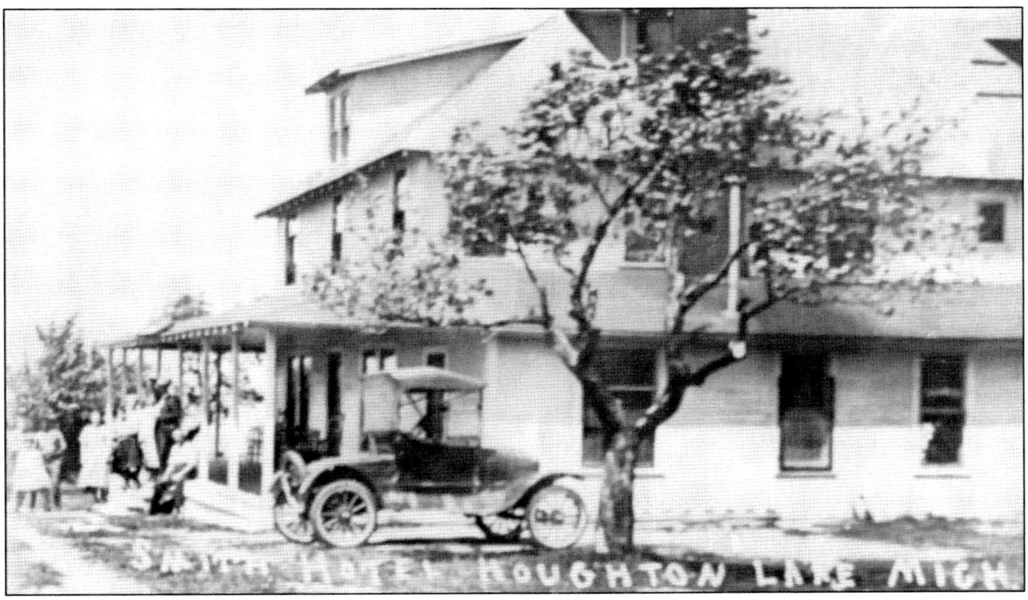

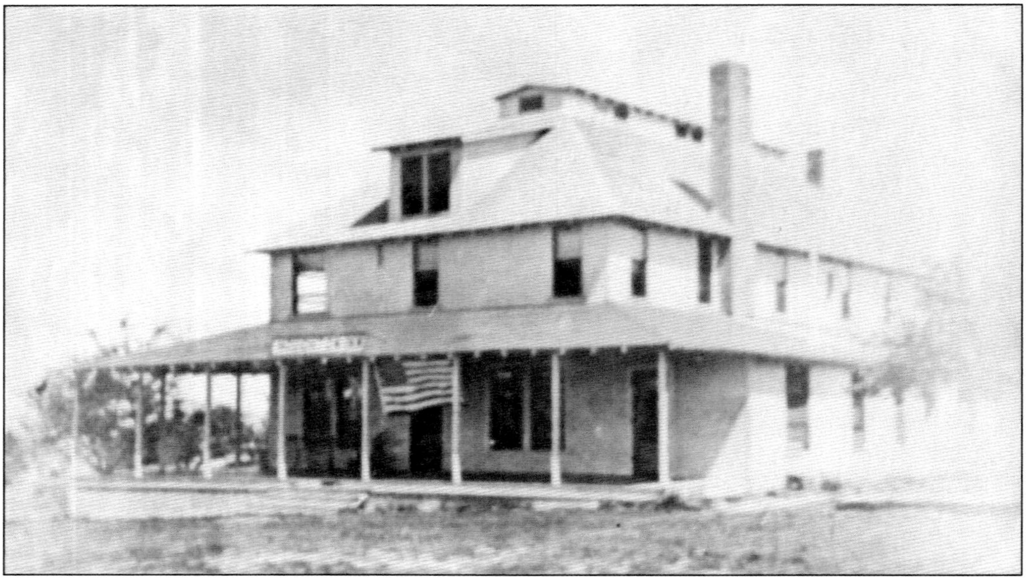

Over the years, the porch was added on to the Smith Hotel and the third-floor rooms were finished by Hazen Randall. By the late 1920s, the porch was screened in and the hotel's name was changed to the Houghton Heights Inn. This building remains standing and is a visual landmark from the water. It is no longer used as a hotel.

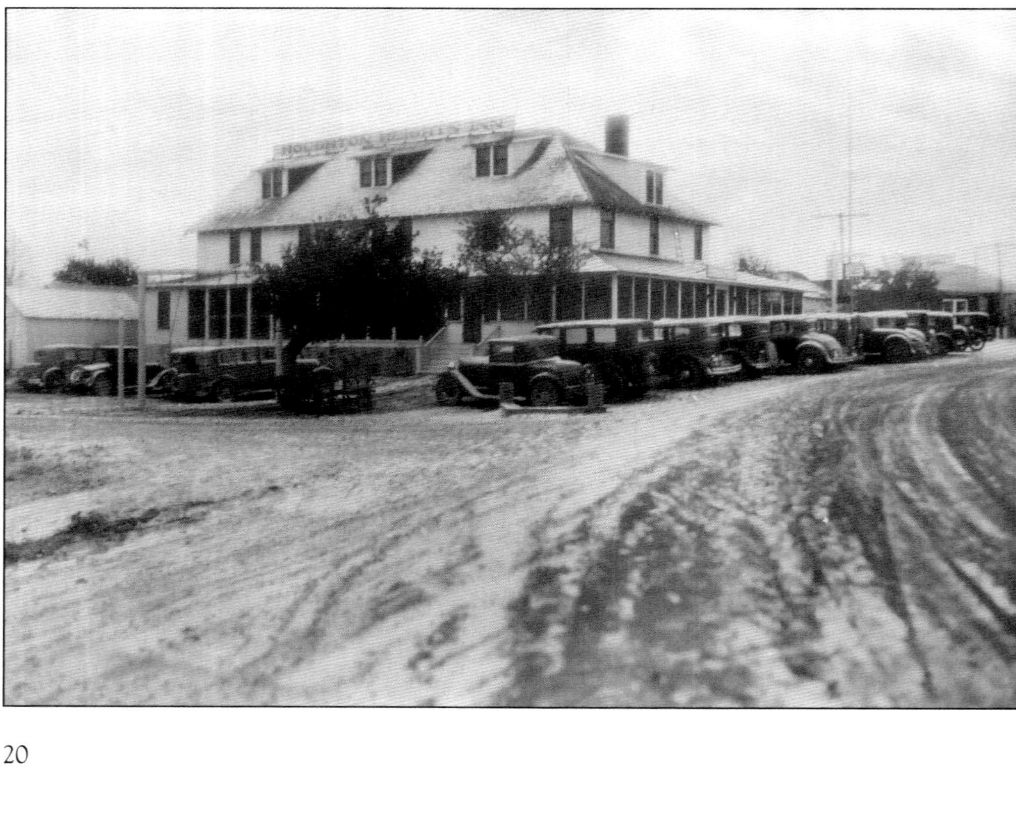

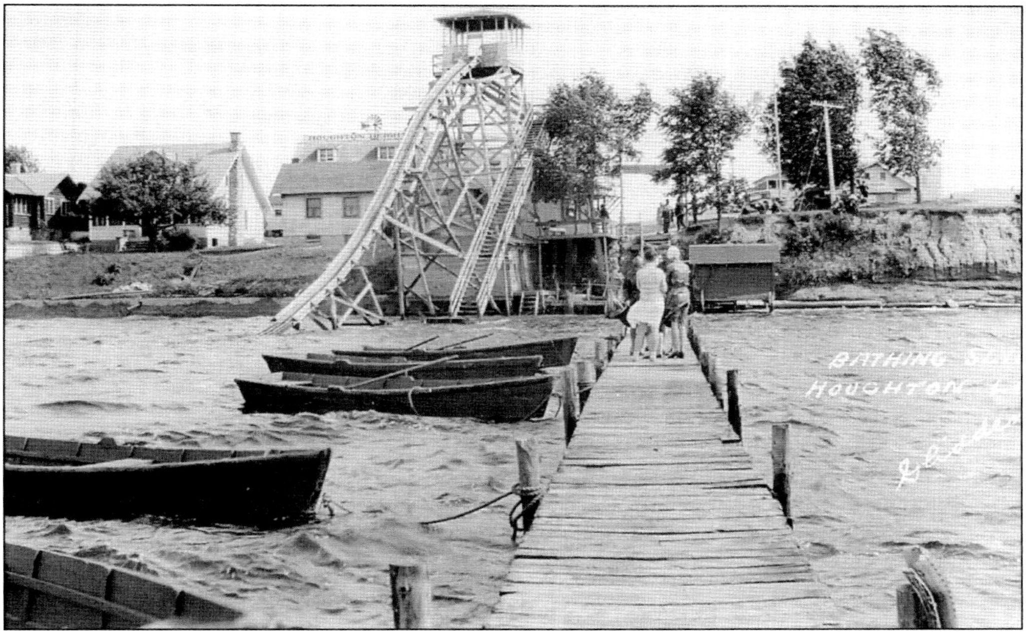

One attraction that visitors to the Houghton Heights Inn enjoyed in the 1920s was a very large wooden waterslide at the Standford dock. Swimmers could climb the stairs from the water and enjoy a cool splash in the lake. There was also an observation deck, where guests could enjoy a clear view of the lake. The slide was stored each winter. The observation deck lasted into the 1960s, but the slide was gone by the 1930s. (Courtesy of Vera Parsons.)

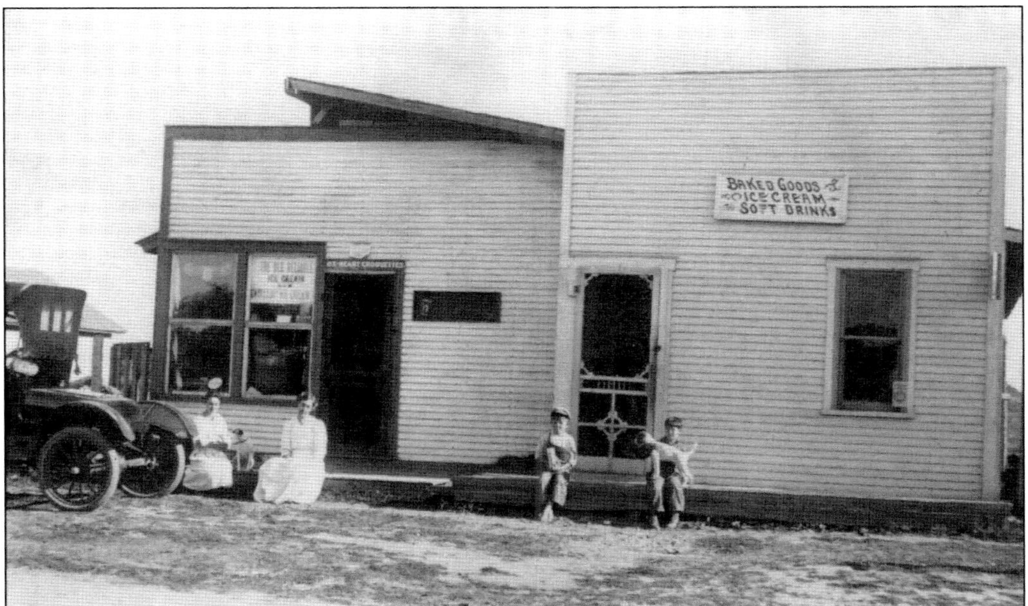

Ox Heart Croquettes was an early bakery and ice cream shop in the Heights in the early 20th century. This photograph was taken in 1916. (Courtesy of Vera Parsons.)

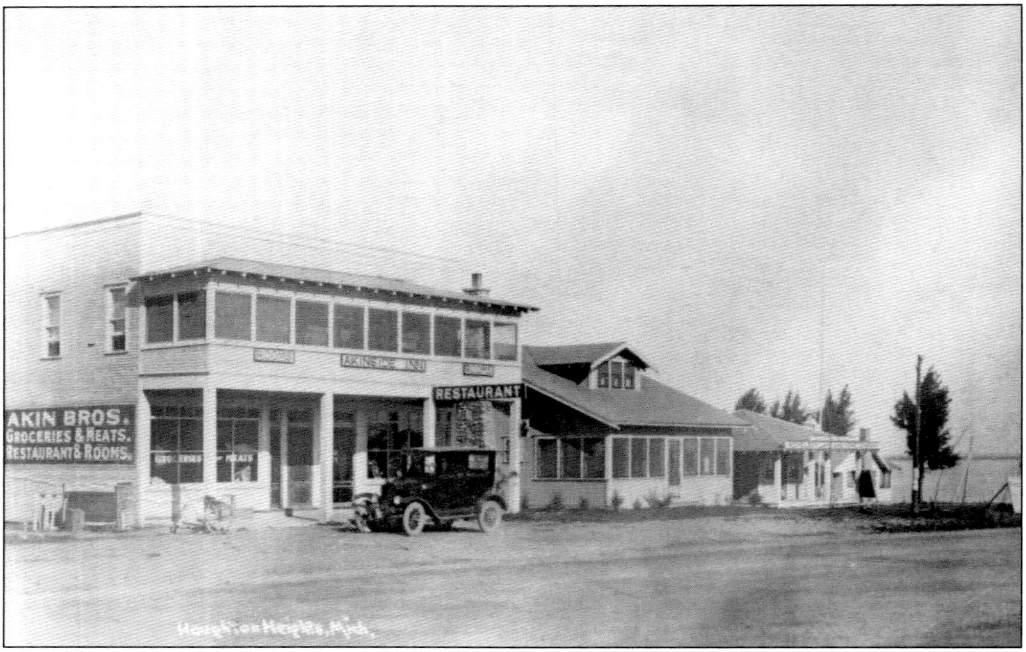

The Akin brothers built a business in the Heights in 1924. The grocery store, restaurant, and hotel (above) served the needs of the growing community. In the photograph below, the Akins family poses in front of their business. They are, from left to right, Nellie, Chester, Ora, Lee, Mildred, and Edith. Chester's dog Chum is in front of them. In 1935, Hazen Randall bought the building.

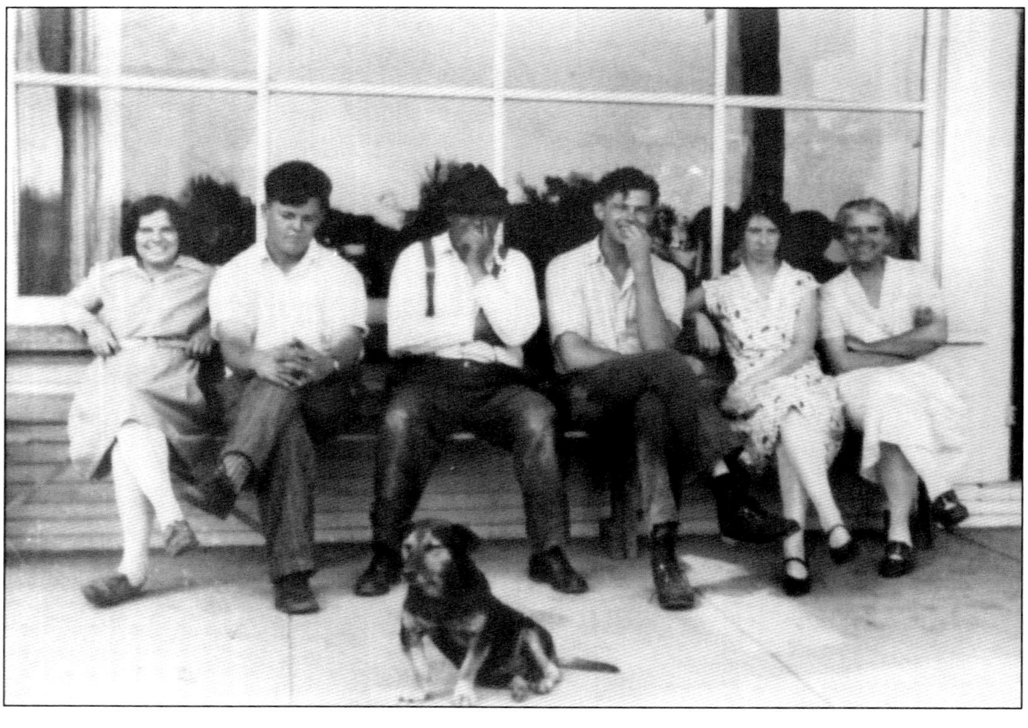

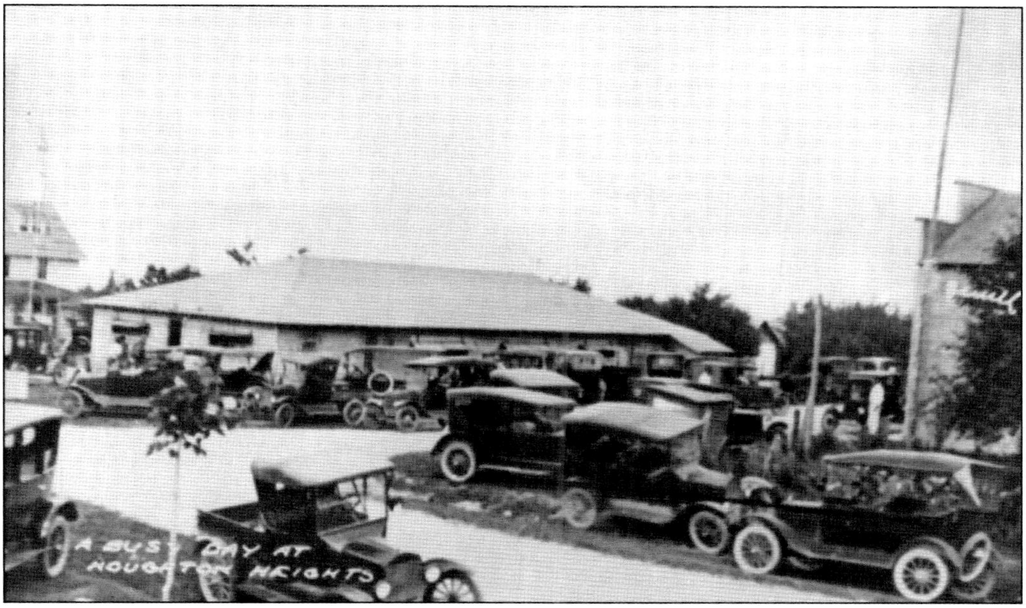

The Heights was the home of Ra-Walla Dance Hall. It was built in 1920 by Ray Walling, who also owned a second venue in the village. For people living in Roscommon Township, Ra-Walla provided a place to socialize. It was not just used for dancing, however. On Labor Day 1922, a boxing match was held at the Ra-Walla, attracting many spectators. During one of the two fights, a boxer was hit so hard that he collapsed and died in the ring. This ended Ra-Walla's foray into boxing.

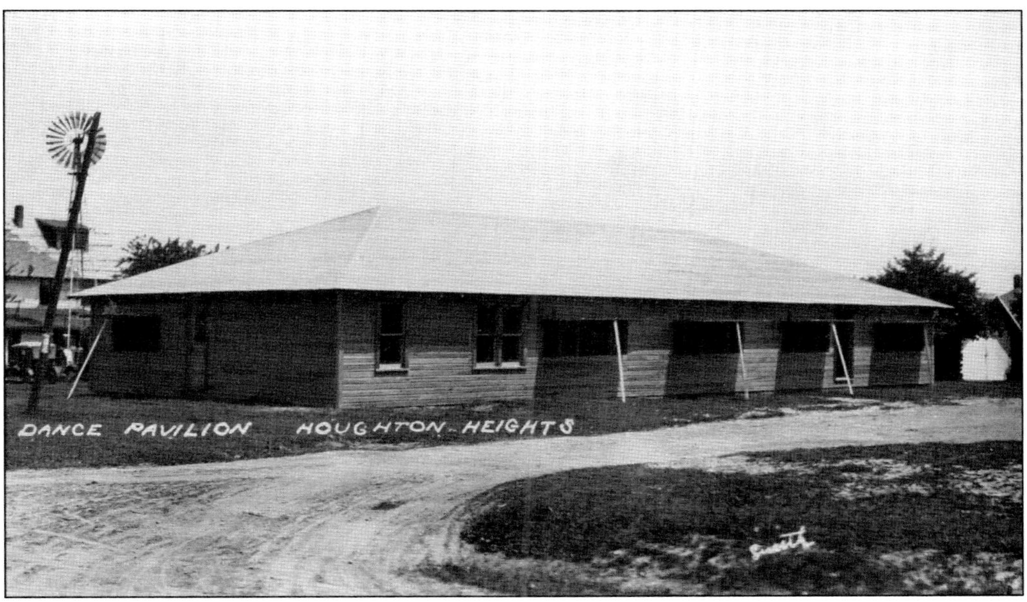

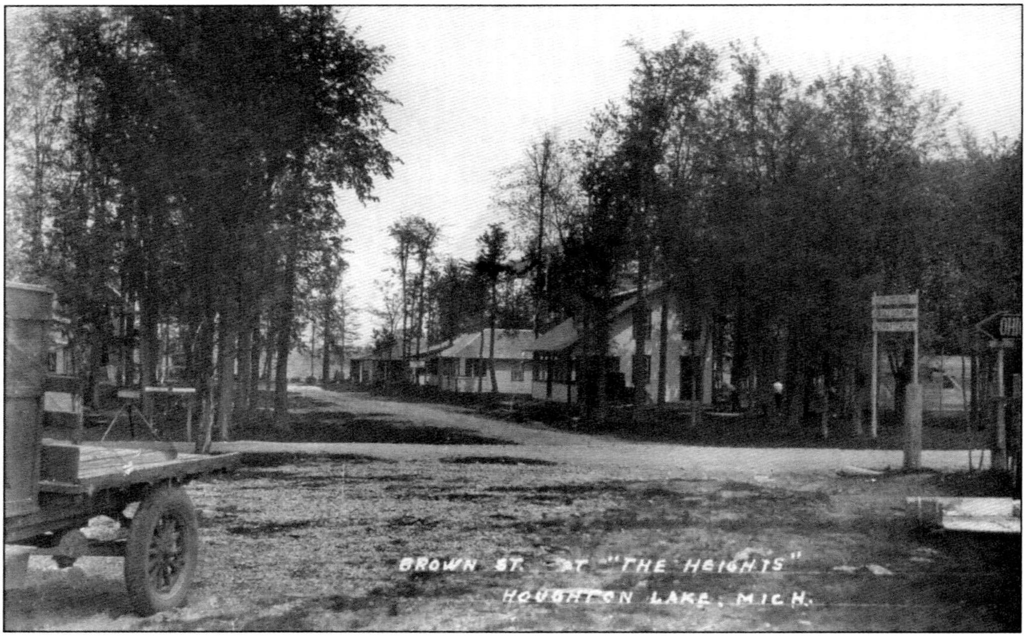

Brown Street in the Heights ran down to the water. In the first decades of the 20th century, cottages were already being built and advertised for sale, as is evident by the sign at right. There were still only dirt trails for roads. W.P. Patterson saw the market for cottages, which could be bought on terms.

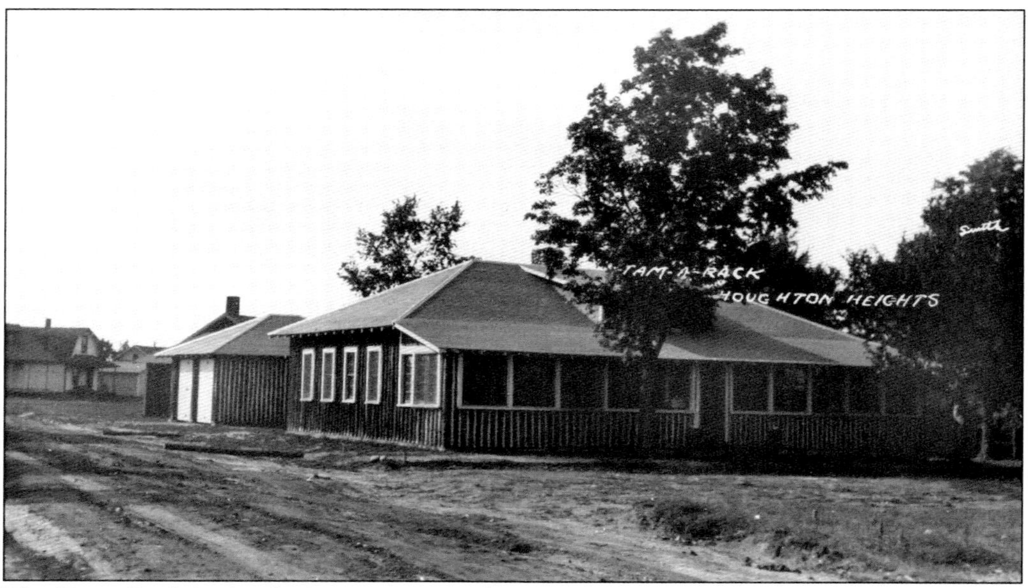

The Tam-a-Rack Lodge, built in 1924, served for many years as a resort. The Tam-a-Rack also had a restaurant, which later became the Eagles Lodge. It was razed in the 1990s.

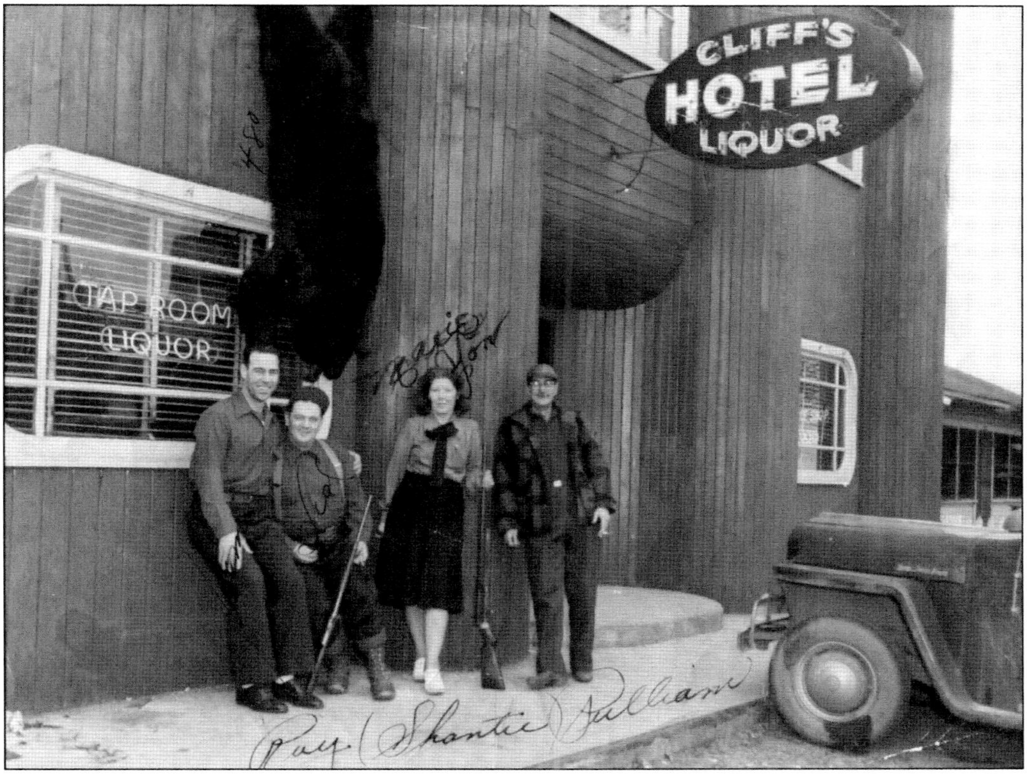

The Akins sold their business in 1933 to Cliff Chapman. The establishment then existed as Cliff's Hotel for the next 52 years. In the late 1960s, Marie Best operated the bar and hotel. She had a beauty parlor in the upstairs. In 1985, the bar was purchased by Savo and Dunsanka Je'Le Stajc. They renamed the business the Velez Country Inn, and, later, Sam's Lounge. At that time, the upstairs rooms were closed. For a short time between 2003 and 2008, it was called the Funky Turtle. In 2011, Clive and Dorothy Clymer bought the bar and named it the Anchor Inn.

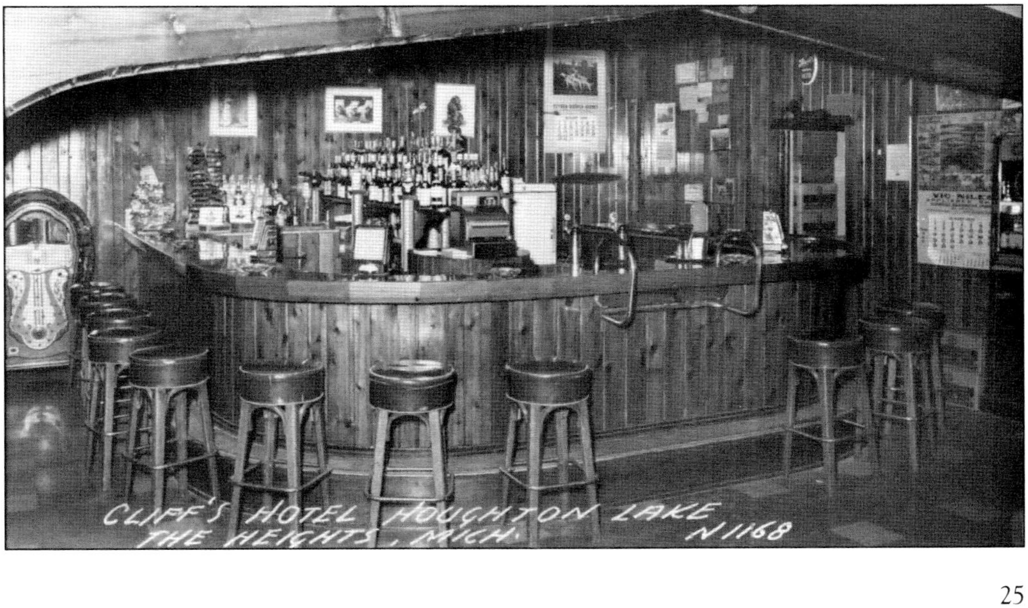

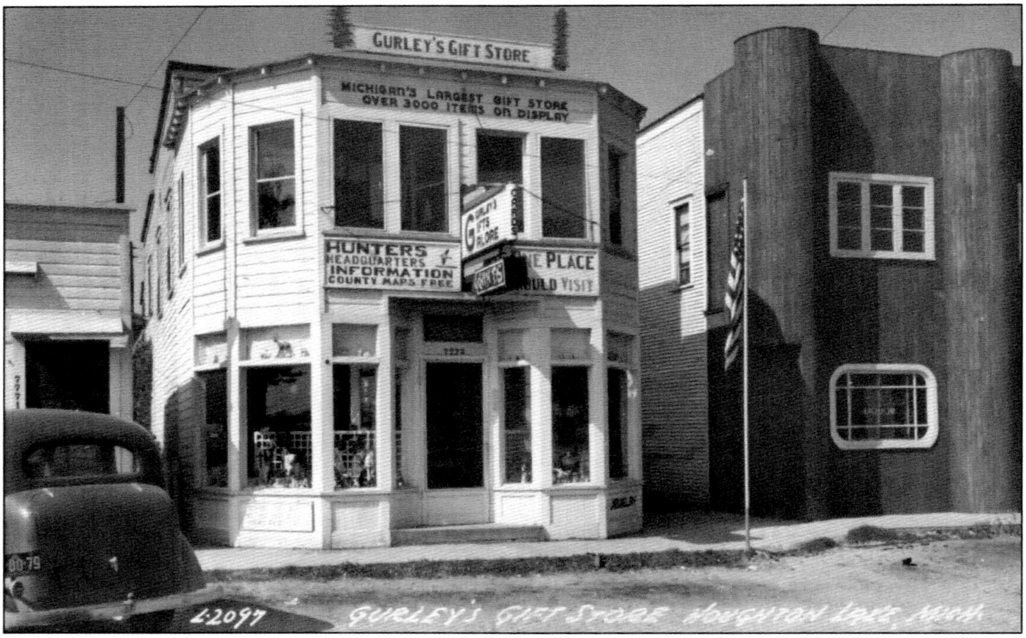

Gurley's Gift Store was built by Rowena and Rupert Gurley in the late 1920s. Advertised as "Michigan's largest gift store," it had over 3,000 different items on display. By the mid-1940s, the front was remodeled with bay windows. The store remained in business until the early 1960s, when the building was razed.

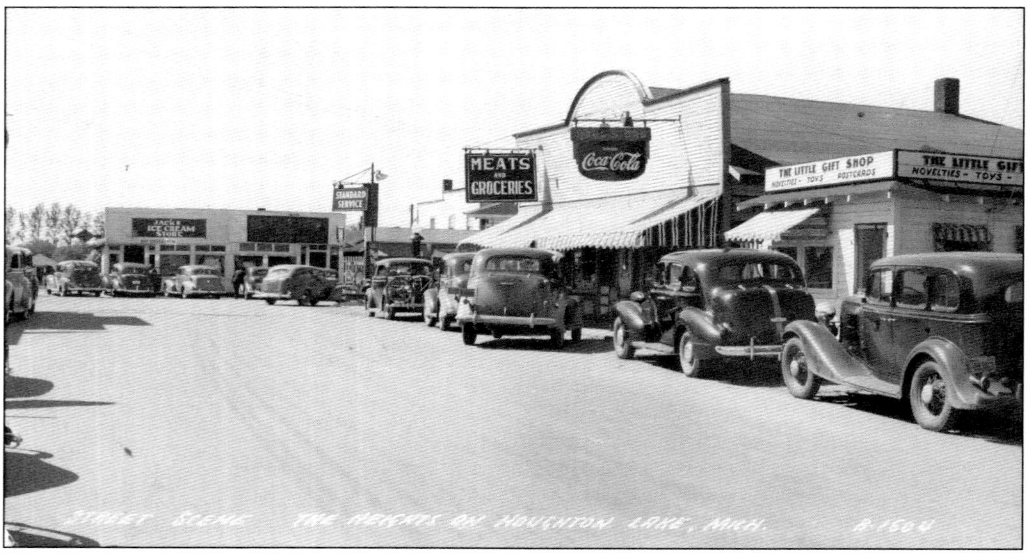

The Heights was a busy place in the 1940s. Shoppers could buy their groceries at the store on the right, owned by Bob Johnson. In 1954, Johnson sold the establishment to Murl "Pinky" Randall. Randall operated his business in the Heights for seven years before building a new store on the corner of Loxley Street and the new M-55. Gift shops were plentiful in the Heights, as merchants catered to the tourist crowd. Within a couple of blocks, there were two stores specializing in gifts and souvenirs. Many of the other stores carried postcards. The grocery store and the Little Gift Shop are no longer in the Heights.

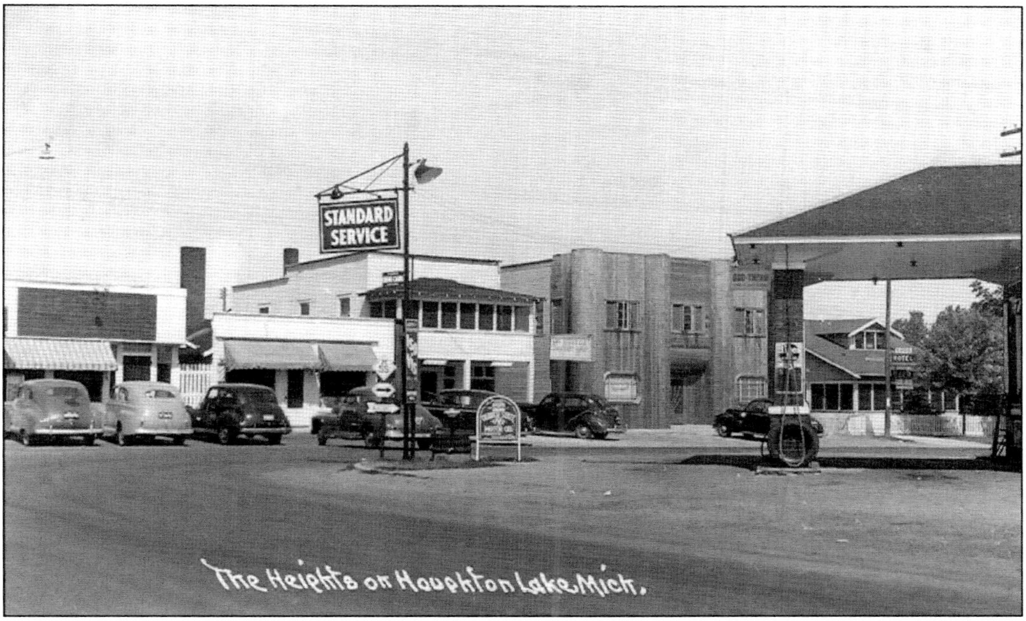

A Standard Oil service station stood on the northeast corner of Loxley Street and Heights View Drive. It was owned by the Post family. In the early years, there was a community drinking fountain by the sign. Looking east from the station, the photograph below also shows Snyder's Drugs, which belonged to Bob Snyder, a pharmacist. His father, Edward, was also a pharmacist. In the 1960s, Terry Elsholtz bought the business and renamed it Terry's Pharmacy. Elsholtz moved the business to M-55 in the 1980s but then closed it completely. The building was then razed. The Northern Bar, visible in the left background below, has enjoyed a long stay in the Heights. The building is still operating as a bar, now called the Old Town Tavern. (Both courtesy of Vera Parsons.)

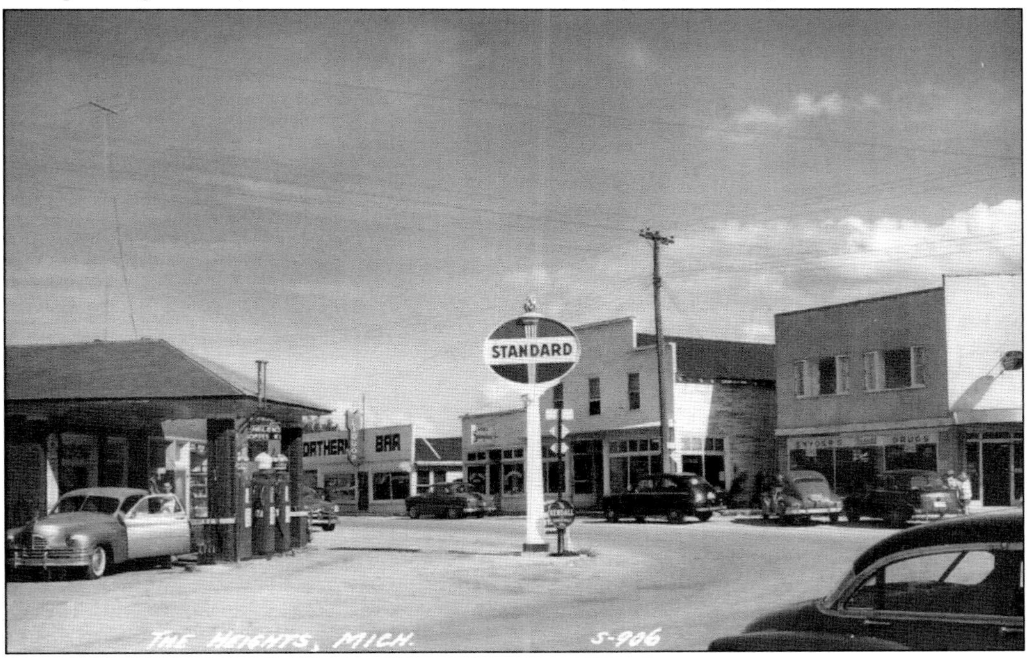

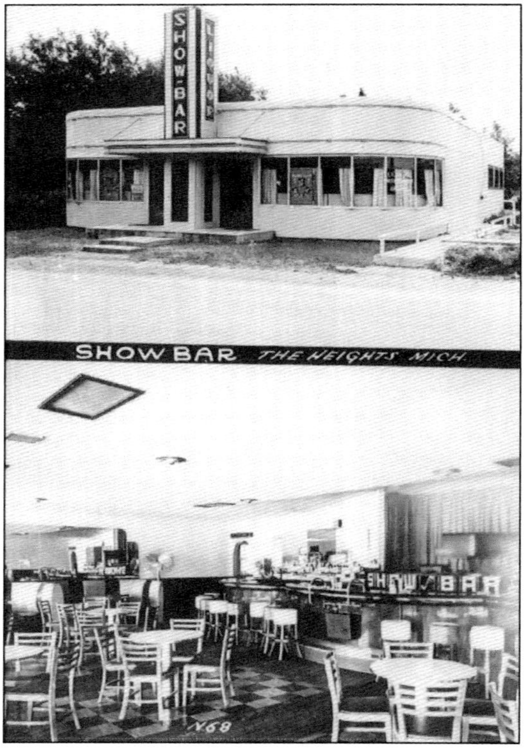

The Show Bar was across the street from the Northern Bar, on the corner of Loxley Street and Byron Avenue. The building no longer exists. (Courtesy of Vera Parsons.)

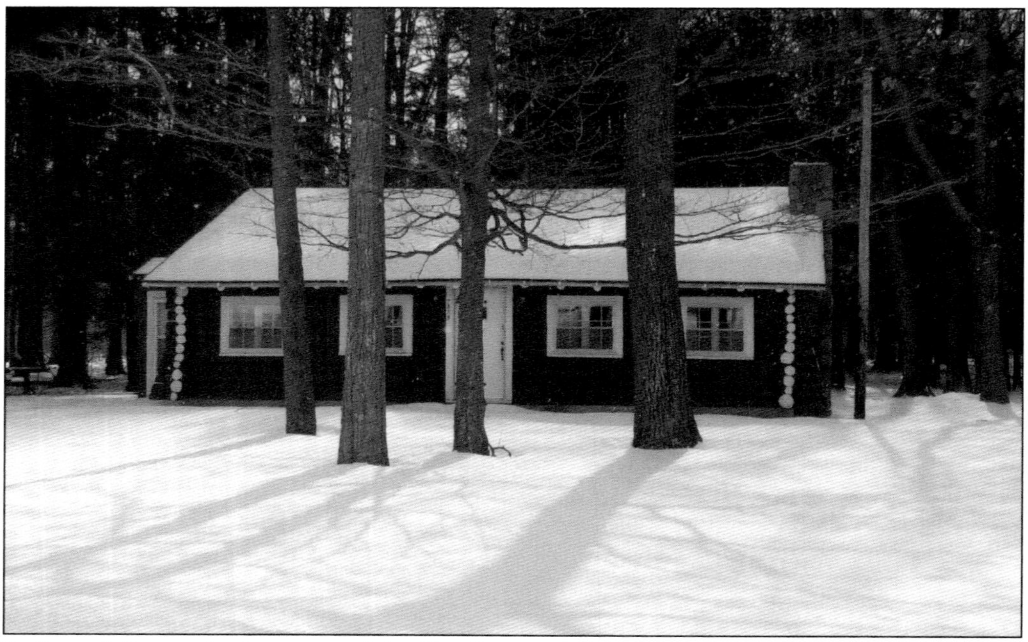

Della and George Larkins started the Boy Scouts and Girl Scouts in Roscommon Township. They raised funds to have the Boy and Girl Scout Lodge built and gave the Scouts a 99-year lease on the building. Built in the late 1940s by Sandy Sanderson, it still stands today, although it is privately owned and no longer used for Scouting. (Courtesy of Vera Parsons.)

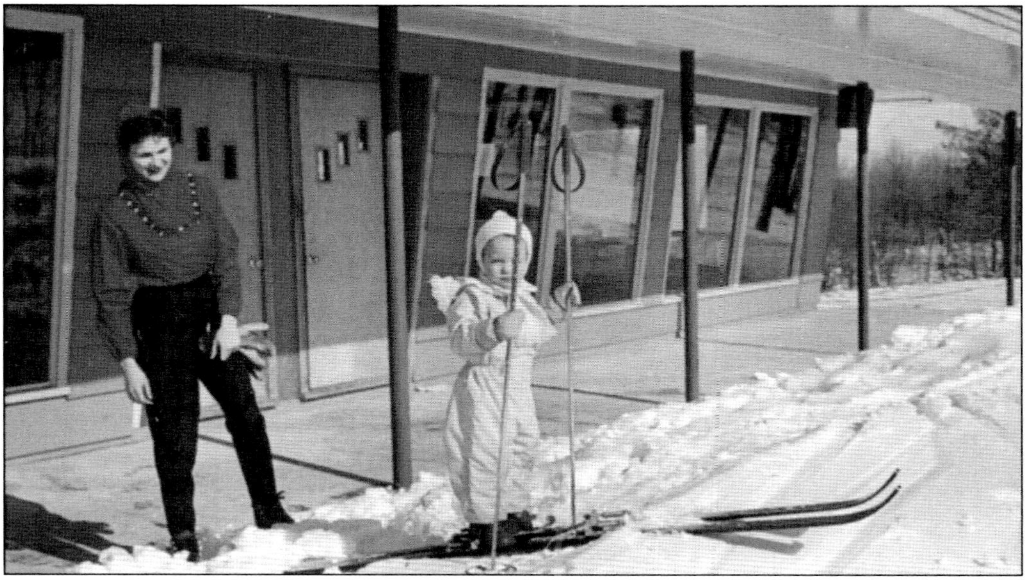

This is an iconic photograph of the Snow Bowl Ski Park. The short-lived endeavor in Roscommon Township was started in 1956 by David Young and Ted Daye. They raised money from the community to help finance the project. The park's opening was delayed due to lack of snow. The business was always rocky, a consequence of weather patterns. In the second year, a new partner was added, Russell La Freinere. He installed more runs and snow-making equipment. Snow conditions forced the park into bankruptcy in 1962, and it closed. It reopened again in 1963 and remained in operation until 1965, which was its last season. The lodge that once stood atop the hill was razed.

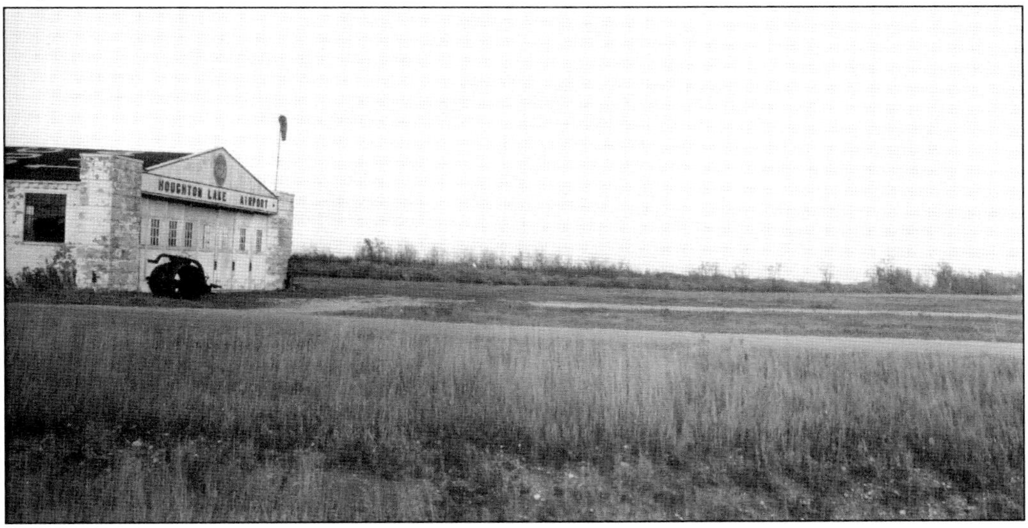

The Houghton Lake Airport was built in 1935, and the hangar was dedicated the following year. Byron Soults was the acting manager. The land was donated to the Michigan Aeronautic Commission by Nels Michelson, and the airport was built as a Works Progress Administration (WPA) project. In the early 1980s, the state wanted to close the airport, but Wilbert Hines III and others worked to keep it open. The airport was turned over to Roscommon Township on May 24, 1984.

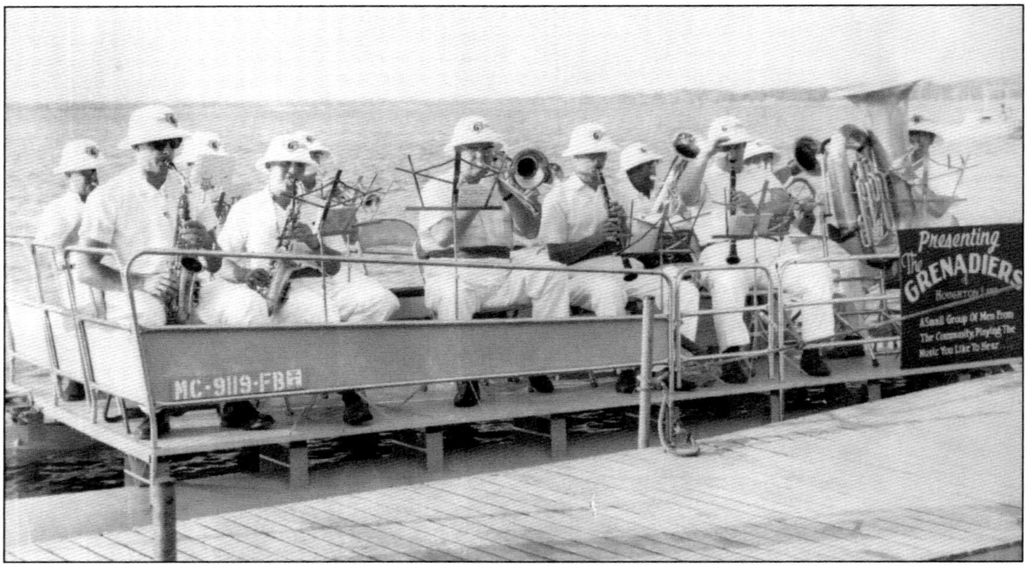

The Grenadier Band was a group of musicians established in 1962 to entertain the masses on a weekly basis. They took their talent to the people by way of the lake. During the summer, they would load onto a pontoon boat and play music while the boat drove around the lake. Residents would sit out by the lake and listen to the beautiful music, which could be heard from a great distance. The band broke up in 1970 because too many members moved away from Houghton Lake. Don Foust, the retired band teacher and motel owner, played clarinet in the group.

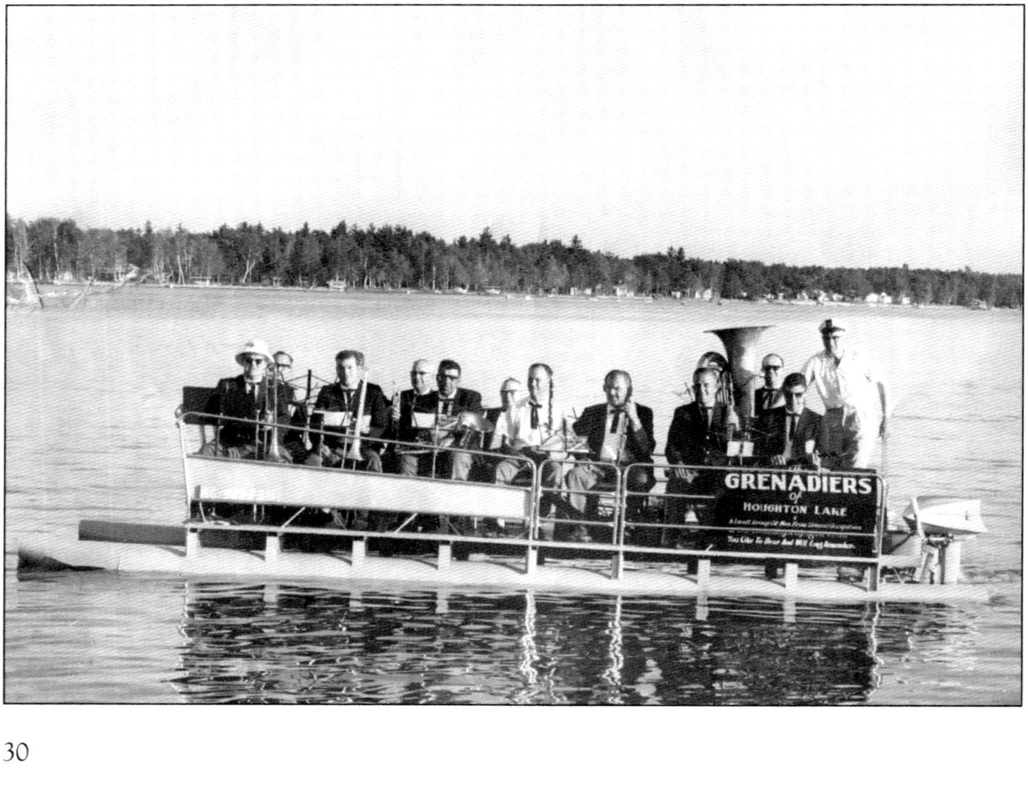

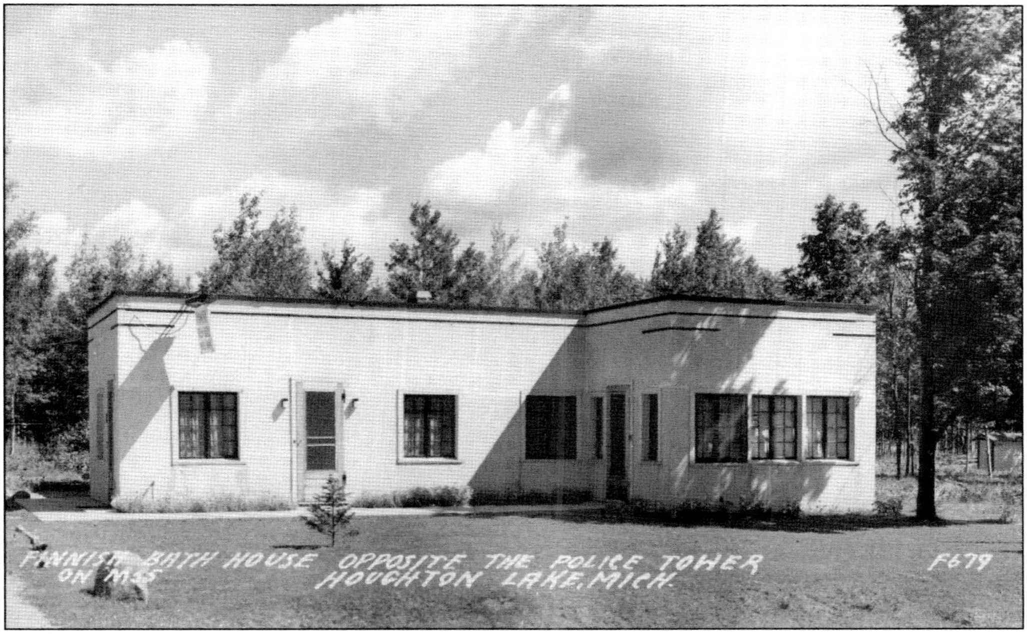

Across from the Michigan State Police post in Lake Township was a Finnish bathhouse (above). Not much is known about the establishment, which operated until the 1940s. After it was razed, Ferguson's Motel (below) was built on the site. A motel, the Chalet, still stands at this location, but it has been closed for many years.

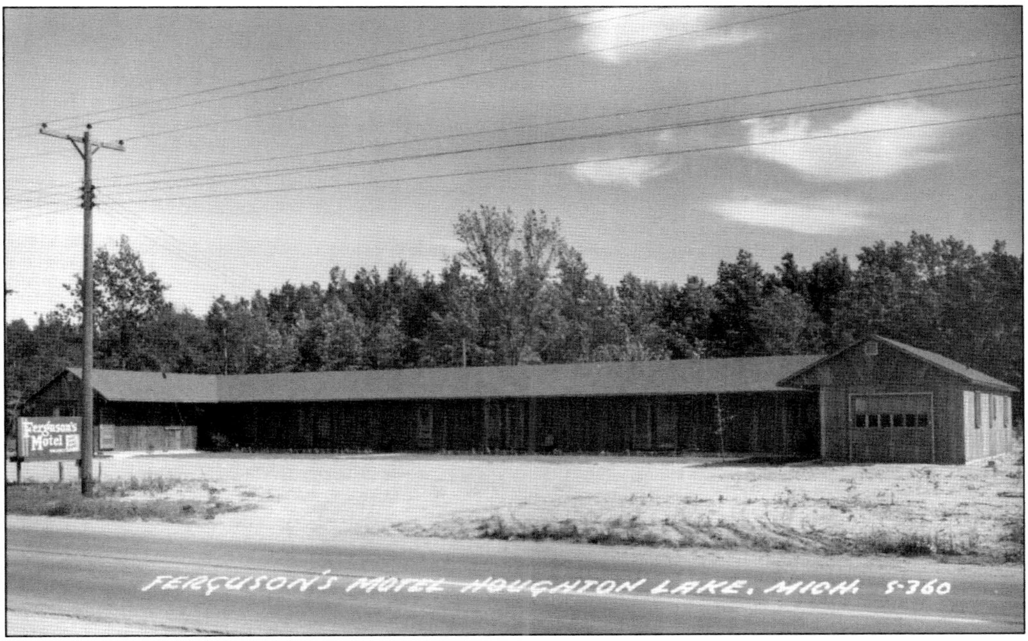

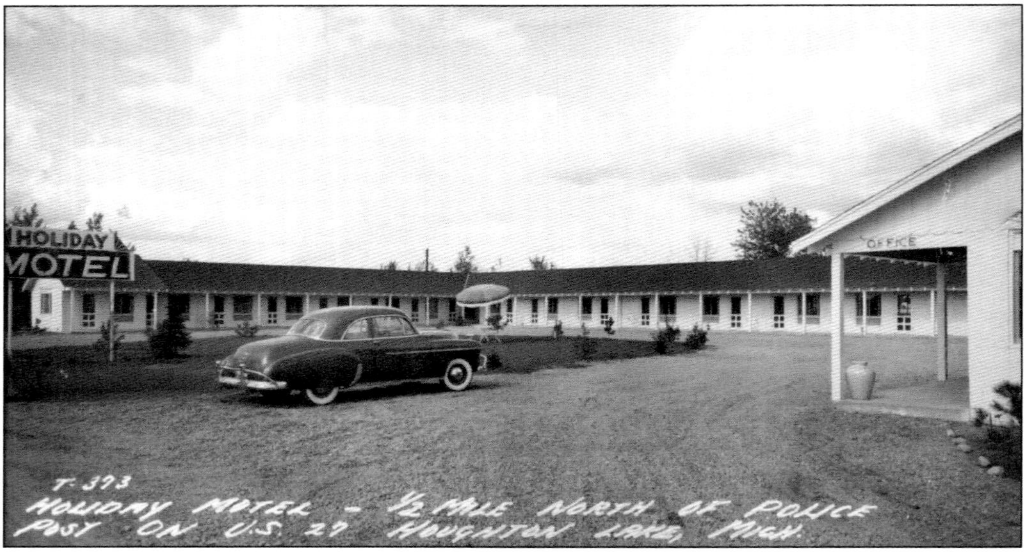

The Holiday Motel was a popular landmark for over five decades. The name changed throughout the years. In the 1960s, it was known as the Holiday Inn. When the national chain built a Holiday Inn at Houghton Lake in the late 1970s, the name was changed to Holiday on the Lake. A dining room was added, and it became a popular place to eat. The bar also had entertainment. Toward the end of the hotel's existence, a patio and large dock were added. The establishment attracted many boaters, who came for the music and the food. It was slated to be razed in the early 2000s when an electrical fire destroyed the building. A three-story Comfort Suites hotel now occupies the site.

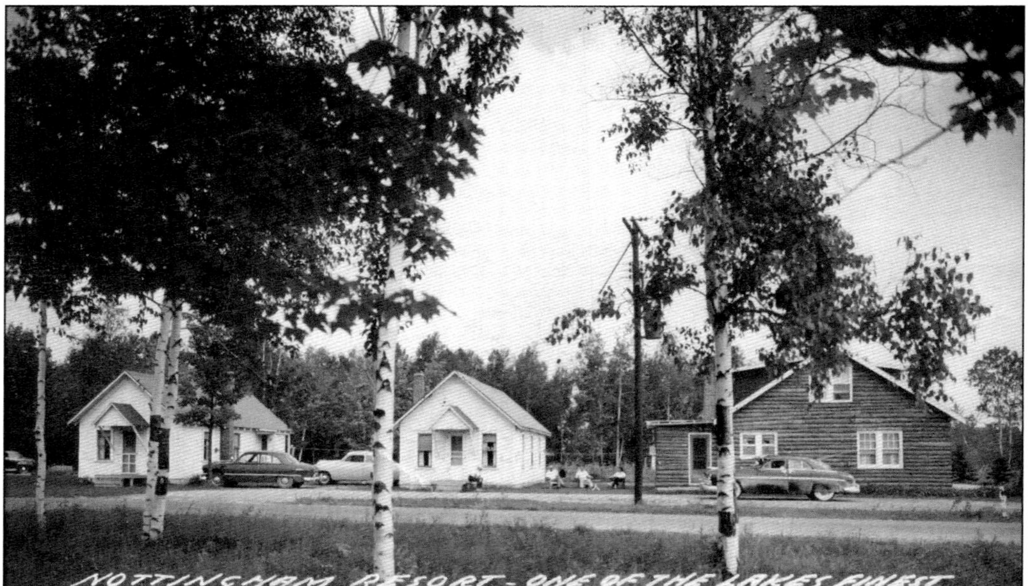

Efficiency cabins were everywhere, including on the west shore of Lake Township. The Nottingham Resort was a typical getaway for people seeking recreation on Houghton Lake. Most of these small resorts have been sold off as either condos or private residences.

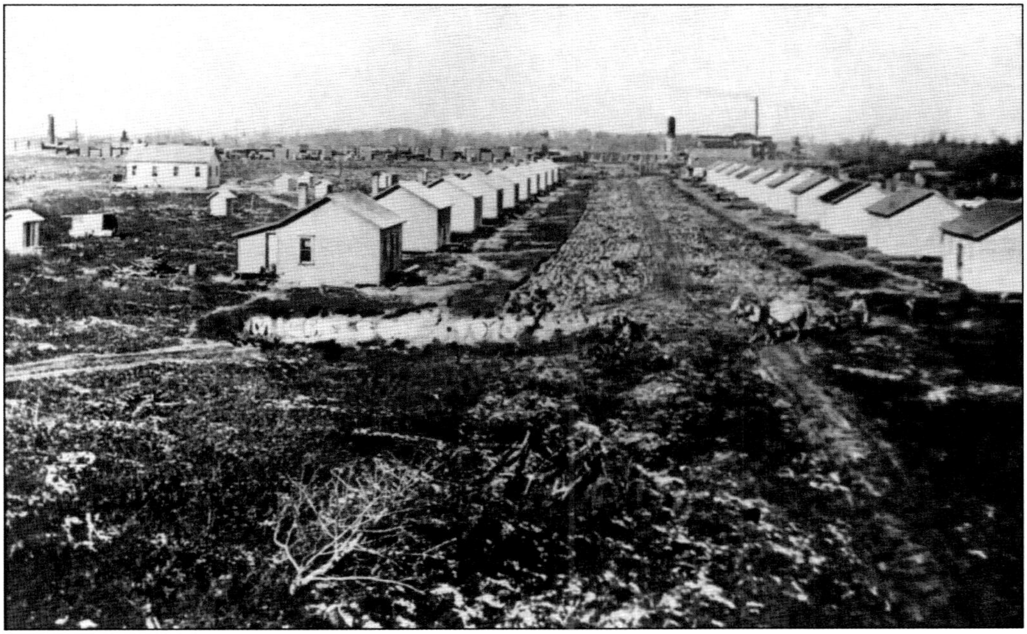

Lake Township is known for its rugged terrain. Much of the township was owned by Nels Michelson, who was in the logging business. This is a photograph of his logging town in 1910. After logging was exhausted, Michelson kept the prime lakeshore property and sold the rest. Lake Township and the northwest shore of Houghton Lake were not accessible by horse or car. It was the last part of Houghton Lake to be developed.

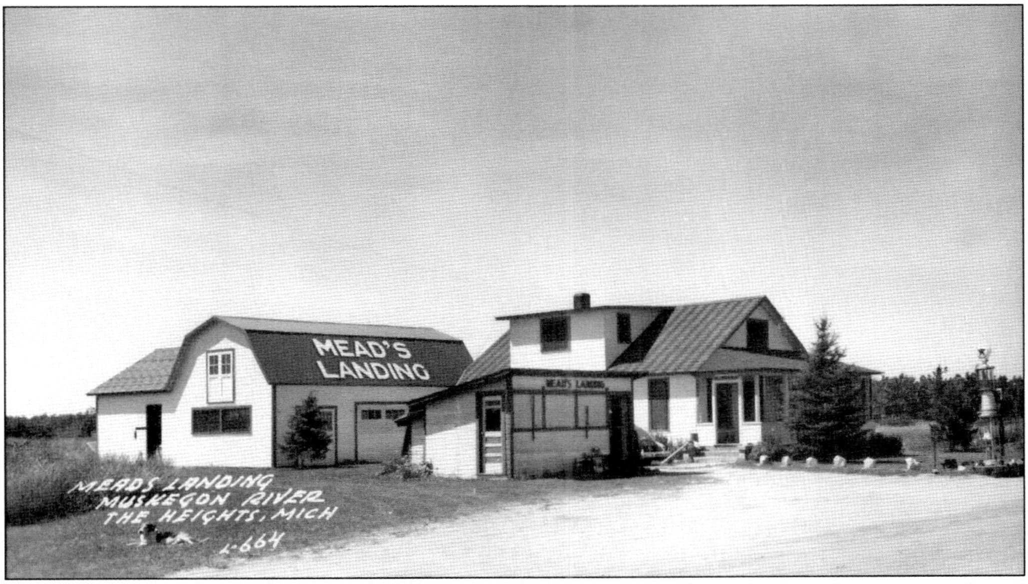

Mead's Landing was known as the old dump site, because it was where the logs that were timbered from around the lake were dumped. It was the starting point of the Muskegon River, on which the logs were driven down to mills, like Michelson's. The Muskegon River gave loggers access to mills farther south in the state. As tourism grew in Houghton Lake, Mead's Landing became a sporting store, where supplies for fishing could be bought.

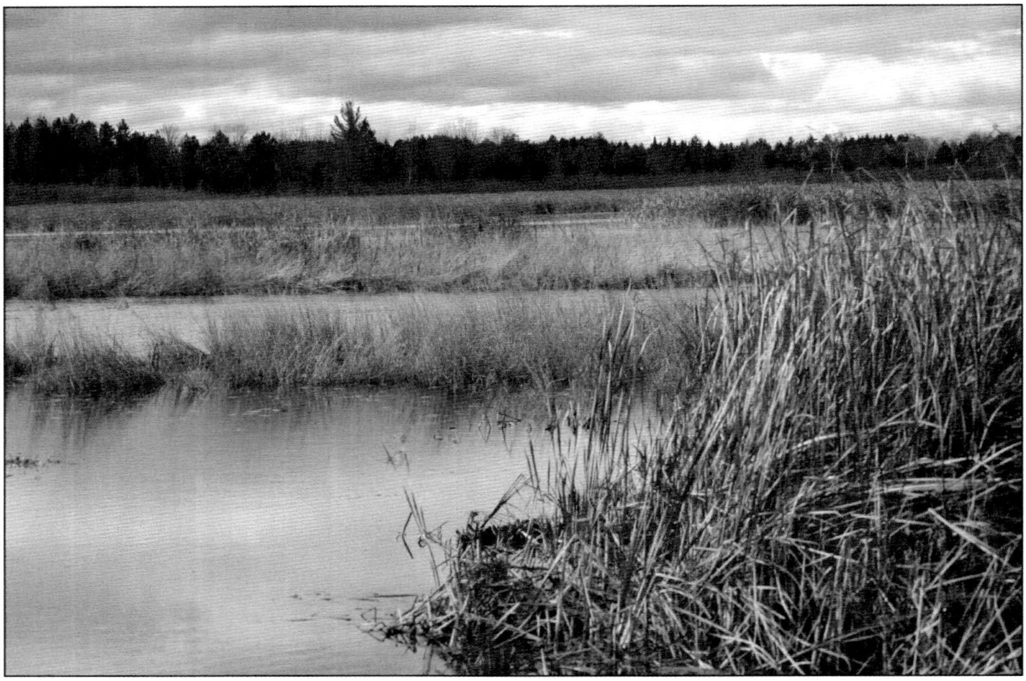

Dead Stream Swamp is a large area that is owned by the state. The name comes from the fact that the stream moves so slowly that it cannot be determined which way it is running. This area is great for hunting all types of game, including bear. There are parts of it that have no road accessibility. It can be a dangerous area for hunters, as one can easily become lost. (Author's collection.)

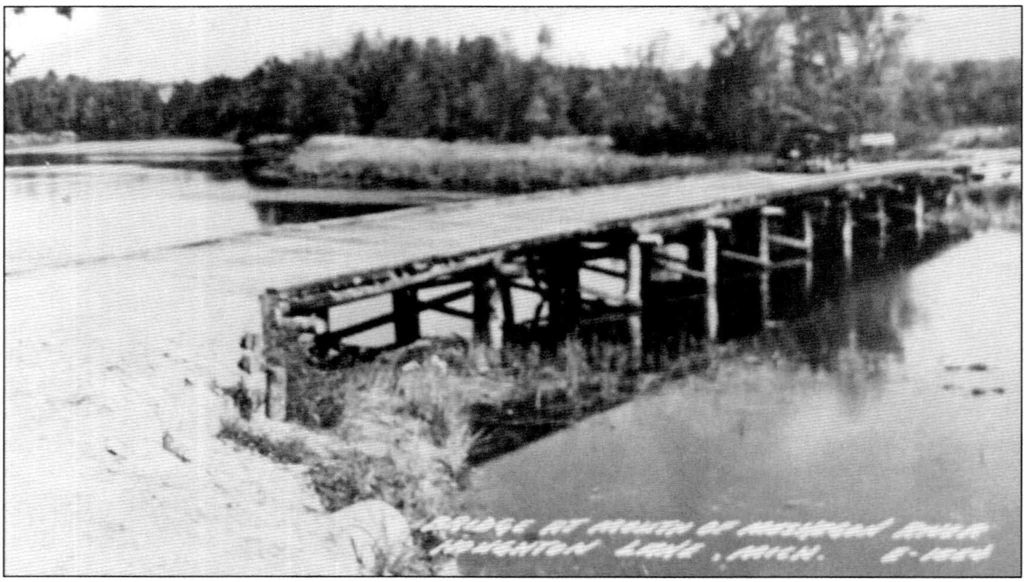

The Civilian Conservation Corps (CCC) built this bridge across the mouth of the Muskegon River, connecting the north shore to the west shore. Emmett Sullivan was a foreman for the CCC. This bridge was removed in the late 1960s, and the road was rerouted just north of the bridge. (Courtesy of Dr. Jim Sullivan.)

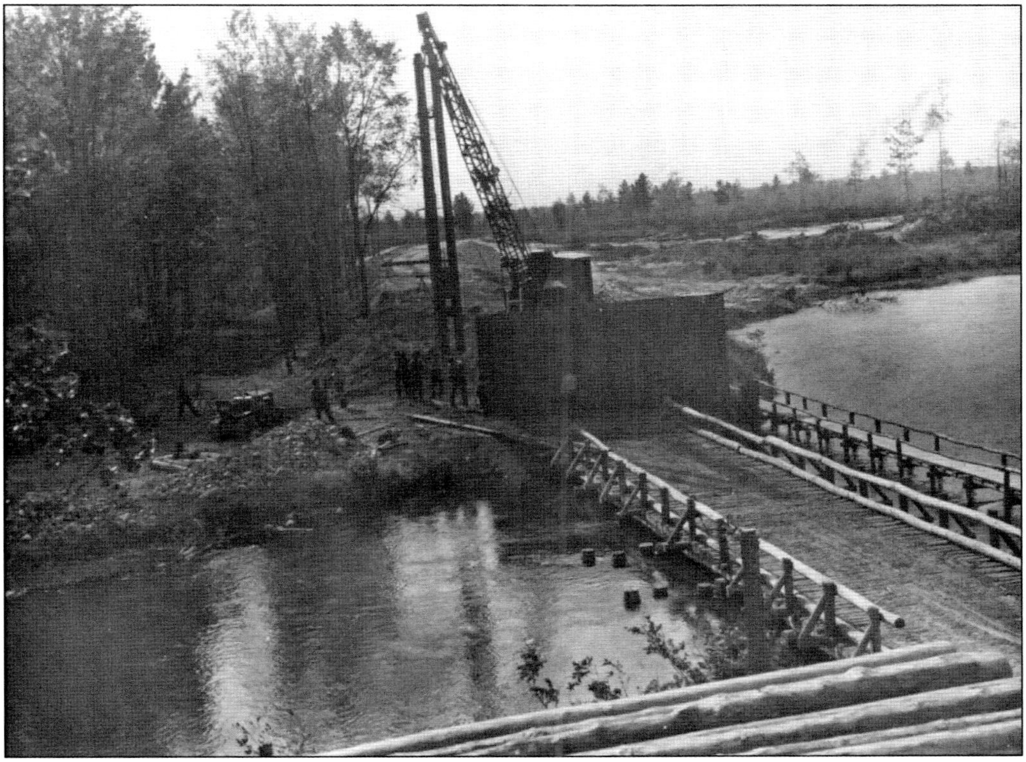

Reedsburg Dam was another very important project the CCC completed in the Houghton Lake area, in 1940. Water levels in the lake could vary seasonally. Residents in a low area could experience flooding during the spring rains, while those at the high part of the lake did not have enough water to float their boats near the shore in the middle of the summer. The dam allows for the level of the lake to be raised and lowered by the insertion or removal of boards. The photograph below shows the dam fully open. Emmett Sullivan was the foreman on this project. The dam still operates today. (Both courtesy of Dr. Jim Sullivan.)

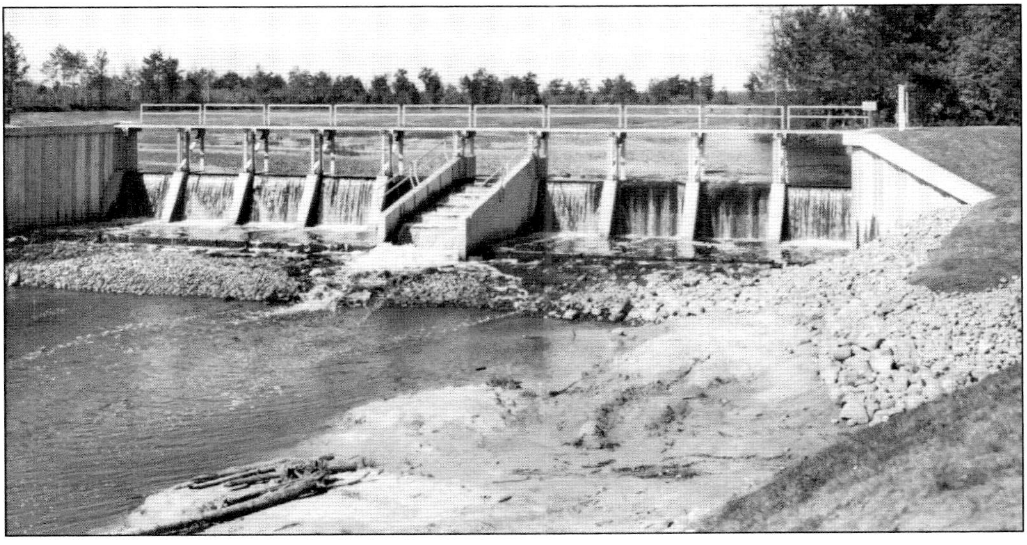

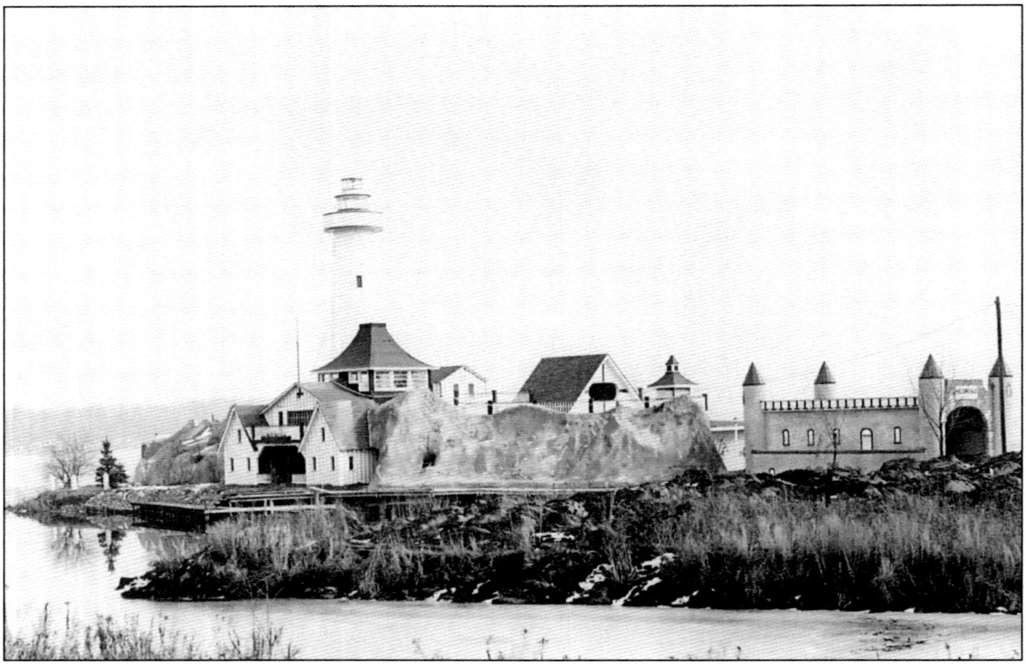

Hazen Isle was a private project of Hazen Randall. He filled in the land on Long Point and built a lighthouse and installed a showboat on his island. He started building it in the late 1950s. He never lived there, but after he retired, he would go to his island every day to work on projects. In the early 1970s, Randall leased it to the Shefflys, who operated a restaurant in the showboat. It was known for its Friday fish fries. Randall sold Hazen Isle in 1977. It was destroyed by fire in December 1990. (Both courtesy of Vera Parsons.)

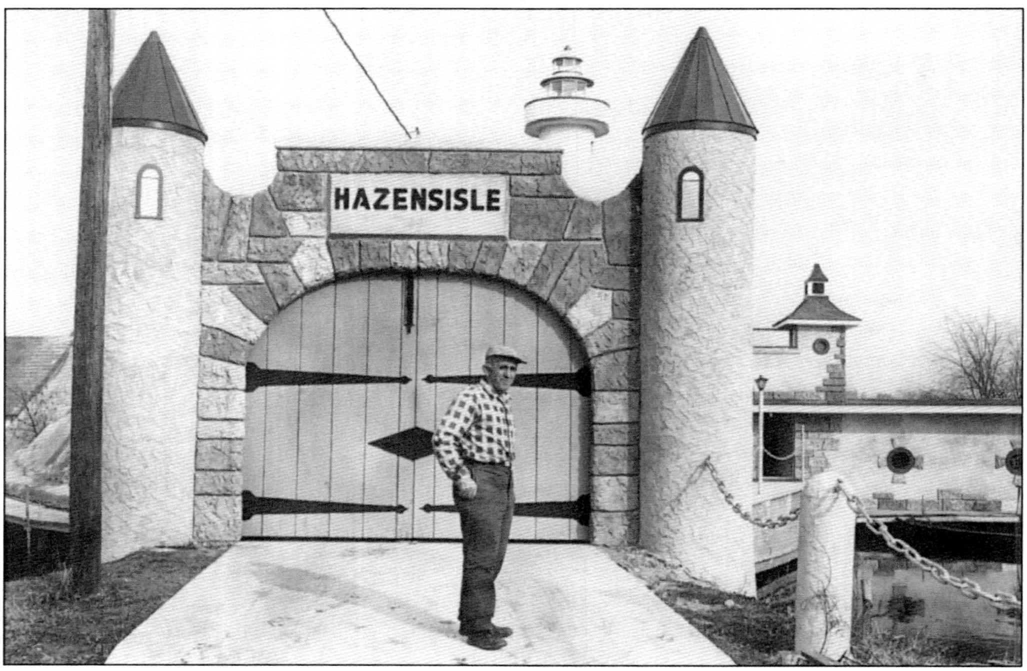

Two

MARKEY TOWNSHIP

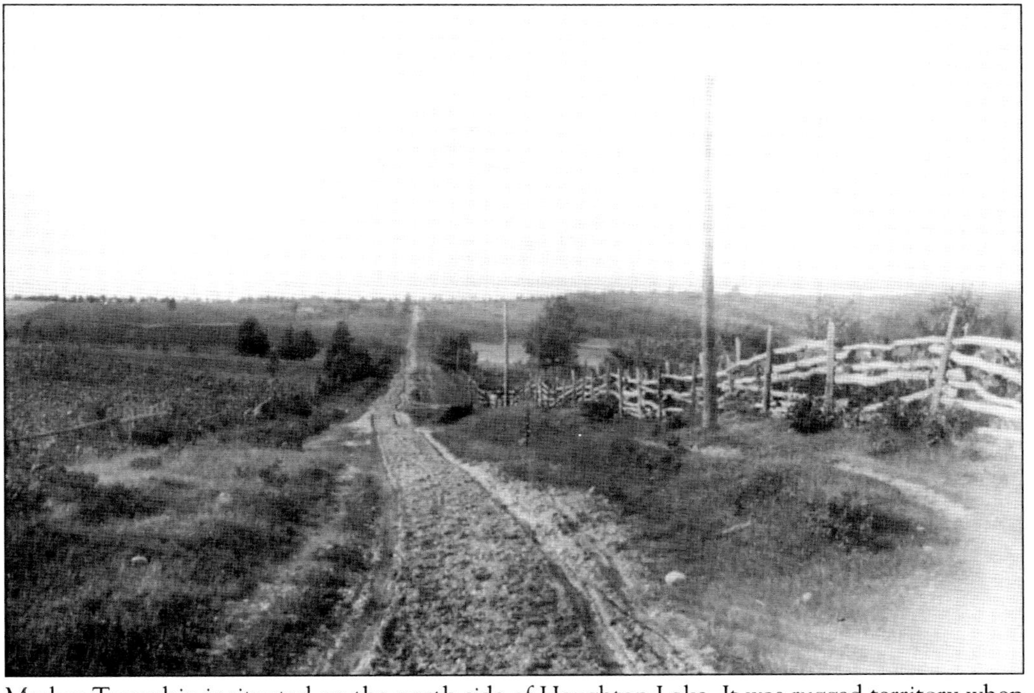

Markey Township is situated on the north side of Houghton Lake. It was rugged territory when the first settlers arrived to timber the land. Among early residents were Nate Carrick, Al Sergeant, and William Doyle. They bought acreage to timber, or they worked for Nels Michelson. These families are still part of the Houghton Lake community. This 1912 photograph of Markey Road shows how rough the trails were. (Courtesy of Markey Township.)

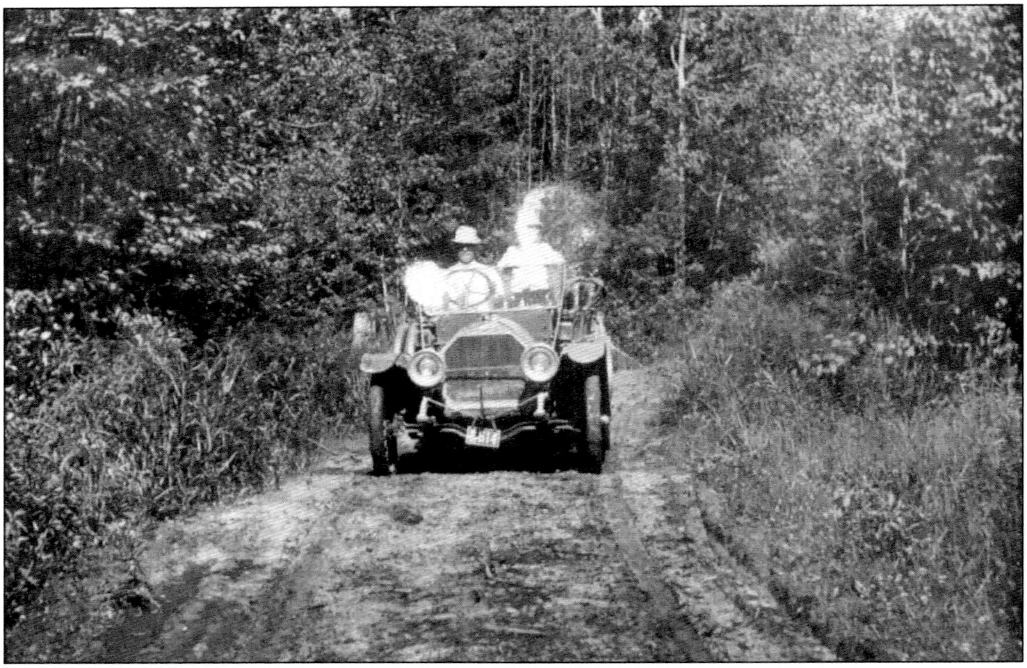

Most of Markey Township was heavily wooded. In the early 1900s, travel was slow and difficult, because the roads were only trails through the woods. (Courtesy of Markey Township.)

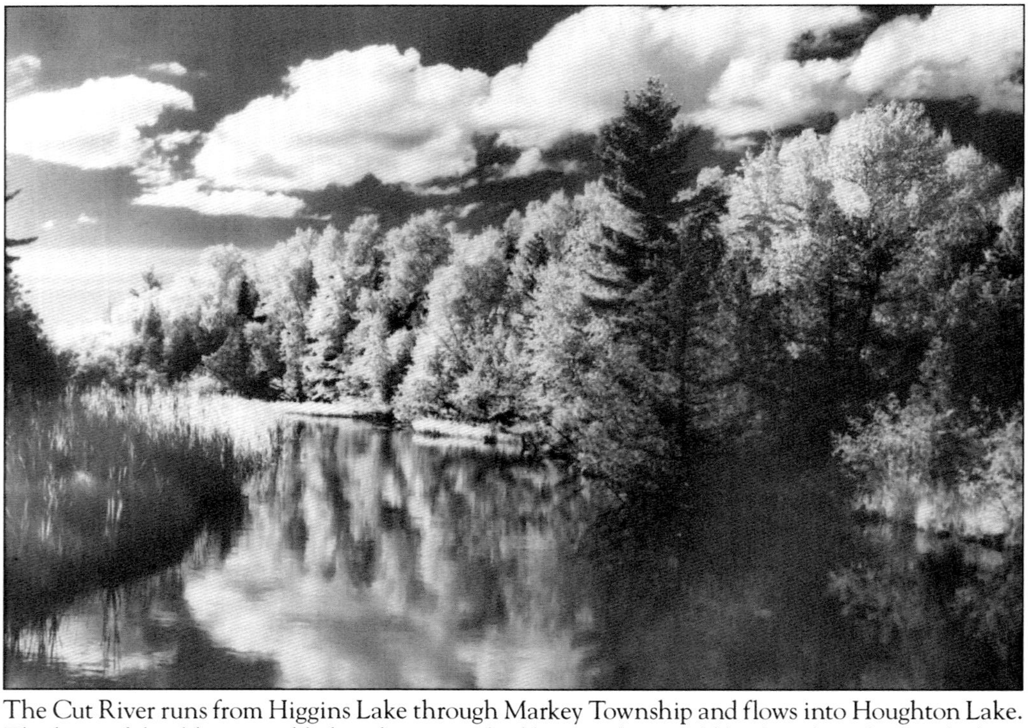

The Cut River runs from Higgins Lake through Markey Township and flows into Houghton Lake. The beautiful wilderness added to the untouched beauty that could be found on the north shore of the lake. (Courtesy of Markey Township.)

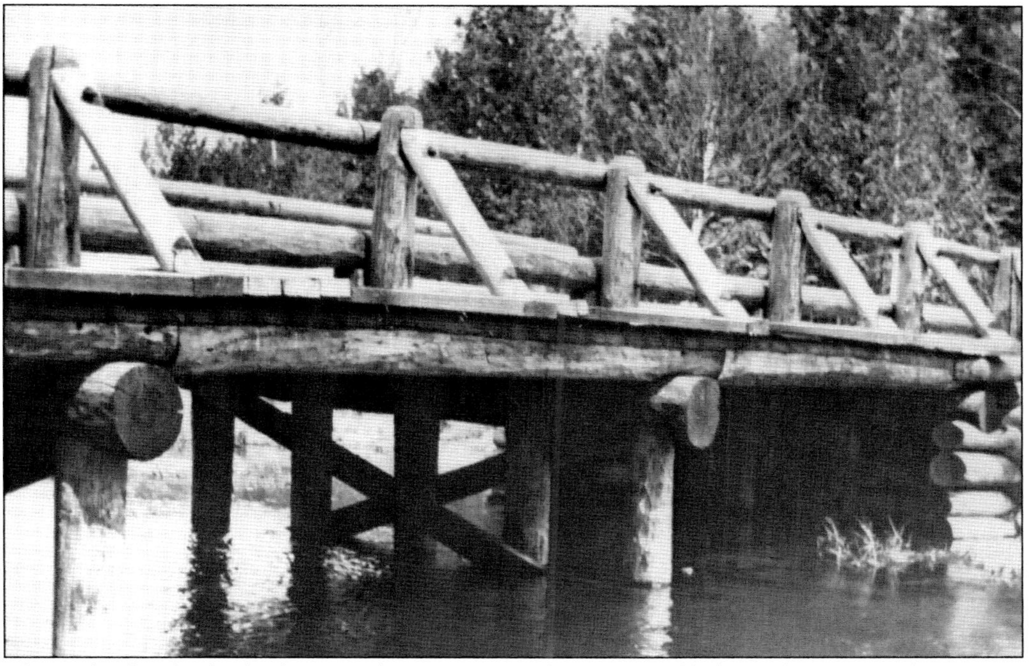

This is the first bridge built across the Cut River. This span enabled people to get to the western part of the township, helping to alleviate some of the isolation of the community. (Courtesy of Markey Township.)

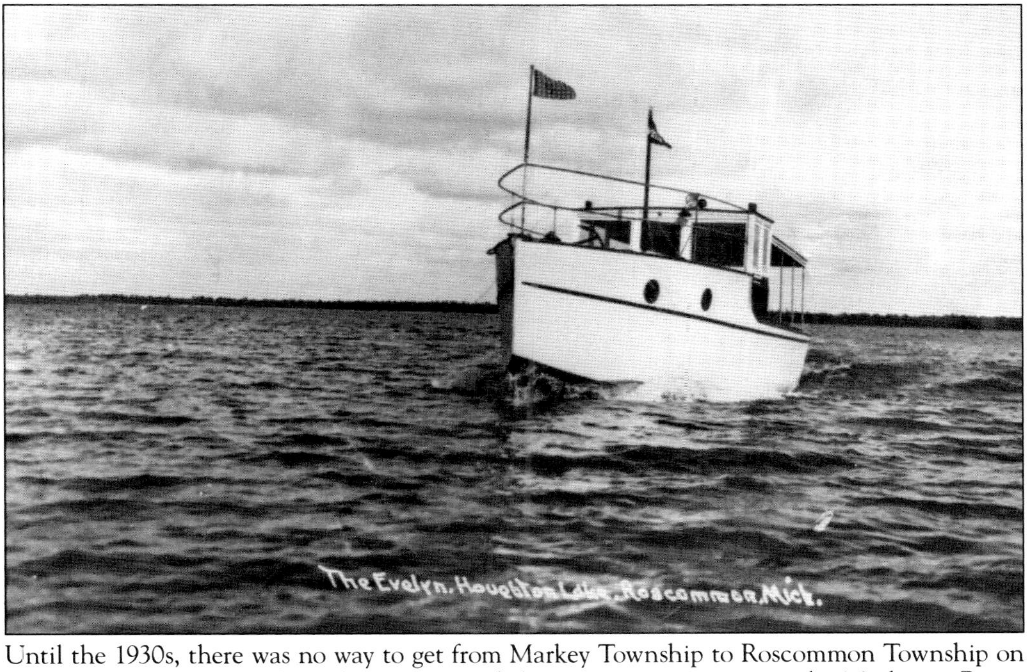

Until the 1930s, there was no way to get from Markey Township to Roscommon Township on land. There were no roads in the swamp, and there was no way to cross the Muskegon River. Boats, like the *Evelyn* (shown here), carried passengers across the water. Boats were also used for sightseeing tours. (Courtesy of Markey Township.)

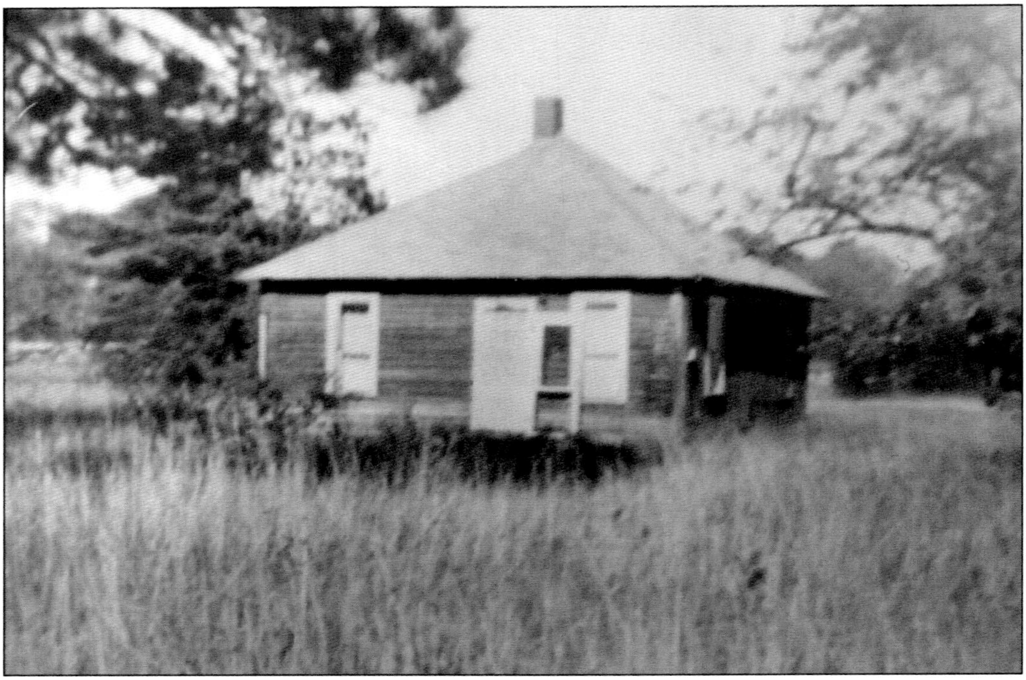

The first post office in Markey was in Mrs. Dewitt's home on Markey Road. Besides running the post office, she also served the community as a nurse and midwife. Eventually, postal service was operated out of Sharp's Corners in Higgins Lake. (Courtesy of Markey Township.)

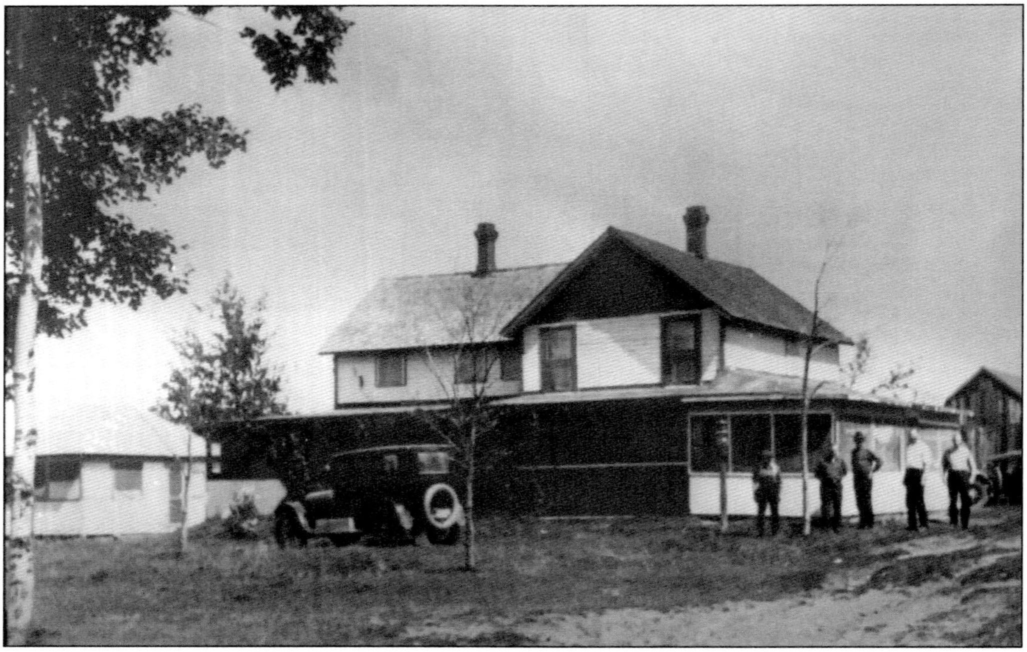

The Breaugh Lodge was built in 1920 by Stan and Mary Breaugh. It was located on a 20-acre parcel on the north shore of Houghton Lake. The lodge attracted vacationers who came to the area to fish Houghton Lake. (Courtesy of Markey Township.)

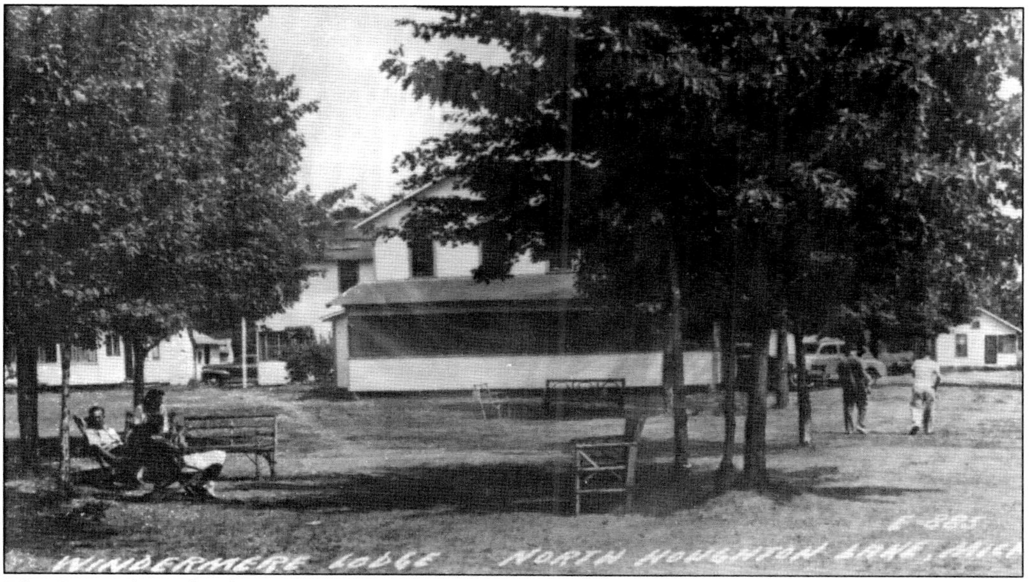

The Breaugh Lodge became the Windermere Lodge, and cabins were added to accommodate guests. The lodge operated on the American plan, and guests took their meals in the dining room in the lodge. Boats and fishing supplies were also available for guests. In 1964, Mary Breaugh sold the Windermere to Russ Kwaiser, who came from Saginaw. He and his family operated it in the summer until 1975, when they installed a natural-gas boiler and opened the lodge for year-round business. Kwaiser's son Joe and his sister Patricia Meyer run the resort today. Some changes have been made to the interior, but the exterior is the same. (Courtesy of Markey Township.)

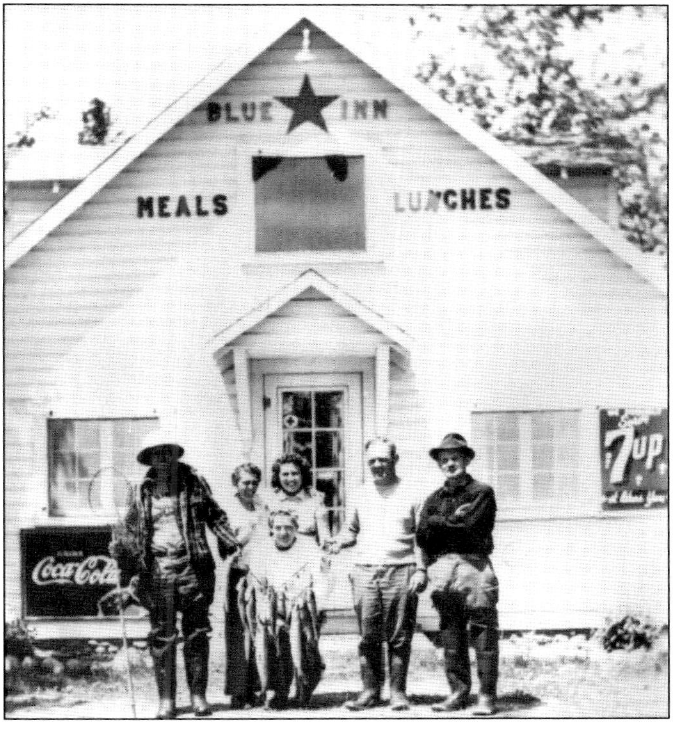

The Blue Star Inn was a small diner in Markey Township. It no longer exists, and little is known about it. In its day, it appeared to be popular with the fishing crowd. (Courtesy of Markey Township.)

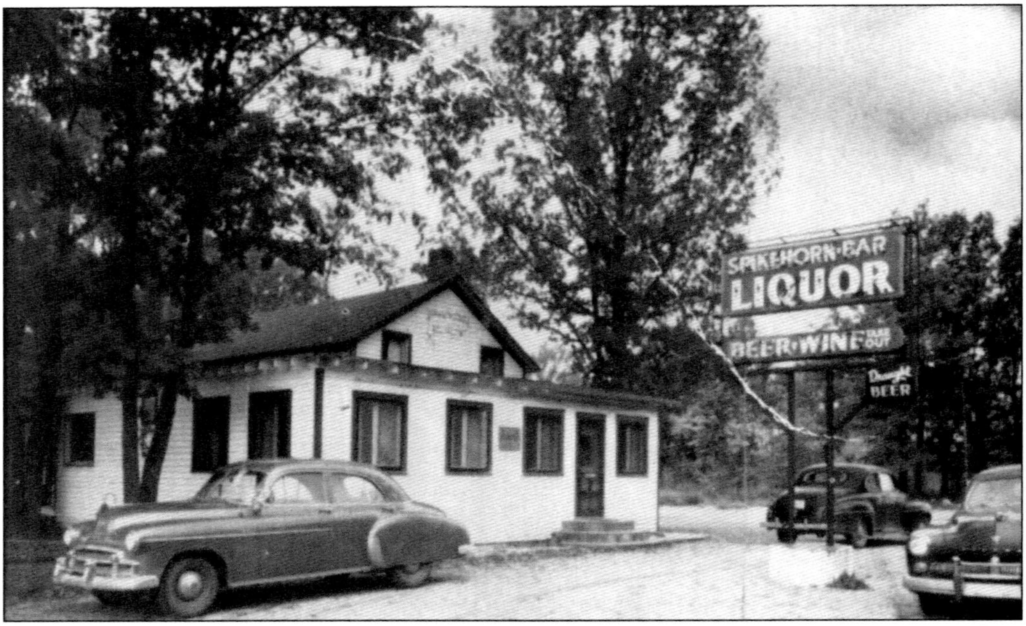

The Spikehorn Bar was built in the early 1930s, before electricity came to Markey Township. It was owned for many years by Bill DuVall. Hank Matulawitz was the second owner, and he in turn sold the establishment to Jack and John Garvin in 1992. The Garvins changed the name to Spikehorn Restaurant and Lounge. They also enlarged the building. (Courtesy of the Spikehorn Restaurant and Lounge.)

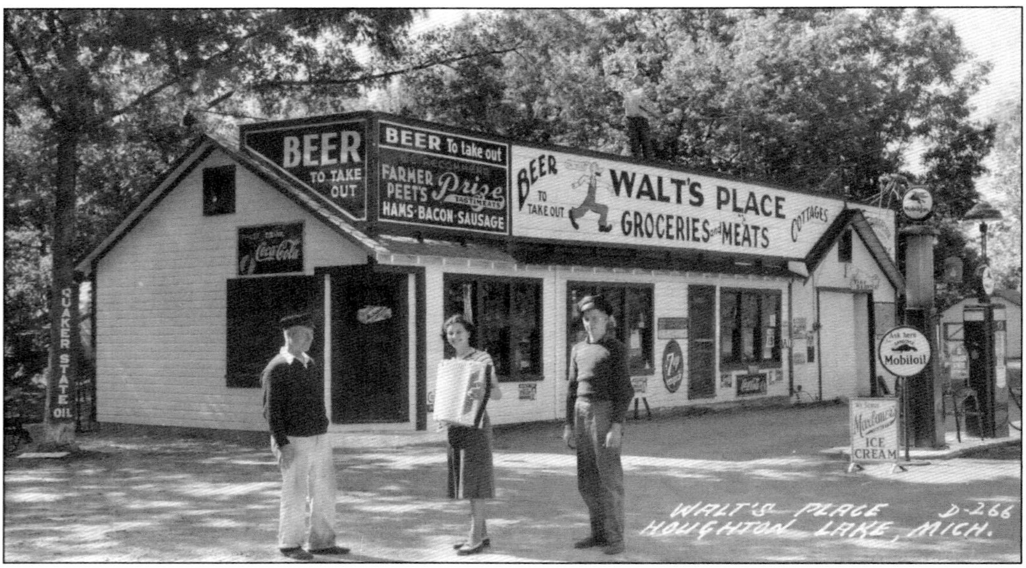

Mini and Walt Davidson owned Walt's Place in the 1930s. It offered many services for its customers, including the sale of groceries, beer, and gasoline. Tires were repaired at Walt's, and the establishment rented cabins. Visible in this photograph is the dummy on the roof, holding a fishing pole dangling a worm over the sign. Walt's became Van's Trading Post in the 1950s. It remained in business into the 1990s, although the ownership had changed. It was closed in the mid-1990s, and it eventually burned down. (Courtesy of Markey Township.)

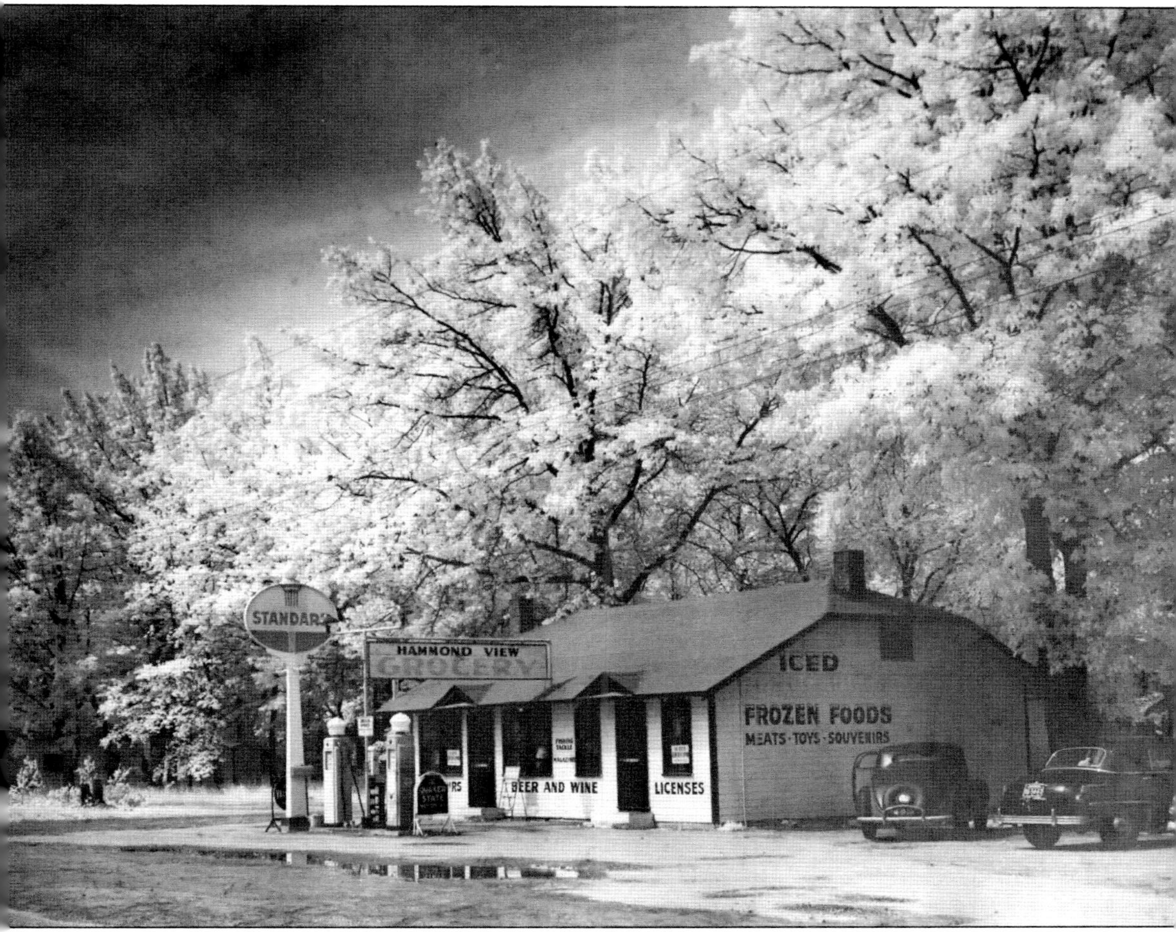

Hammond View was across the side street from Walt's Place. A Standard gas station, it also sold groceries, beer, and wine, and it rented cabins. The store also sold souvenirs, which were always a hit with vacationers. Hammond View is still in operation as a convenience store. (Courtesy of Markey Township.)

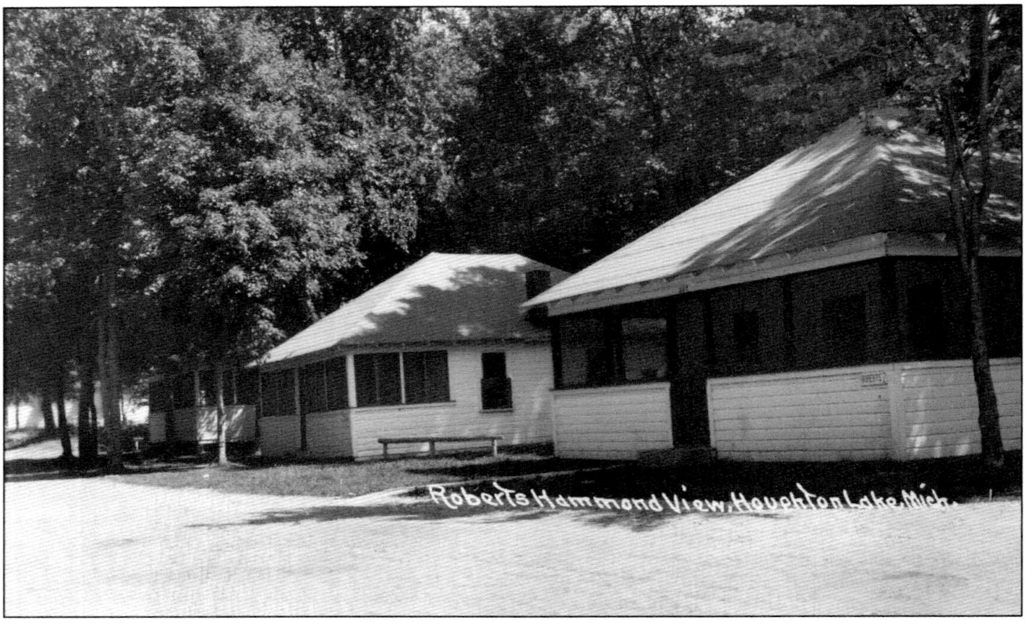

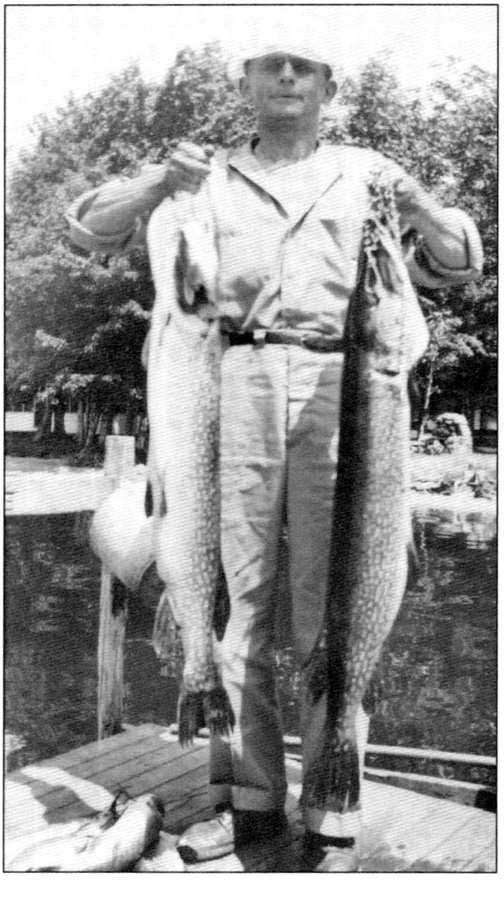

The Hammond View cabins were near the grocery and had lake access. Many guests came in pursuit of the fishing, hoping to catch the big one. The photograph at left shows Al Schear and the 40-inch northern pike he caught on Houghton Lake in the 1950s. (Both courtesy of Markey Township.)

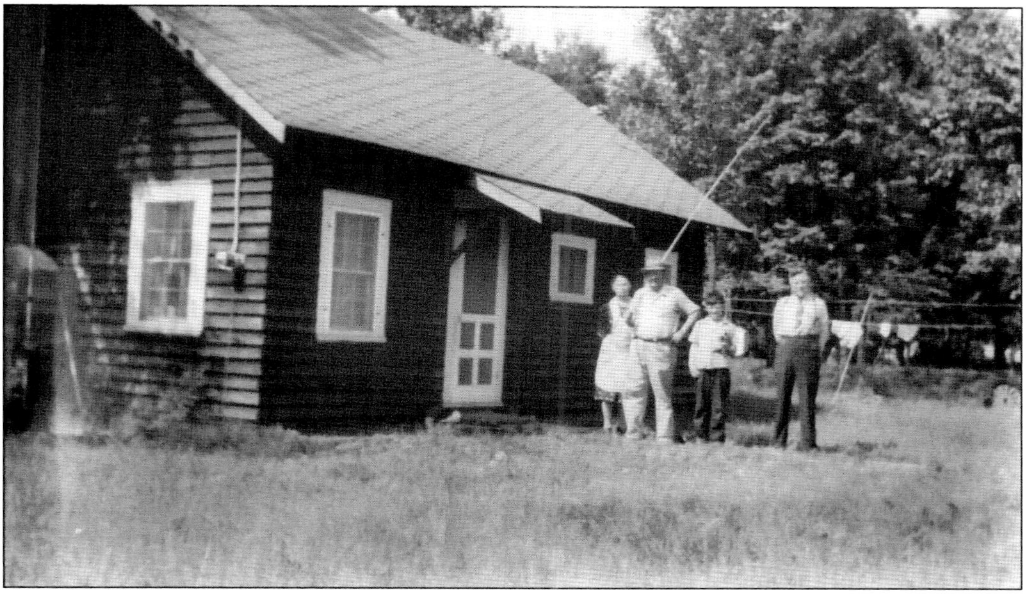

Many people built cottages to get away from the city. The photograph above shows the Foxworthy cottage. Posing in front of it are, from left to right, Mr. and Mrs. Ira Foxworthy, Fritz Hanson, and an unidentified man in June 1941. Below, the Hanson children pose with the Foxworthys and a great catch of northern pike in 1938. The Hansons are, in front from left to right, Fritz, Peter, and Bea. (Both courtesy of Markey Township.)

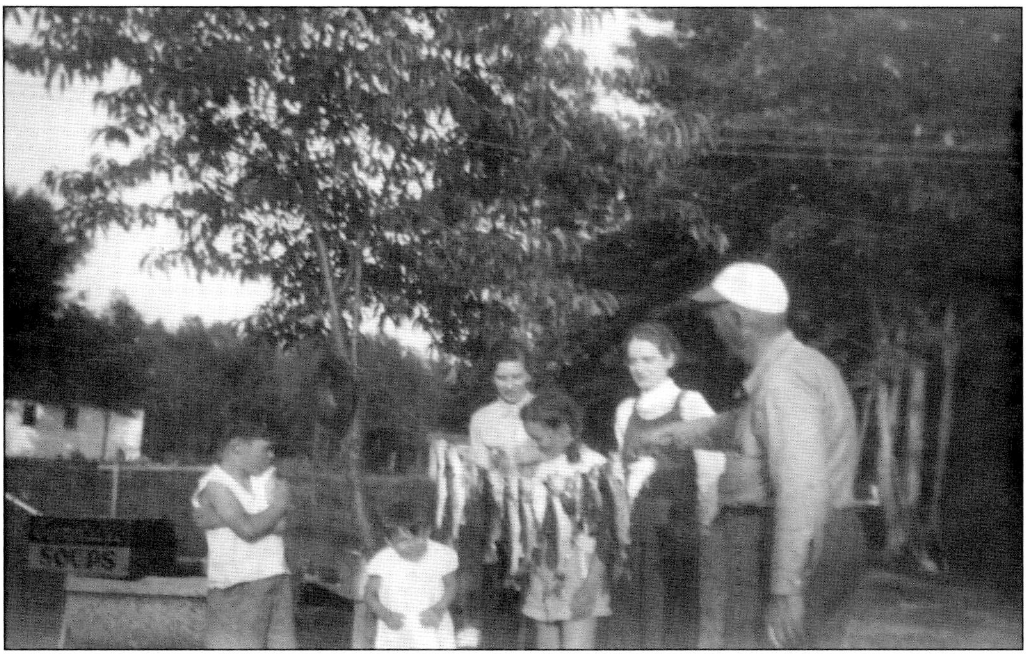

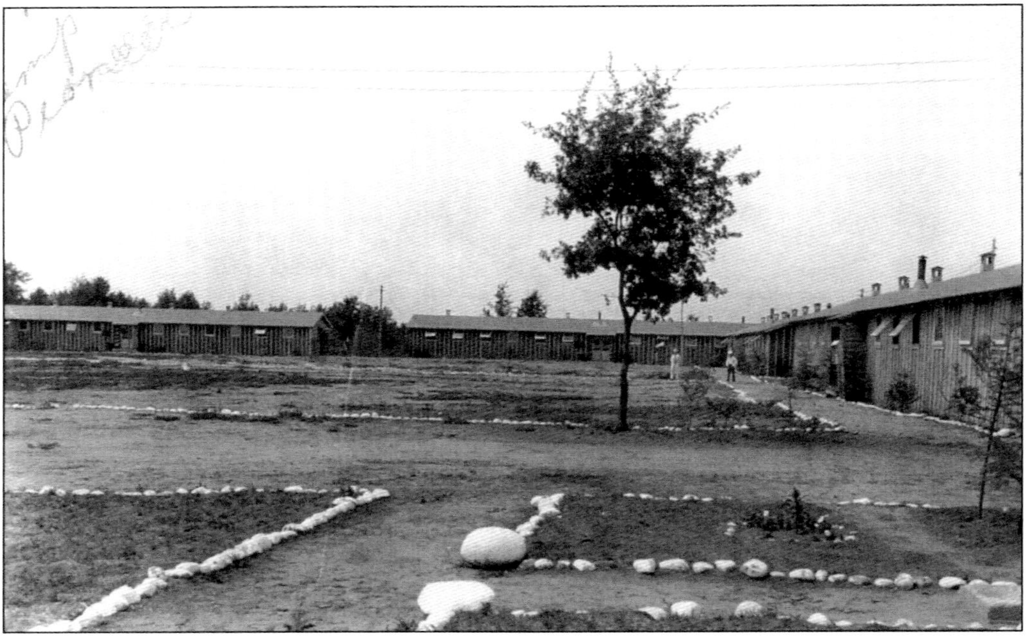

Markey Township, like all communities, felt the pain of the Great Depression. The Civilian Conservation Corps (CCC) was a welcomed work program in the area. Not only did it give local men employment, it also made many improvements to communities, like building bridges and helping with the State of Michigan's reforestation project in the 1930s. Camp Pioneer (above) was in Markey Township. The photograph below shows CCC workers at Camp Pioneer. (Both courtesy of Markey Township.)

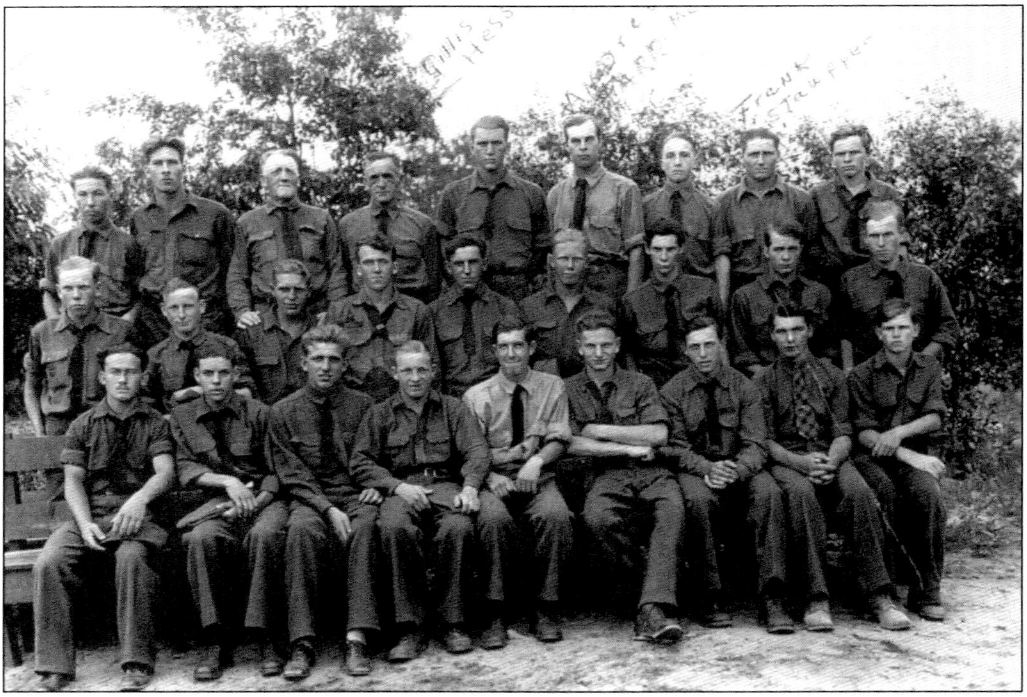

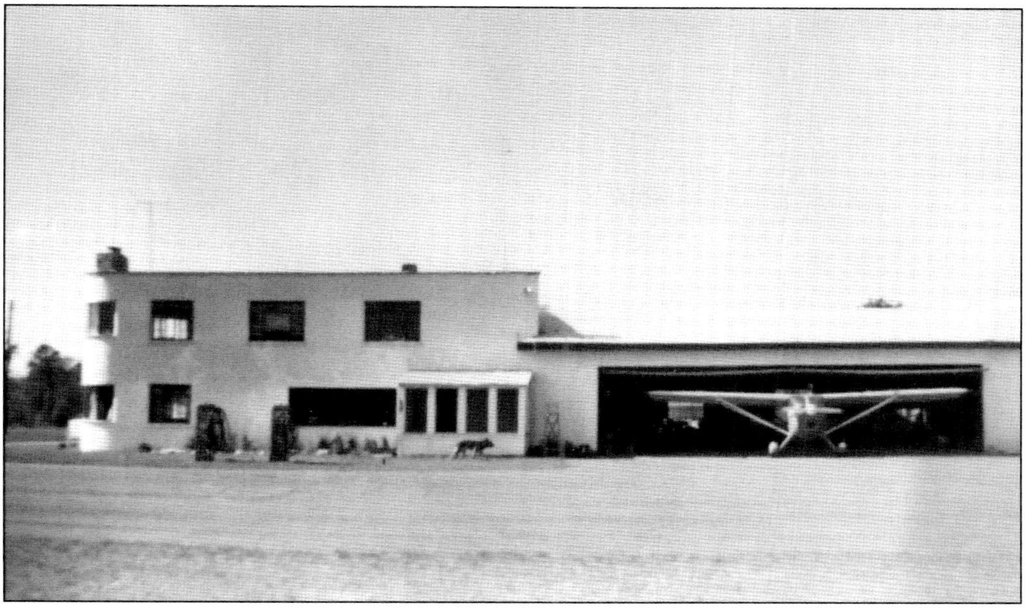

An airport was sought, to make access easier to Markey Township. The township officials worked with the county board of commissioners to start the airport. The runways were built in 1946, and Milton De Potty was the first fixed base operator. He had a 10-year contract, after which the county had to purchase the airport and continue to run it. With a grant of $5,000 from the state, the county took over the Roscommon County Airport in 1957. Francis Blodgett became the fixed base operator and ran Blodgett Aviation at the airport. Blodgett retired in the late 1970s, and Dan Hamp became the operator. He ran the airport for a few years, before Francis Blodgett's son Terry took over the airport, remaining in that capacity until his death in the late 1990s. The airport was renamed Blodgett Memorial Airport. In 1954, the US Weather Bureau built a weather station at the Roscommon County Airport. It was closed in the 1980s. (Both courtesy of Markey Township.)

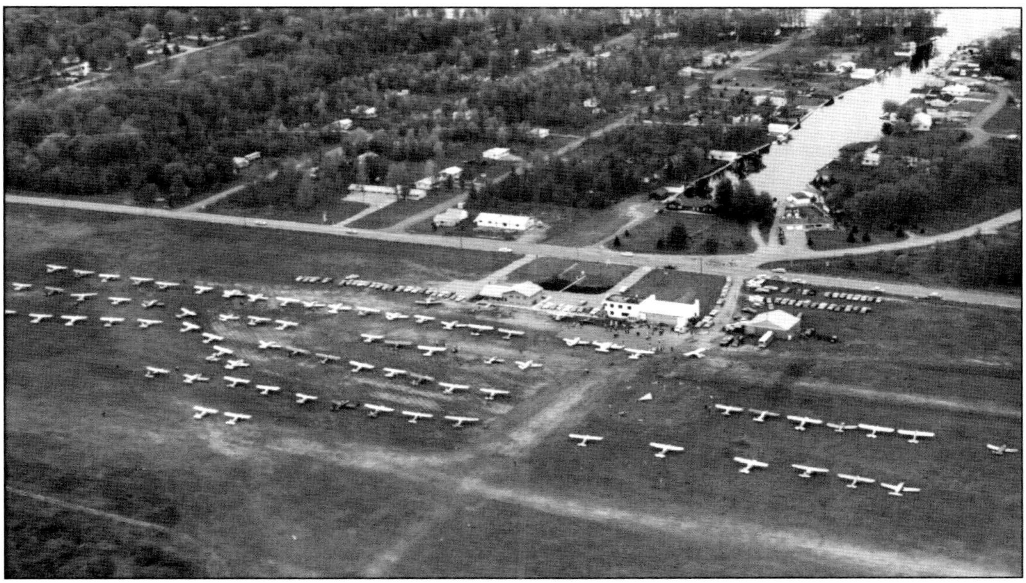

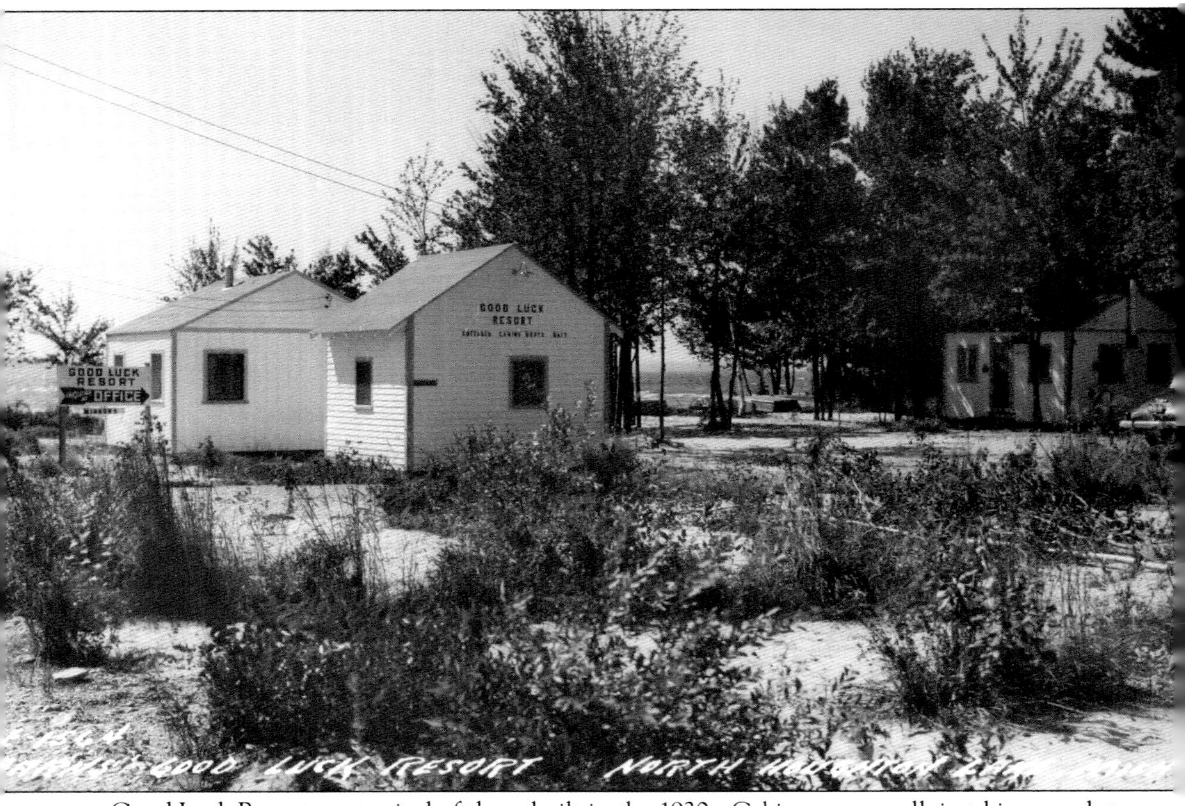

Good Luck Resort was typical of those built in the 1930s. Cabins were small, just big enough to accommodate sleeping, as most of the day was spent on the lake. The land around the cabins, like much of this side of Houghton Lake, was swampland. Sand sucker holes were dug in the lake to backfill the swampy land to build on it. These holes get their name because the machine used on the land sucked the sand out of the lake. The holes are still there today. The locals fish them, but they are controversial, because people have drowned in them. The holes do not suck their victims into them, however. Swimmers come upon them, unaware that they are there, and panic, because the sandy bottom drops off suddenly to very deep water. (Courtesy of Markey Township.)

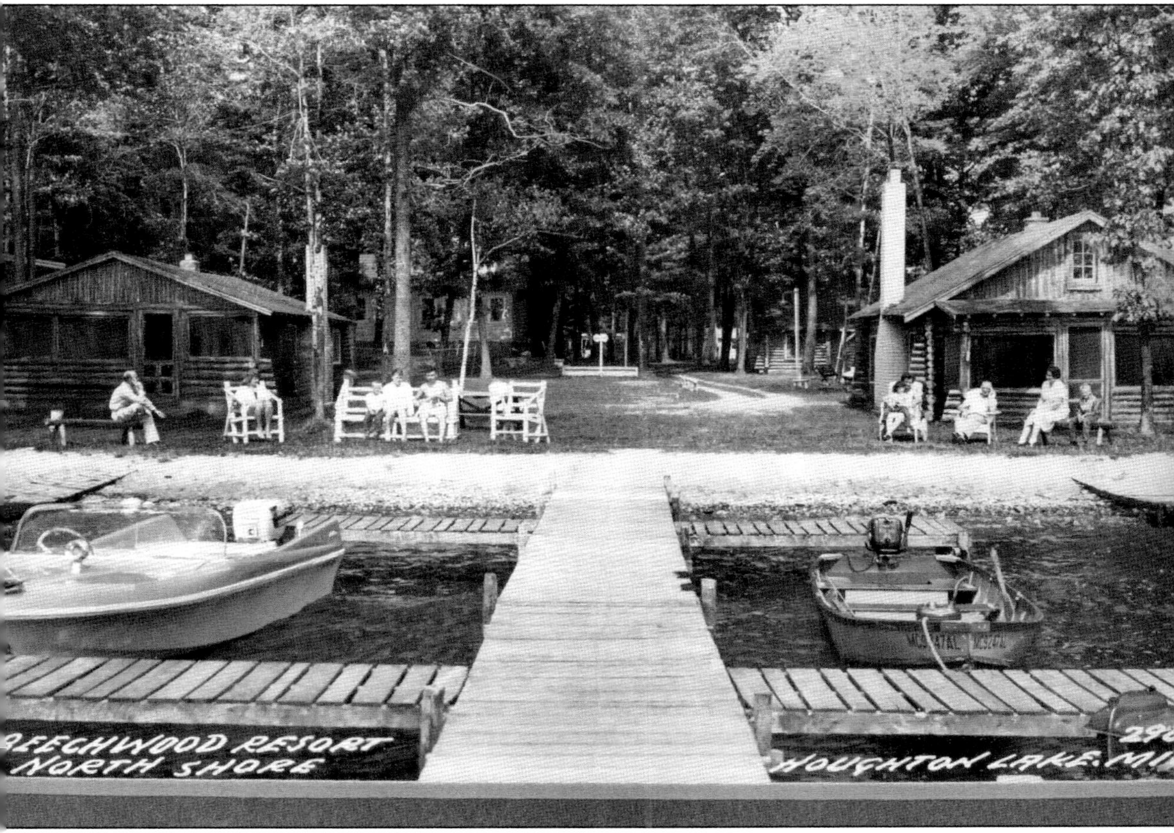

Beachwood Resort offered cottages that were right on the beach. Cottages were always full in the 1950s and 1960s. Fiberglass boats was just becoming popular in the mid-1950s. Soon, fiberglass speedboats were rapidly replacing wooden boats, including on Houghton Lake. They became the boat of choice because of their low maintenance. (Courtesy of Markey Township.)

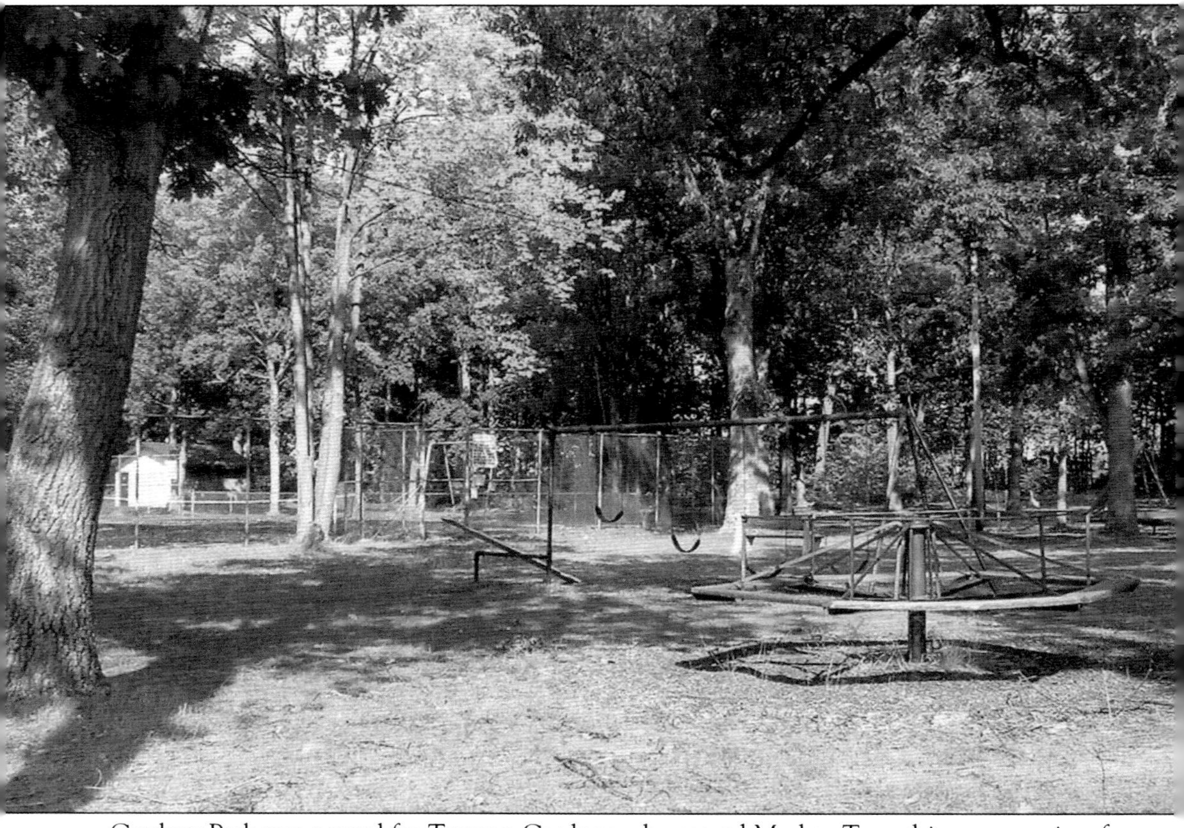

Gardner Park was named for Truman Gardner, who served Markey Township as supervisor for more than 40 years. The park is on County Road 100, across from the Hammond View store. It has playground equipment for children and a tennis court. (Courtesy of Markey Township.)

Three

Denton Township

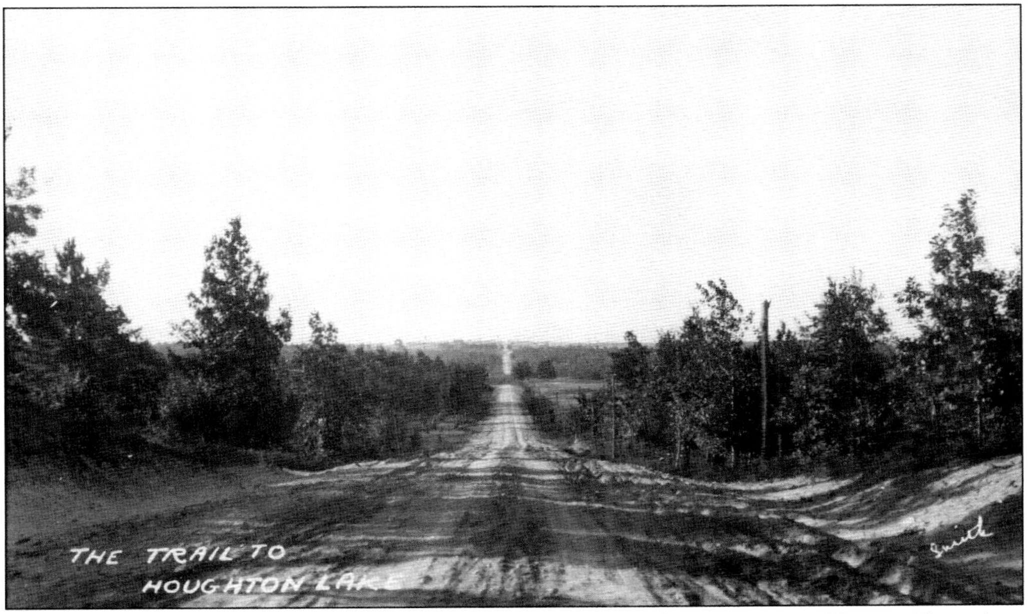

For those who wanted or needed to go to Prudenville, the main business area in Denton Township, travel was hard. M-18, the main road to Houghton Lake from Roscommon, was a corduroy road making a trail through the swamps and forests that separate Houghton Lake from the county seat in Roscommon.

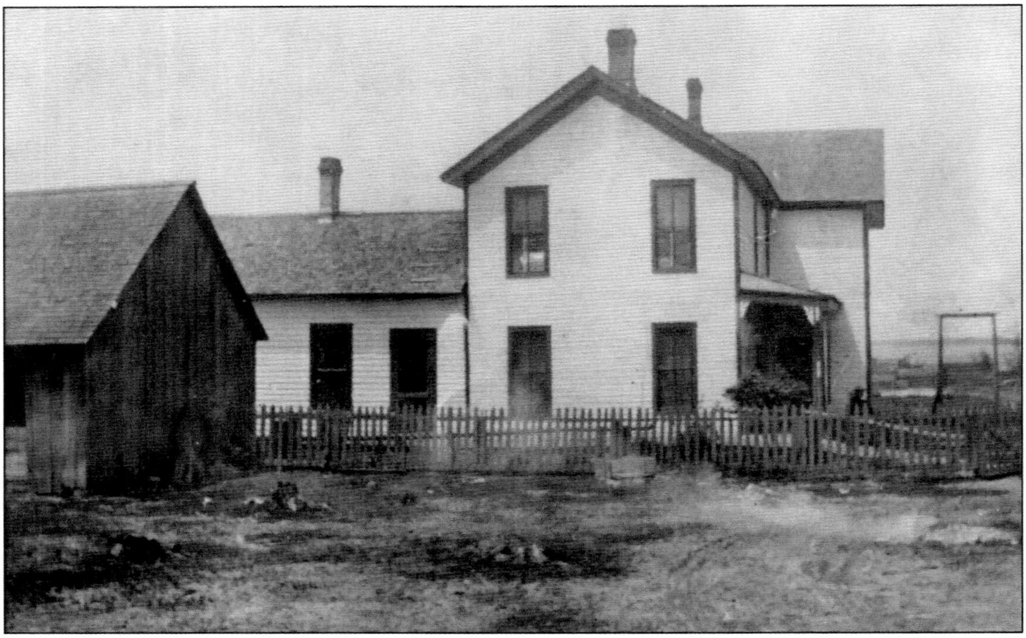

Following the end of the timber industry, folks who did not mind the rugged surroundings of Houghton Lake came for the abundant fish. The Decatur House was the gathering place for the Houghton Lake Fishing Club, a group of people from Decatur, Illinois, who came each summer. The club, which dates to 1905, bought the former Harcourt House, which was owned by Tom Harcourt and Bridget Sullivan. It was located in Prudenville, where Eddie's Bar is today. (Courtesy of Dr. Jim Sullivan.)

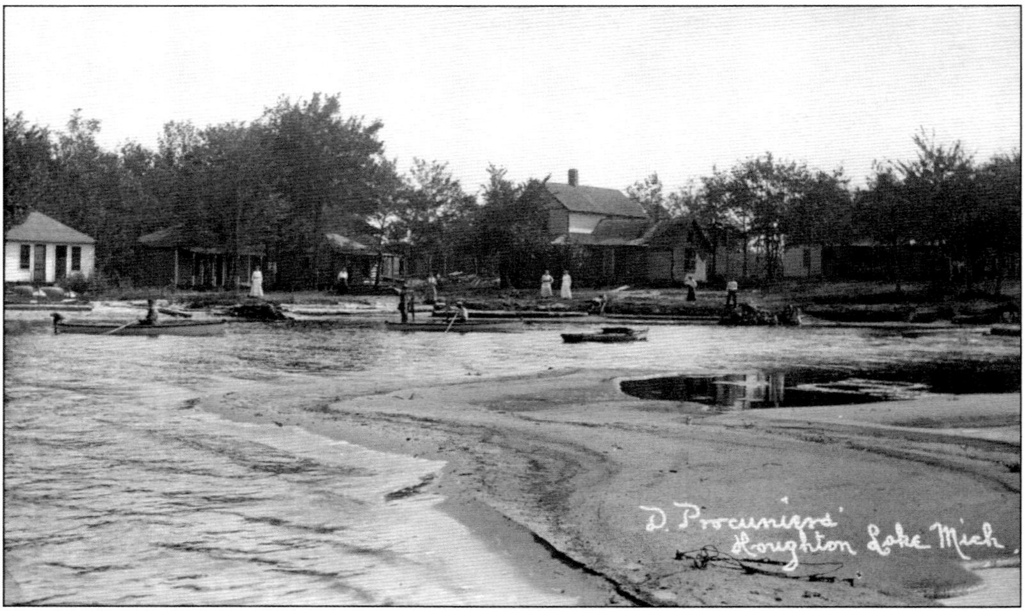

The Procuriner Hotel began its existence as the repurposed log schoolhouse in Prudenville. A second story was later added to the building. The Procuriner also had cottages on the lakeshore, providing its guests with access to the lake for fishing. (Courtesy of Dr. Jim Sullivan.)

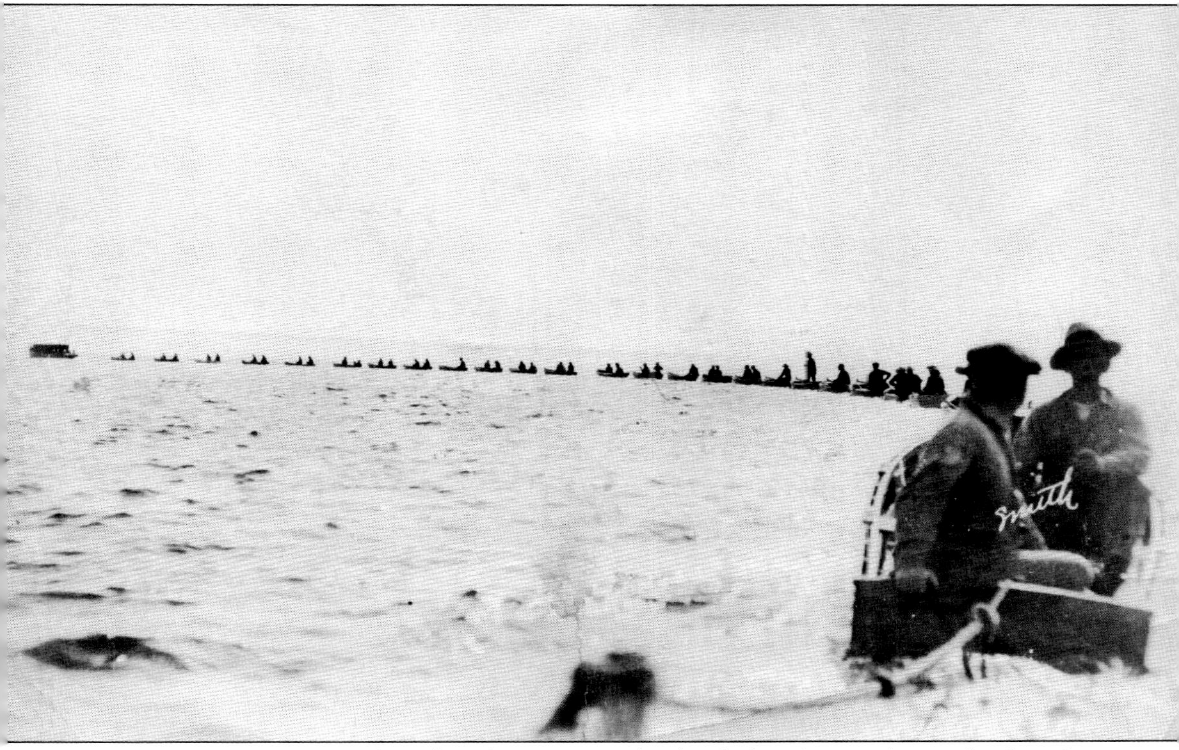

Fishing brought visitors to Prudenville. About 1919, in the days before the popularity of outboard motors, there were only two ways to get to the fishing grounds: row the boat or be towed. The latter was the preferred method, devised by a local resident. A large boat, like the *Adventurer*, would tie a string of boats to each other and haul people out for a day of fishing. It would then return to pick the boats up. This became so popular that tow service was available all around the lake. Unfortunately, in 1933, the method's shortcoming was realized. On a June afternoon, a bad storm kicked up. Waves were reported as high as 10 feet. The launch operators scrambled to get the fishermen off the water, but four people drowned in the storm.

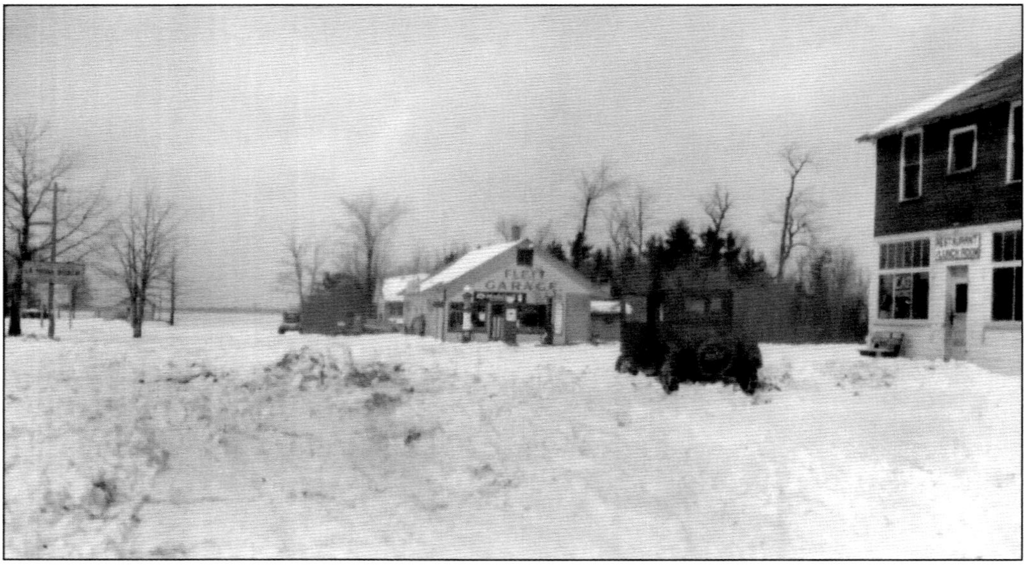

Winter in Denton Township could be just as hard as summer storms. The Flett Garage stood at the corner of what would become M-18 and M-55. Detmer's Hotel was on the opposite corner. The hotel was built in the 1920s, after the Ontario Hotel, owned by John E. Harcourt and his wife, Elizabeth Sullivan, was moved to Denton Creek.

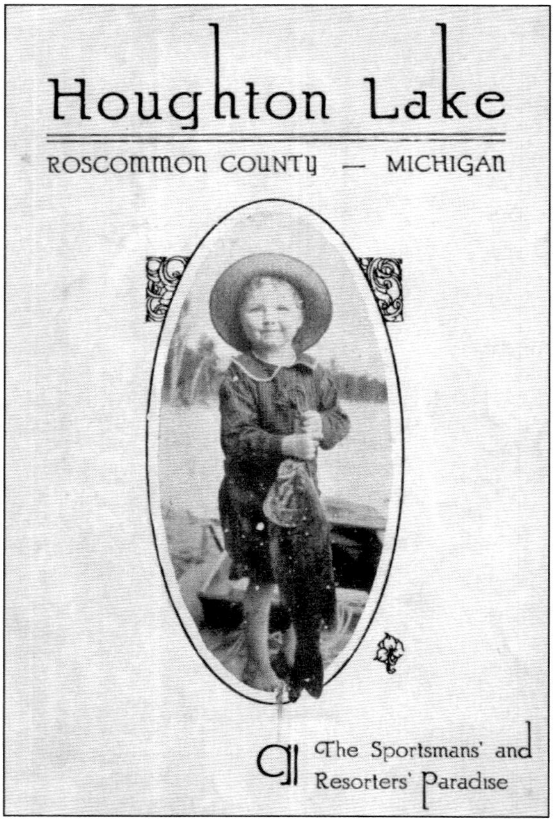

With the end of the lumber industry, speculators began to subdivide tracks of land around the lake. Hiram R. Smith of Roscommon and Glen Smith of Detroit were two men who saw the value of the cutover lakeshore land, buying property on the north side of the East Bay.

The Smiths called their subdivision Trails End and created the marketing booklet shown here to sell their land. The subdivision featured high ground on the lakeshore, which were desirable lots. The Smiths set aside an area on the lakeshore, called Smith Park, to allow back-lot owners to have a beach. Over the years, this park became part of the property adjacent to the park. Farther down Old Trail Drive, a second subdivision was created, called Sandy Shores. These lots, located in the low ground, were made by backfilling the land from sand sucked out of the lake. The holes left in the lake are still good fishing spots today.

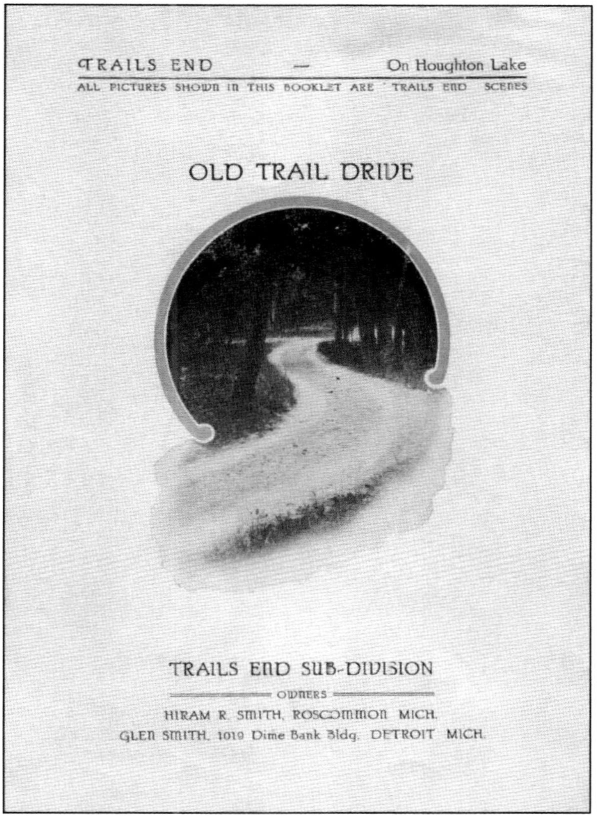

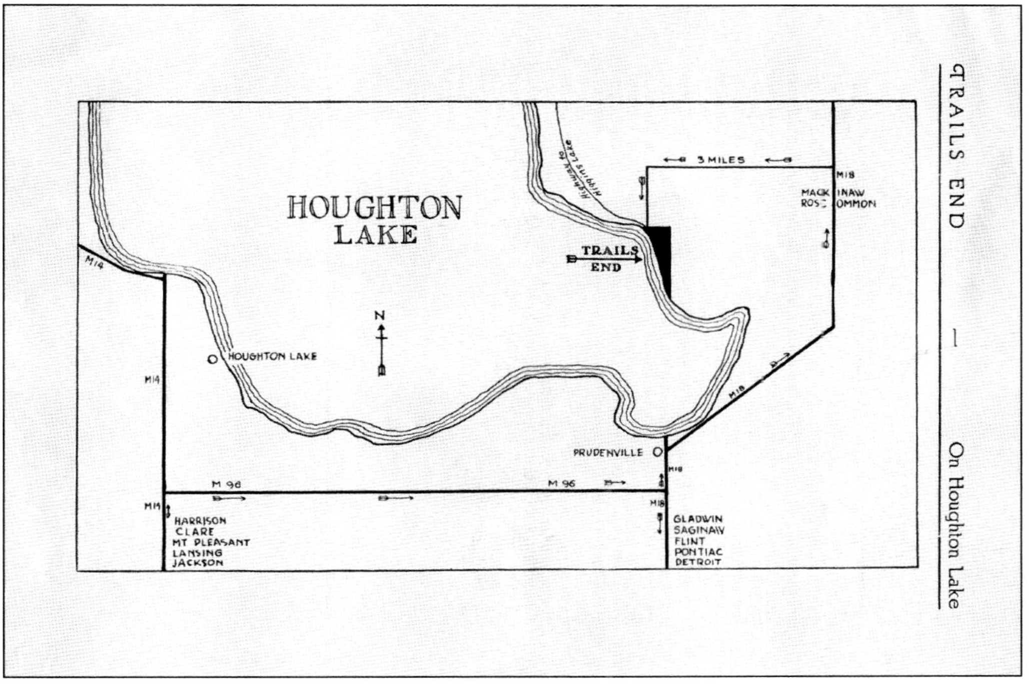

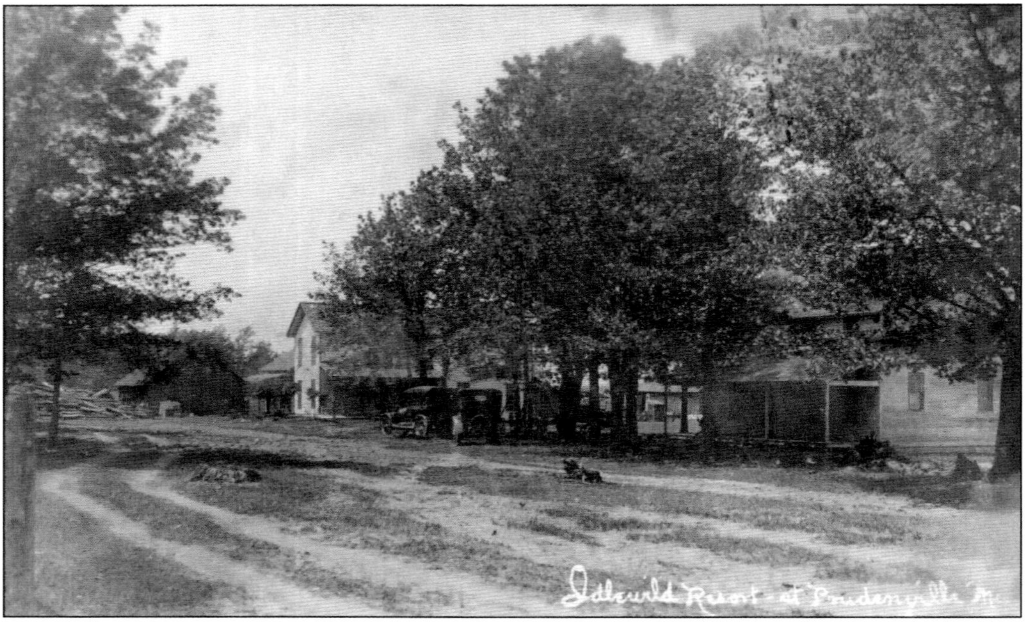

Across the East Bay in Prudenville, the Idlewild Resort was built by Roy McKibben. It operated well into the late 1950s. It fell victim to fire but was rebuilt. Like in many places, a dance hall was part of a well-appointed resort in the early 20th century. Until Frank Johnson built Johnson's Rustic Dance Place, the Idlewild was the only dance hall in the village of Prudenville. (Both courtesy of Dr. Jim Sullivan.)

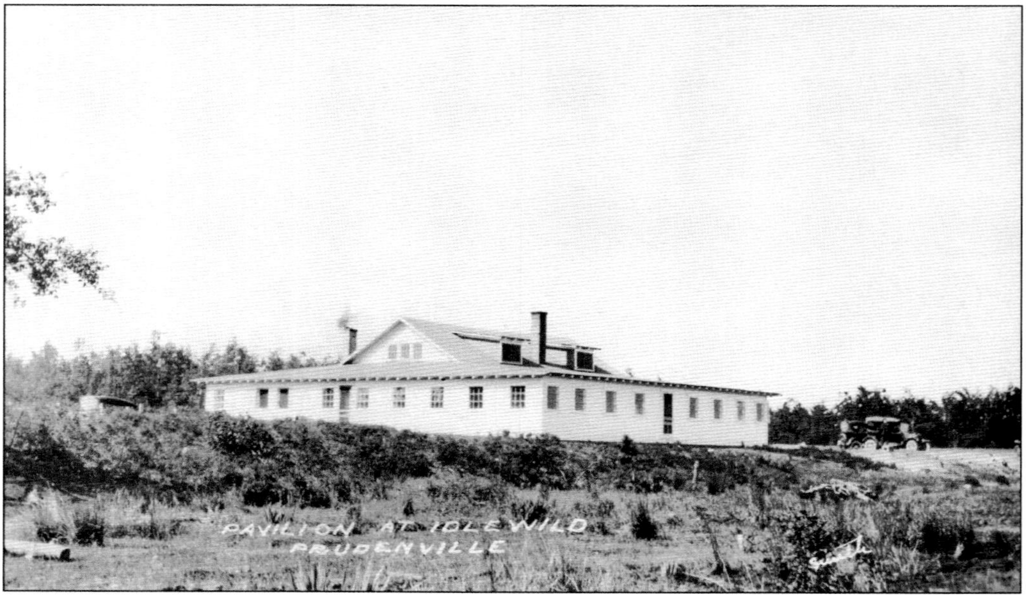

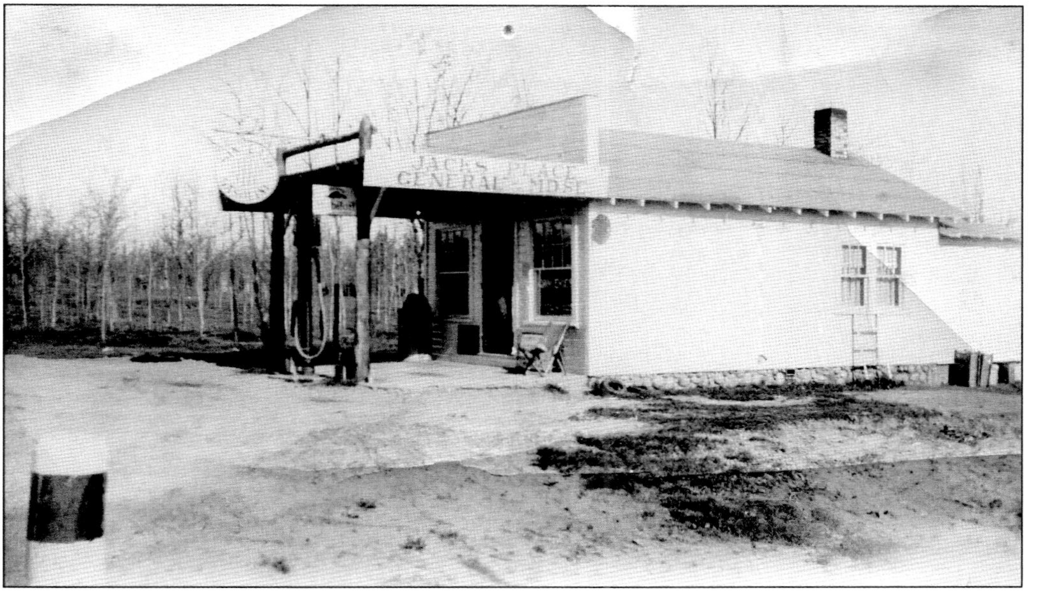

The Wickham family settled farther down M-55, in the area of Guernsey Street. Jack's Place (above) was a one-pump gas station that stood on the corner of these two roads. William Wickham kept a small bear, called Teddy, at this location (below). Many people in the area kept bears as tourist attractions. (Both courtesy of Bob Zavitz.)

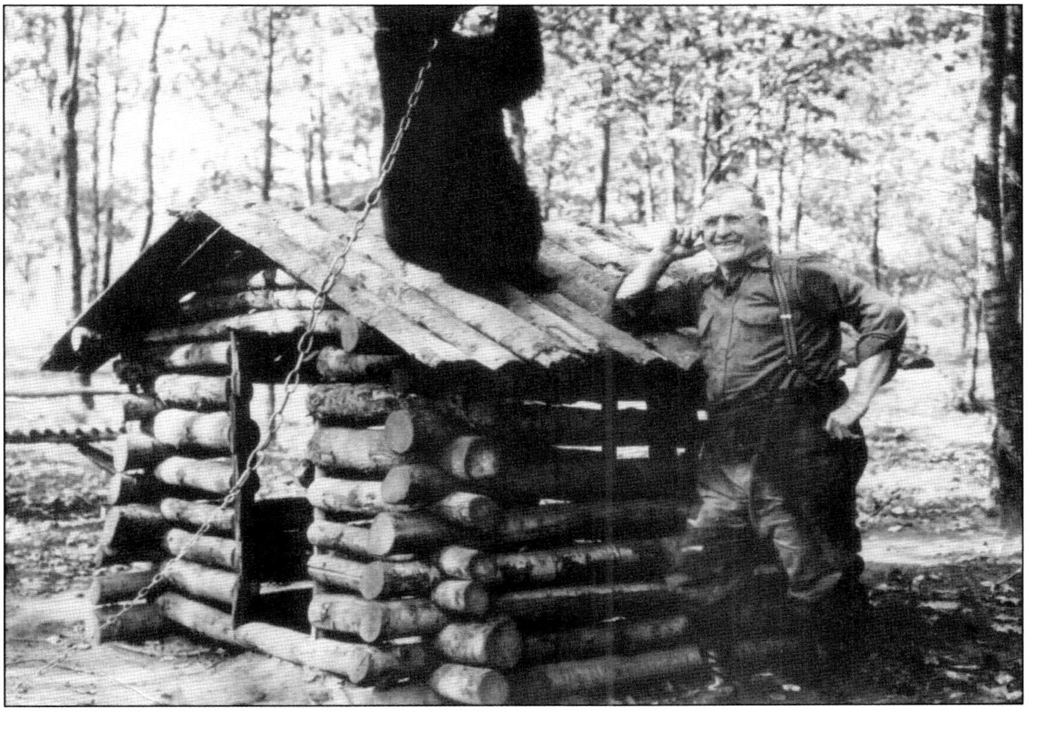

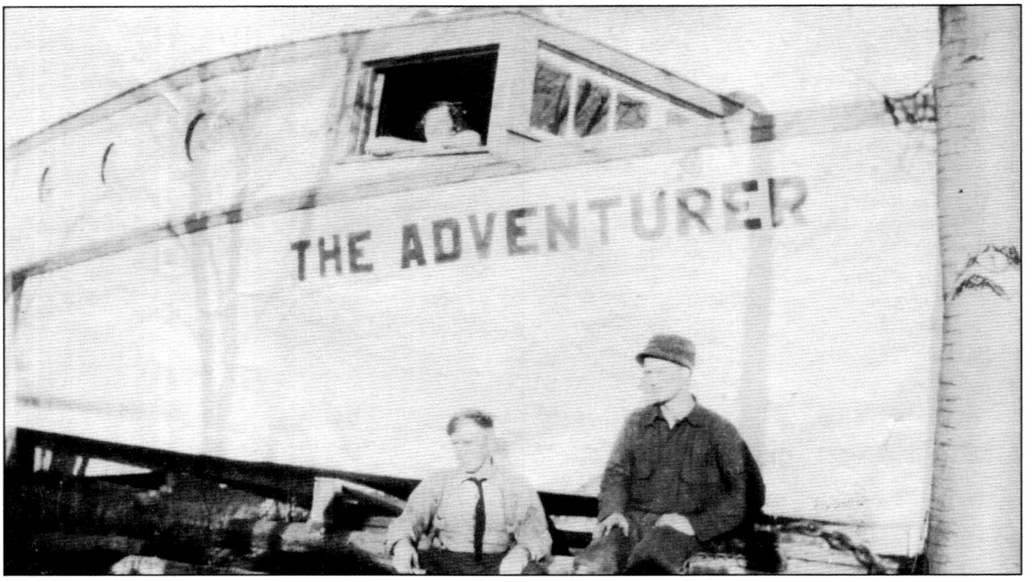

The Wickham family was in the boating business. It owned the launch the *Adventurer*. Bob Zavitz and Albert Wickham had the first dealership for the Star Tank & Boat Company. They would haul their boats on the back of their truck, delivering them to Sullivan's Landing in Prudenville. (Both courtesy of Bob Zavitz.)

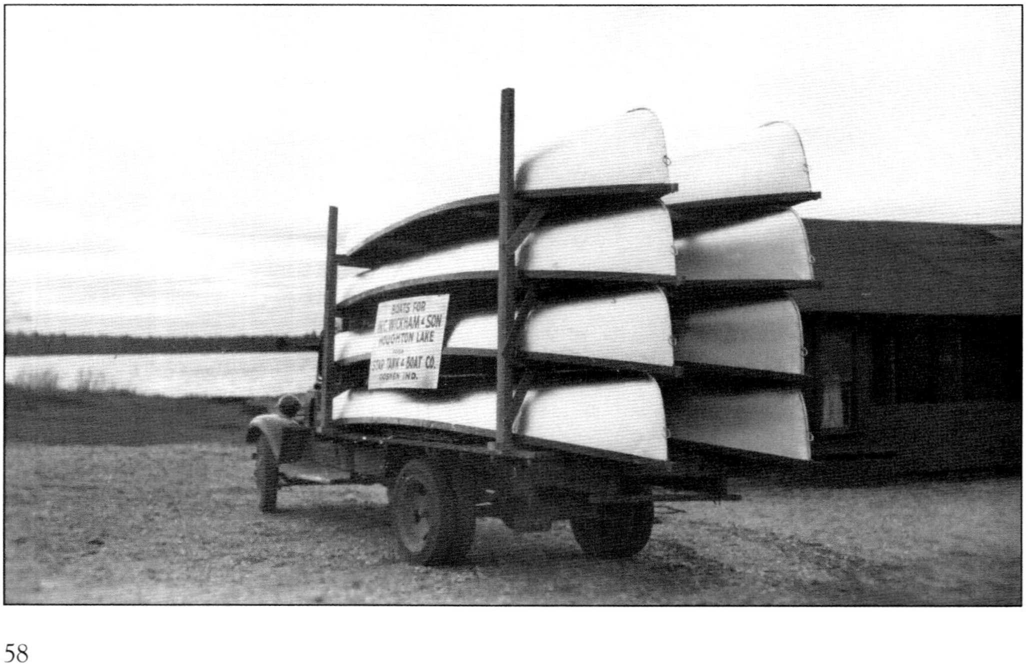

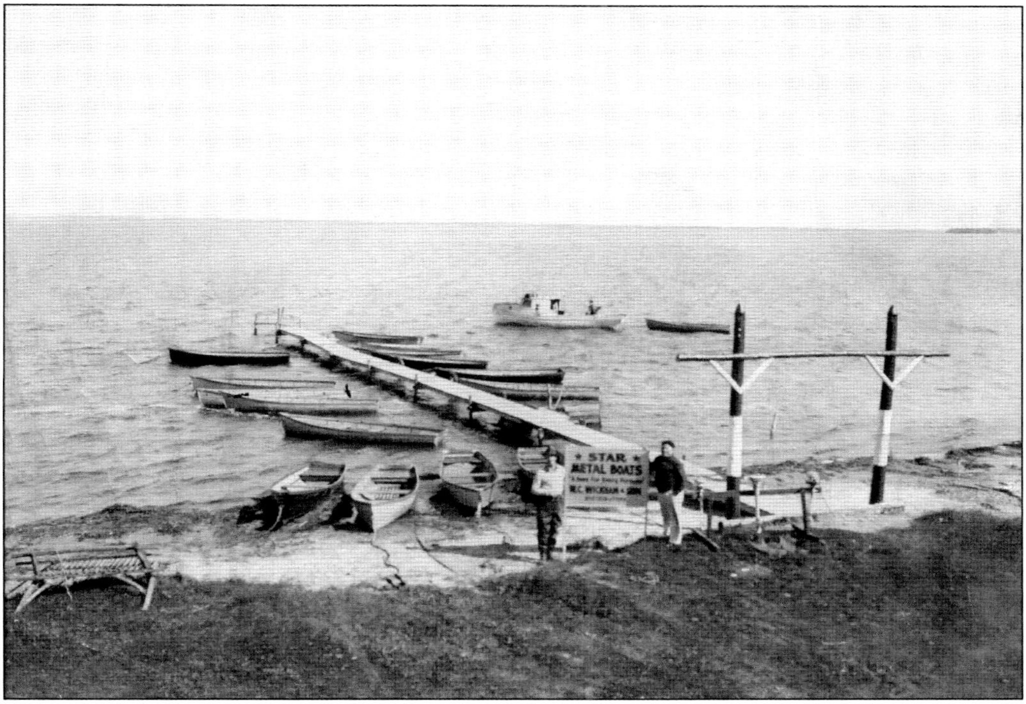

Wickham's resort was at the end of Guernsey Street, off of M-55. It offered rowboats for its guests and great fishing. Below, William Wickham shows off a great northern pike caught at the resort. (Both courtesy of Bob Zavitz.)

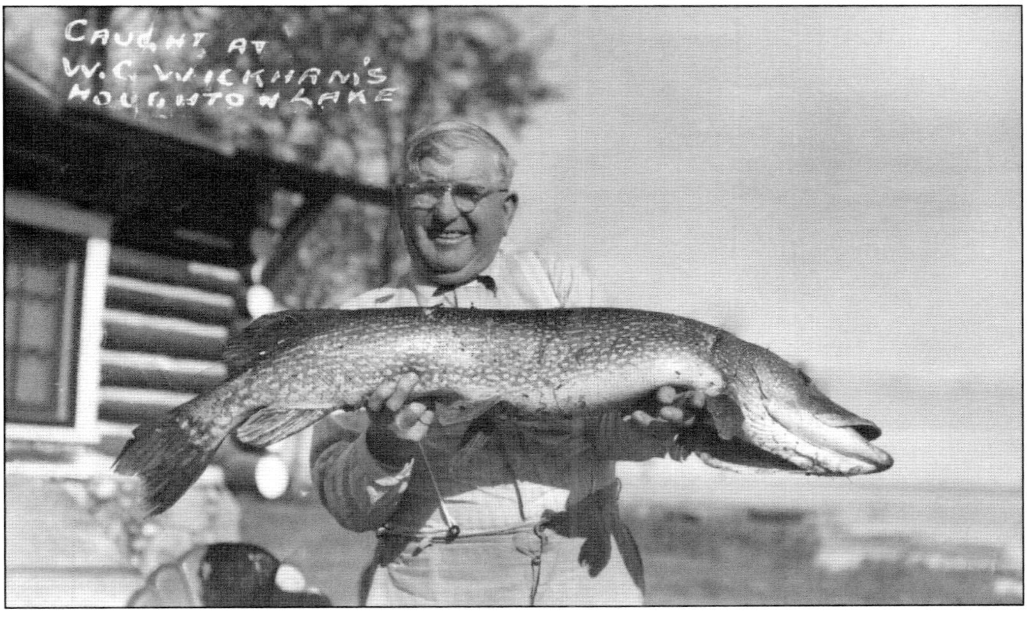

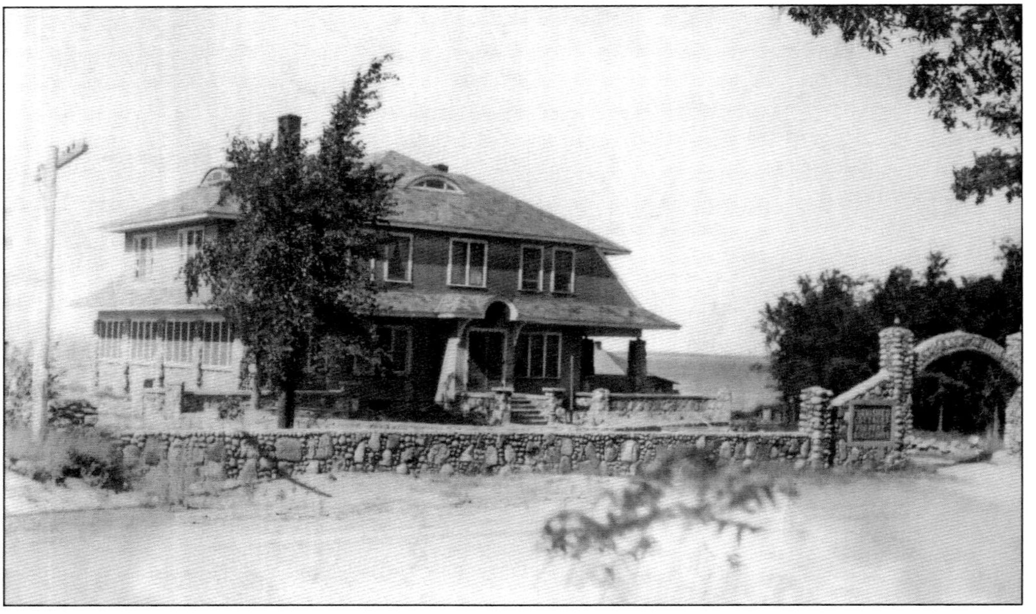

The Limberlost Inn has a long and varied history. It began as the private home of Dr. Arthur Sturge. People came to his home for treatment, and he sometimes kept them there if they needed more care. Over time, the building was sold and became a hotel and bar. It operated for many years, but it suffered several fires, the last in the late 1960s, when the establishment burned to the ground. In the early 1970s, a new building was erected, but the name remained. It became one of the premiere nightspots at Houghton Lake. It is the sponsor of the Bud Bash, a summer party on the lake. (Both courtesy of Dorothy Sunman.)

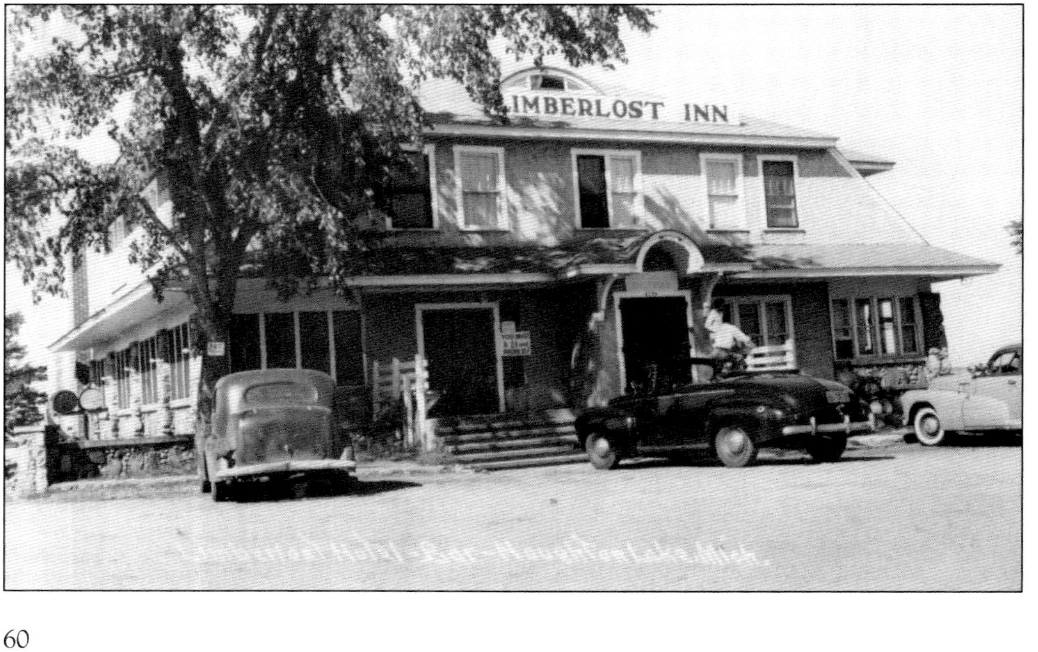

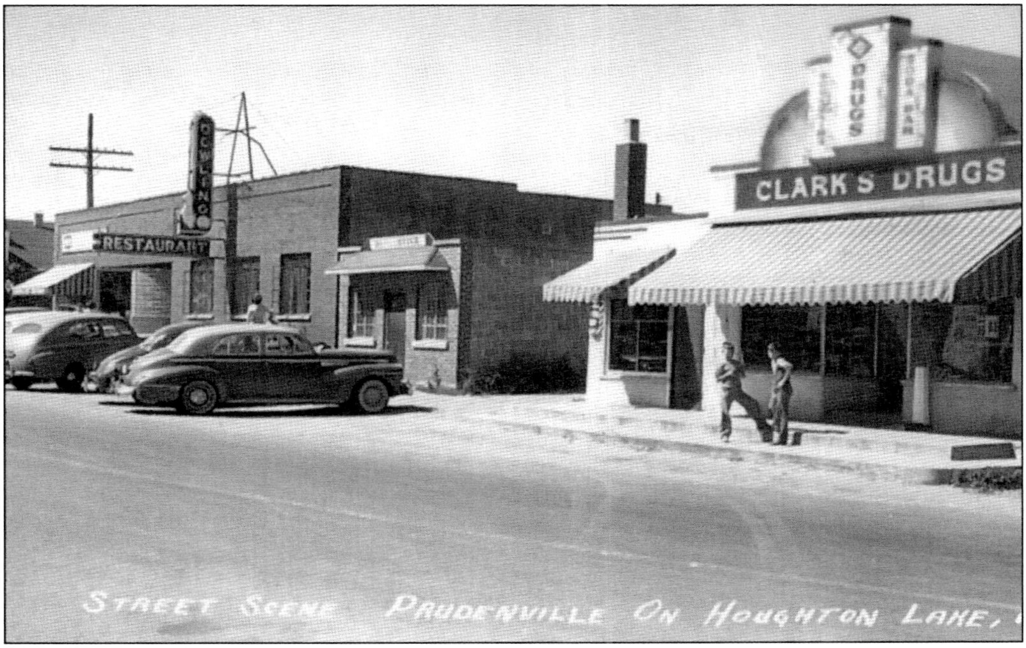

The northwest corner in Prudenville was occupied by a drugstore. In the late 1930s and early 1940s, it was Clark's Drugs. A few doors down the block was the bowling alley, owned by Harold Bowman. It was an entertainment mainstay in the village of Prudenville. Bowman's wife ran Lola Bell's Restaurant, next to the bowling alley. (Courtesy of Vera Parsons.)

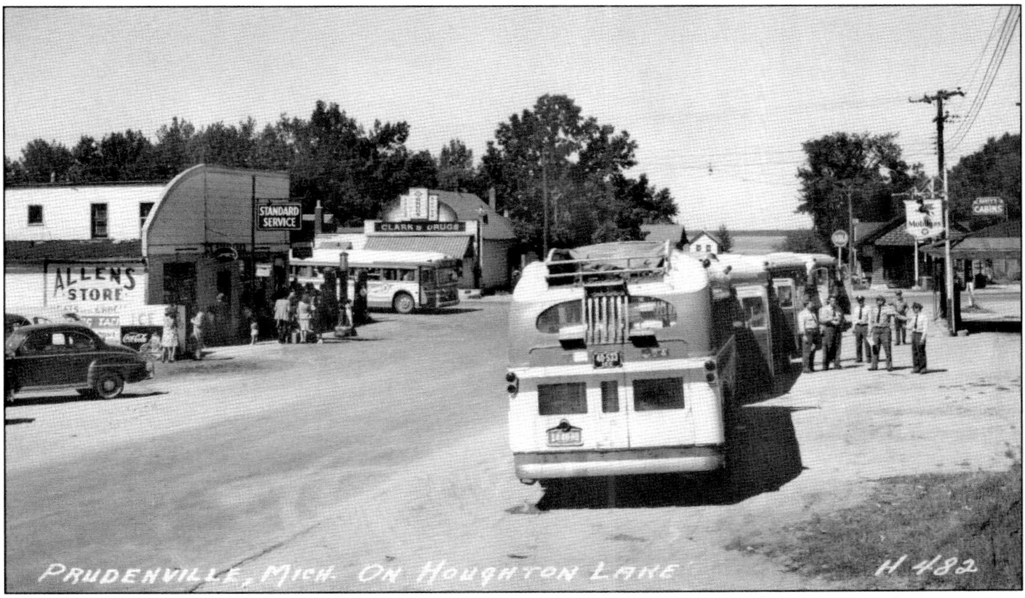

The Greyhound bus service was a popular way to travel in the early 20th century. The corner in Prudenville was where buses dropped off and picked up passengers. There were three gas stations on the corner in the 1940s. Hasty's (right) had the Mobile station, along with cabins and a restaurant. The Flett Garage owned the Gulf station, and Allen's Store (left) ran a Standard service station. The Greyhound bus depot was at Allen's Store. (Courtesy of Judy and Casey Kronner.)

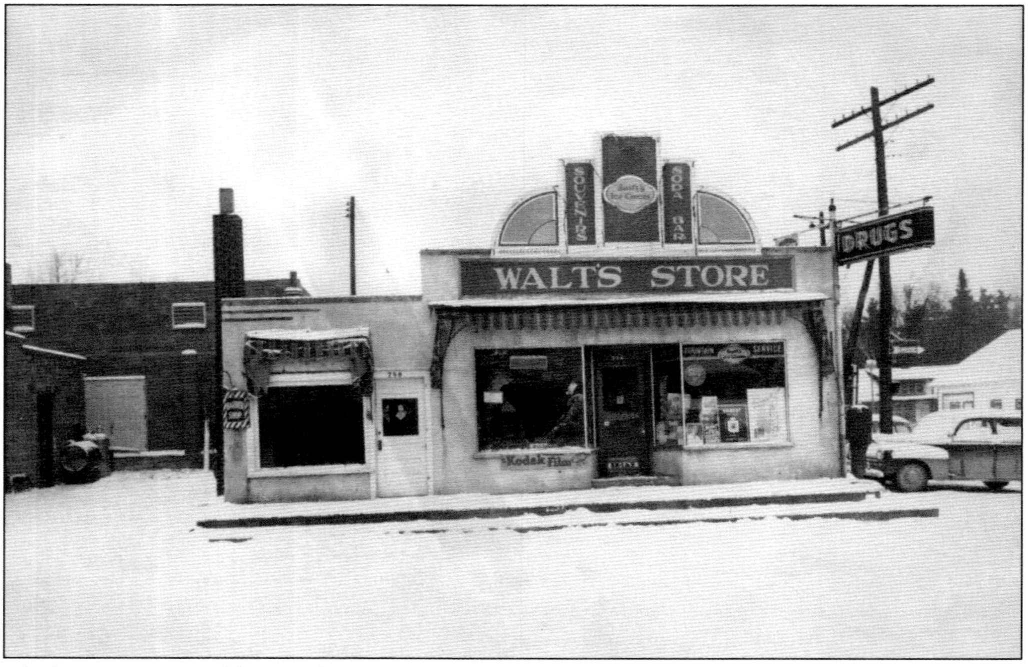

Clark's Drugs was sold to Walt Wintringham, who in turn sold the business to Francis "Frank" Kronner in April 1951. Kronner used this building for two years. Mr. Frosch ran the barbershop attached to the pharmacy. (Courtesy of Judy and Casey Kronner.)

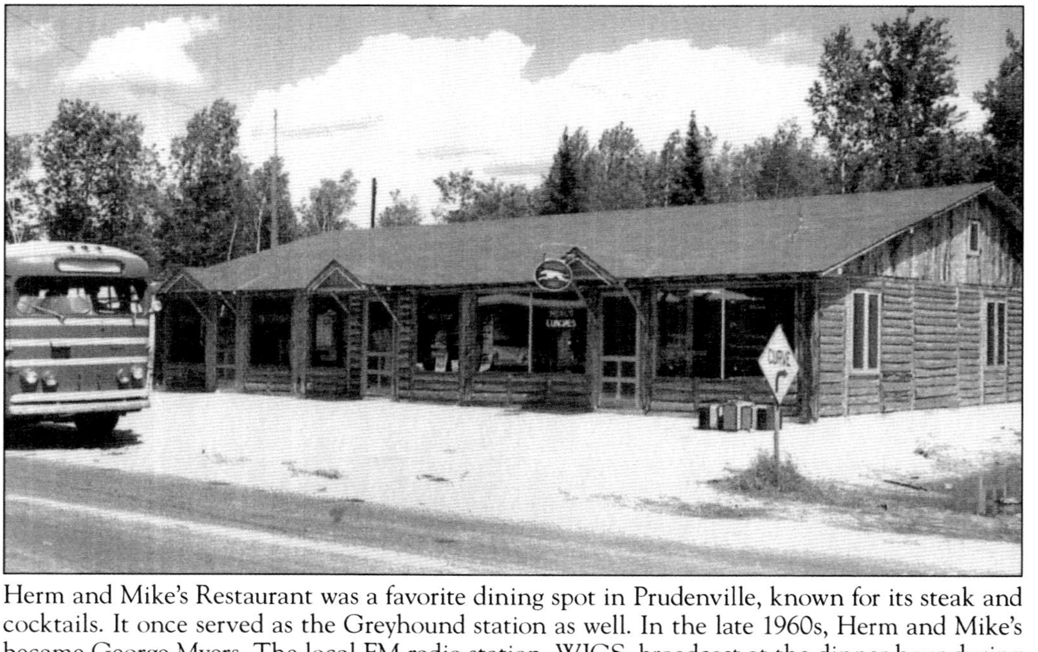

Herm and Mike's Restaurant was a favorite dining spot in Prudenville, known for its steak and cocktails. It once served as the Greyhound station as well. In the late 1960s, Herm and Mike's became George Myers. The local FM radio station, WJGS, broadcast at the dinner hour during the summer. In the early 1970s, it was sold again and became the Brass Lantern, which remained a favorite for the more than three decades Ken Yaklin owned the restaurant. Yaklin sold the property to Walgreen's, and it was razed in the late 2000s.

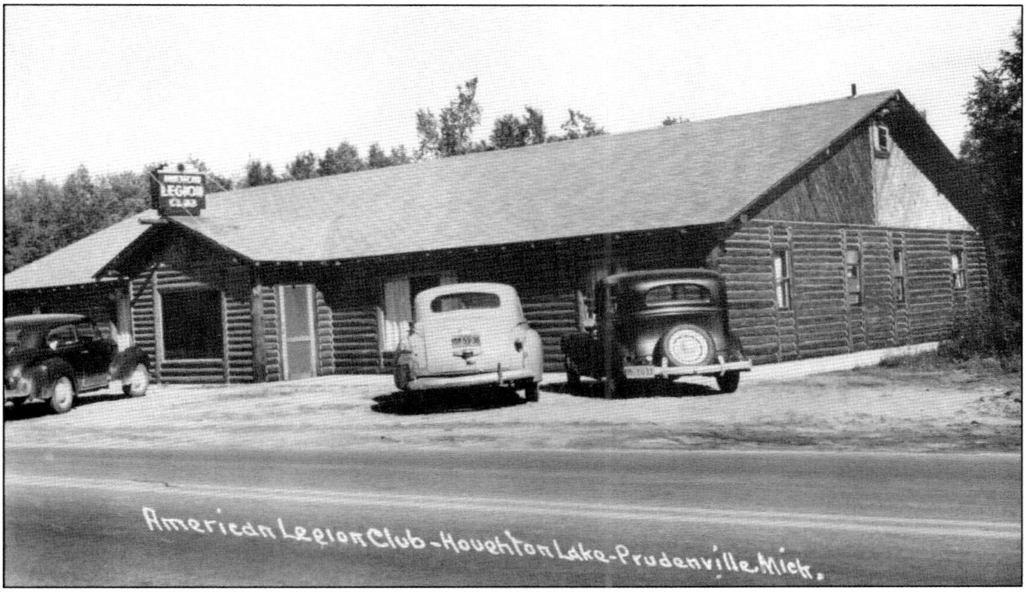

The American Legion's first location was this log building just northeast of the corner in Prudenville. It was next door to Herm and Mike's Restaurant. Each year, the Legion sponsored a Christmas party for children on Christmas Eve. Santa would arrive about 8:00 p.m., and there was always candy and toys for the children.

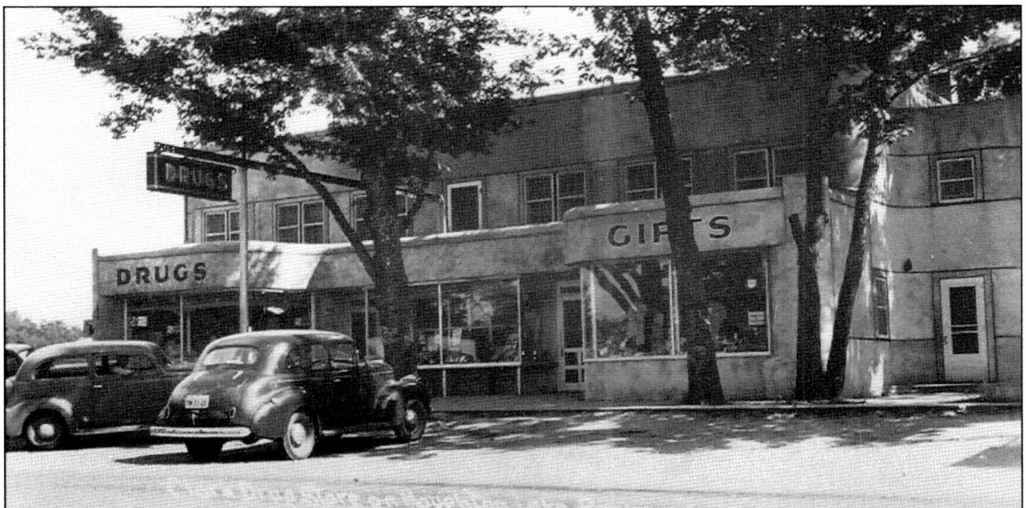

Hazen T. Randall owned this large building in Prudenville. Located on the south side of M-55, it was known as the Randall Block. The building housed a drugstore, a gift shop, and apartments on the second story. The *Houghton Lake Resorter*'s December 23, 1943, edition reported that the building burned down around 11:30 the previous evening. The children of Mr. and Mrs. Toby Frankfurth were at home alone. Their mother was working at the bowling alley. Randall's two sons, Murl and Herbert, were also at the business. The boys were able to escape, but Shirley, the six-year-old daughter of the Frankfurths, perished in the fire. It was said that the smoke could be seen in Roscommon. The building was never rebuilt. It was determined that the older Frankfurth son started the fire. (Courtesy of Vera Parsons.)

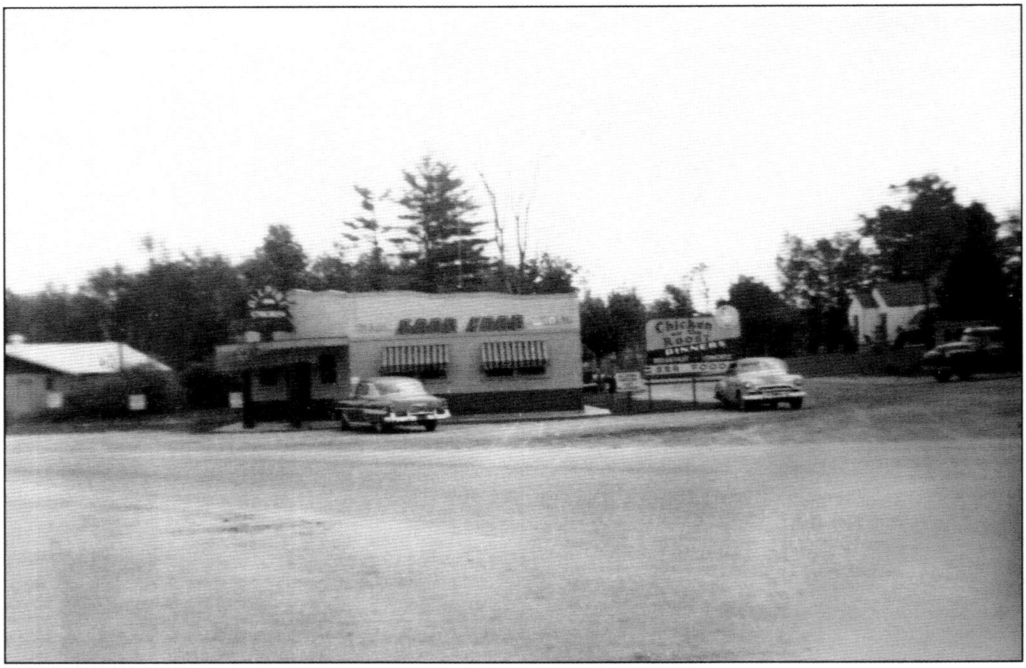

Restaurants were very busy places in the summer. Many of them had resort licenses for liquor and could only be open seasonally. Owners made good livings catering to the summer crowd. The Alpine Inn (shown here) was one such place. Edith and John Wycoff bought it in 1940, and they owned it until the early 1970s. It was then expanded and renamed the Bavarian Haus. The building was destroyed by fire in October 1992. A small bar and restaurant, built behind the original site, was sold when the Brass Lantern sold to Walgreen's. The new building was then razed.

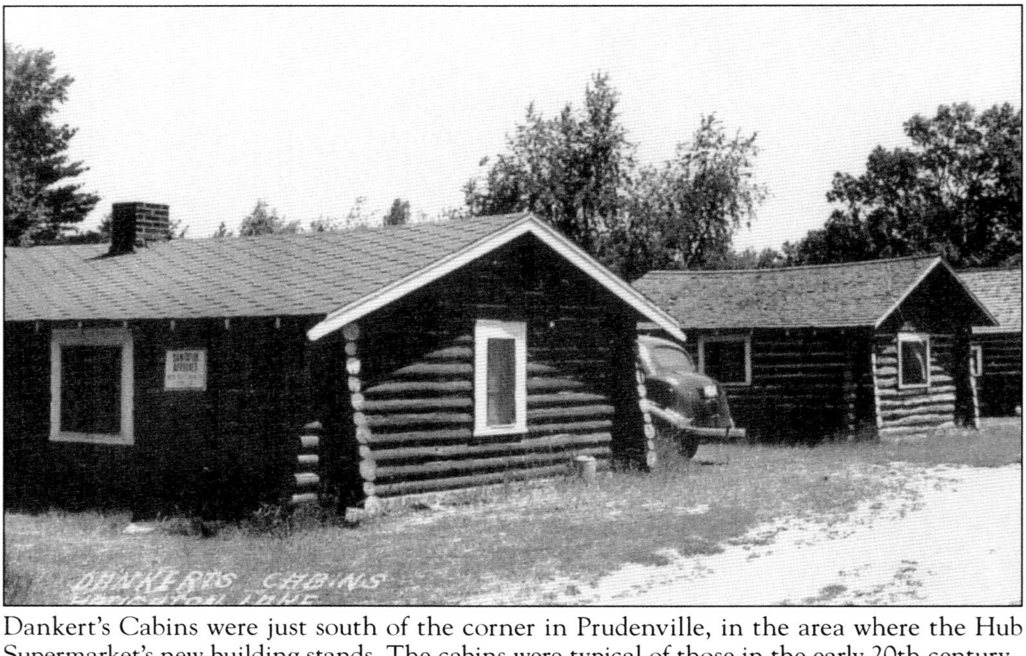

Dankert's Cabins were just south of the corner in Prudenville, in the area where the Hub Supermarket's new building stands. The cabins were typical of those in the early 20th century.

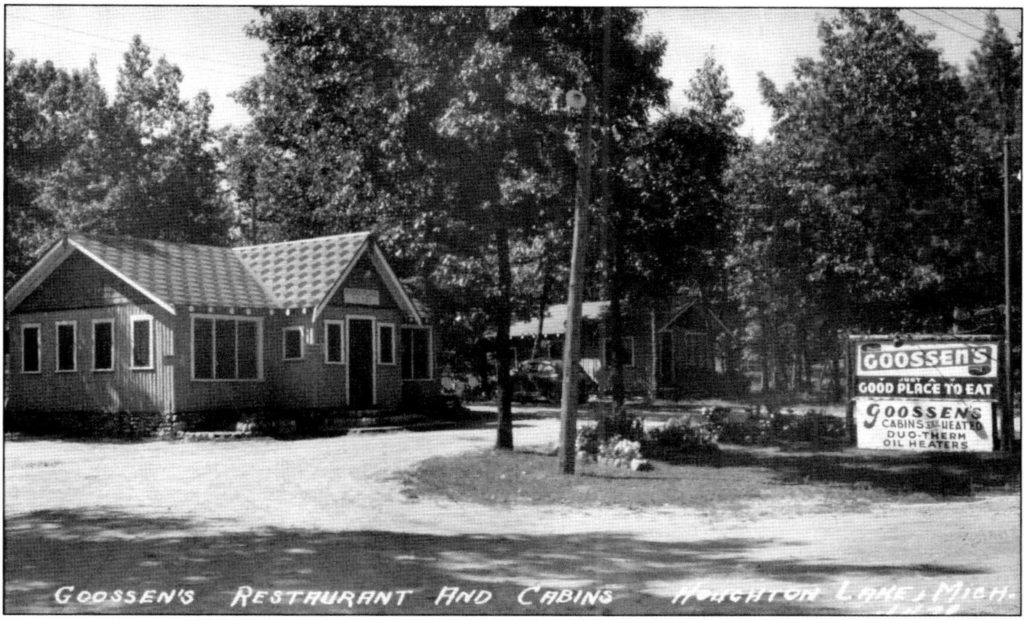

West of Prudenville, Mac Goossen built his restaurant and cabins (above) in 1935. It is the oldest continually operating restaurant in Houghton Lake. Over the years, the name has changed, and the cabins have been removed. At one point, it was called the Deer Track Inn. Currently, it is Powell's Restaurant (below). One thing that has not changed is the good food. Patty and Bill Randall now run the restaurant for Patty's mother, Gerri, who bought it with her husband in the late 1970s. (Both courtesy of Powell's Restaurant.)

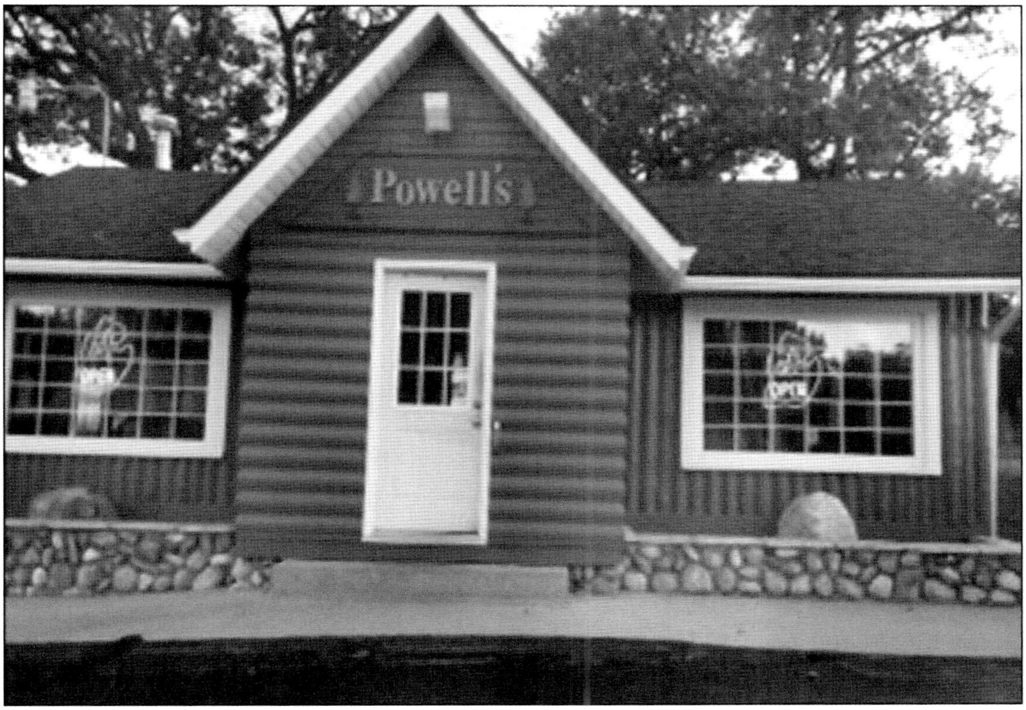

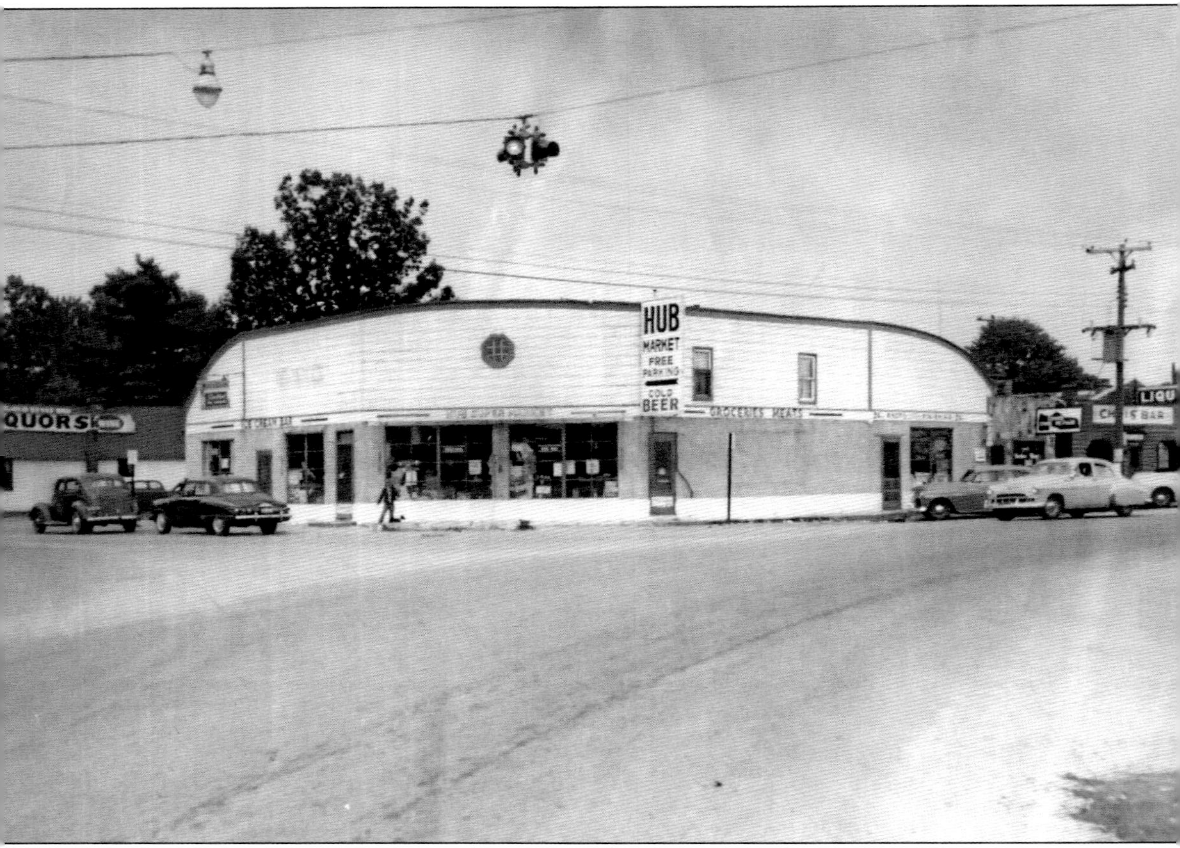

Archie Moore bought the former Allen's Store in October 1951. By then, the gas pumps had been removed. Moore's market, called the Hub, was known for its fresh meat counter. Moore built a new store across the street from this one in the late 1960s. For a time, the Kronners operated Shoppers Korner, a department store, at this location. They eventually built a department store behind the pharmacy. Moore then ran a surplus store at this location into the first decade of the 21st century. Behind the Hub was the Old Style Bar, which later became the Sand Bar. It is still in operation.

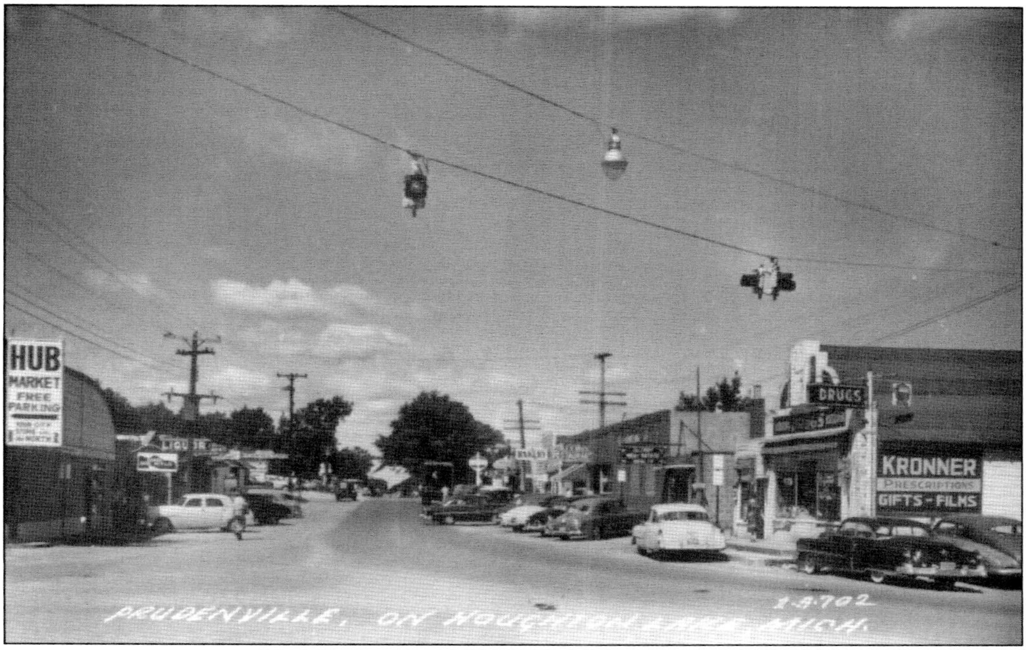

These photographs show M-55 in Prudenville before 1953. The road was still composed of two lanes, and there were many small businesses on both sides of the street. These businesses remained into the late 1970s. A community revitalization grant paid for the removal of the old buildings on the north side of the road. (Both courtesy of Judy and Casey Kronner.)

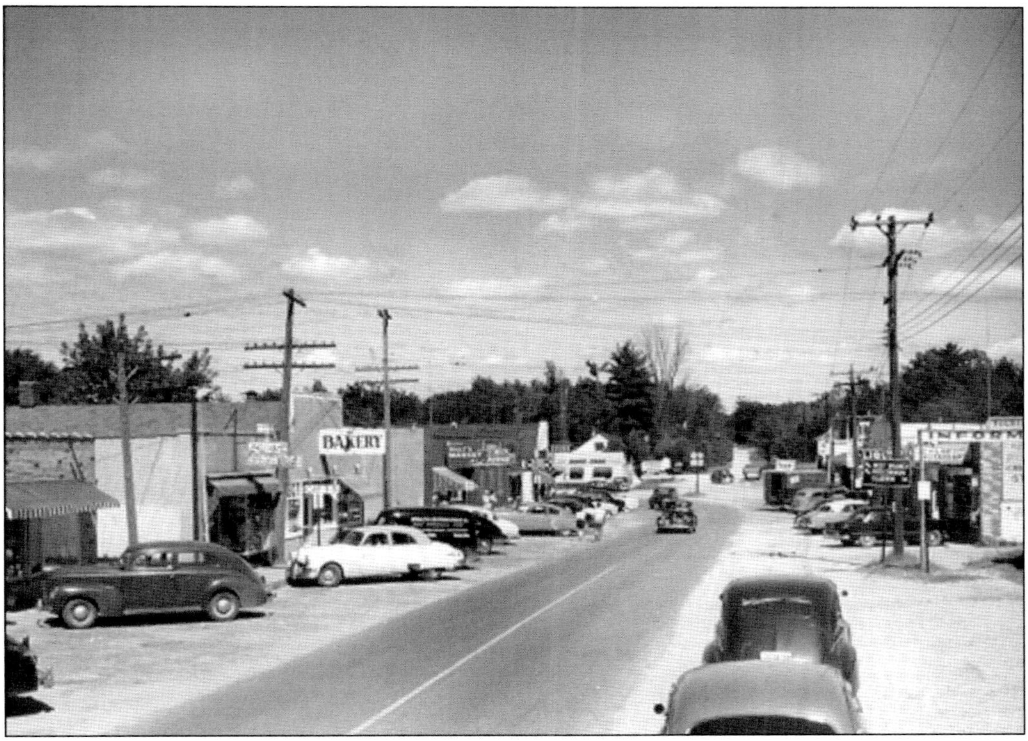

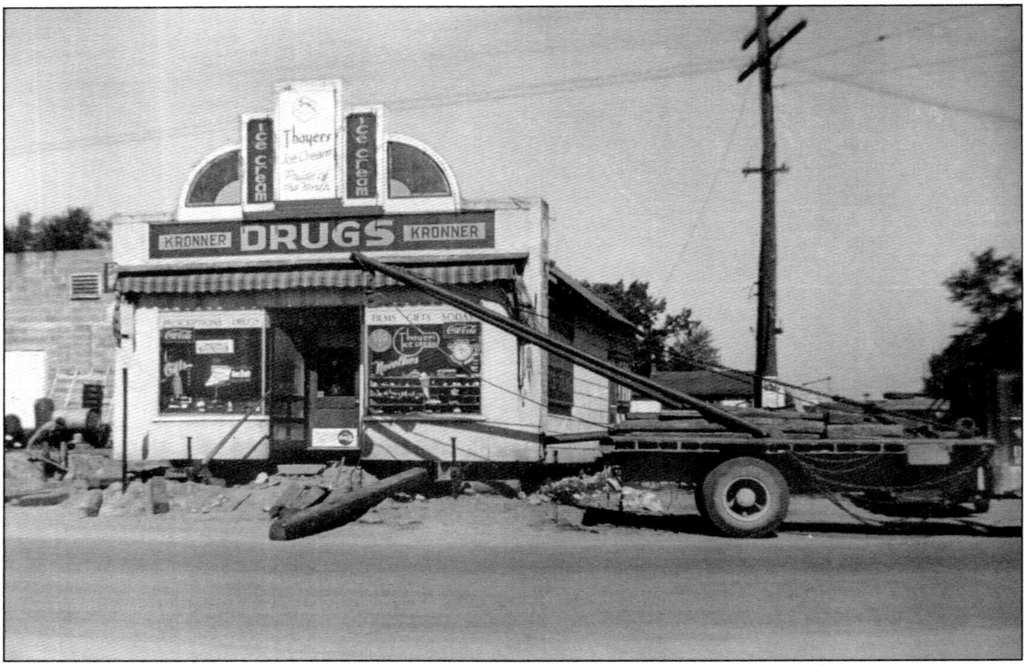

The northwest corner of Prudenville was drastically changed when Frank Kronner had his drugstore moved around the corner, behind its original location. Kronner was preparing to build a new, modern drugstore on the corner. (Courtesy of Judy and Casey Kronner.)

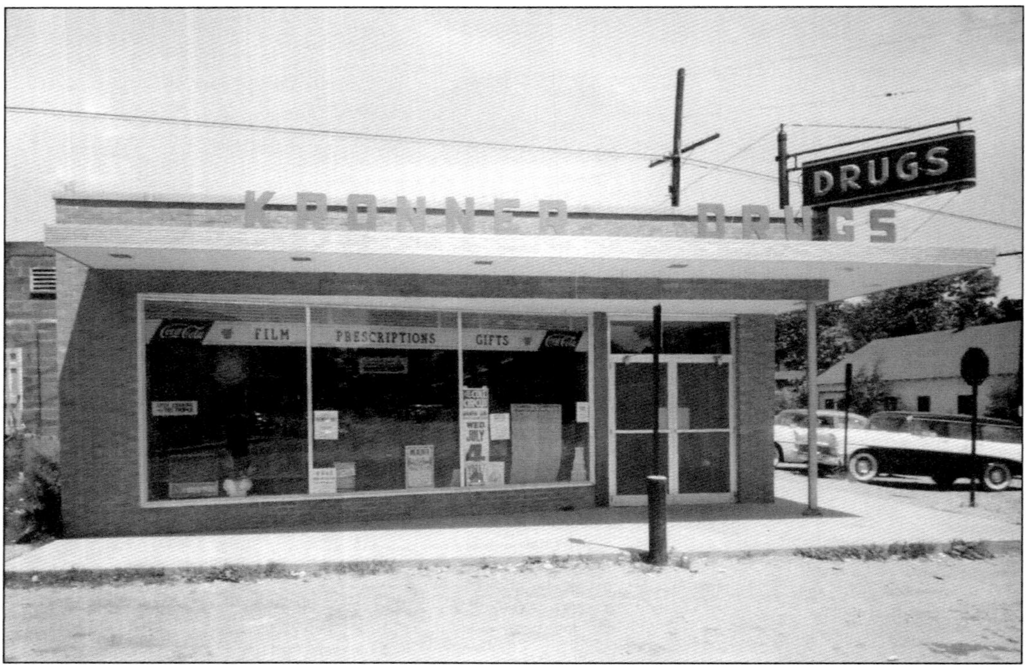

Frank Kronner built a new pharmacy in 1953. The brick-faced building was larger than the frame building it replaced. The east side of the building was painted orange. (Courtesy of Judy and Casey Kronner.)

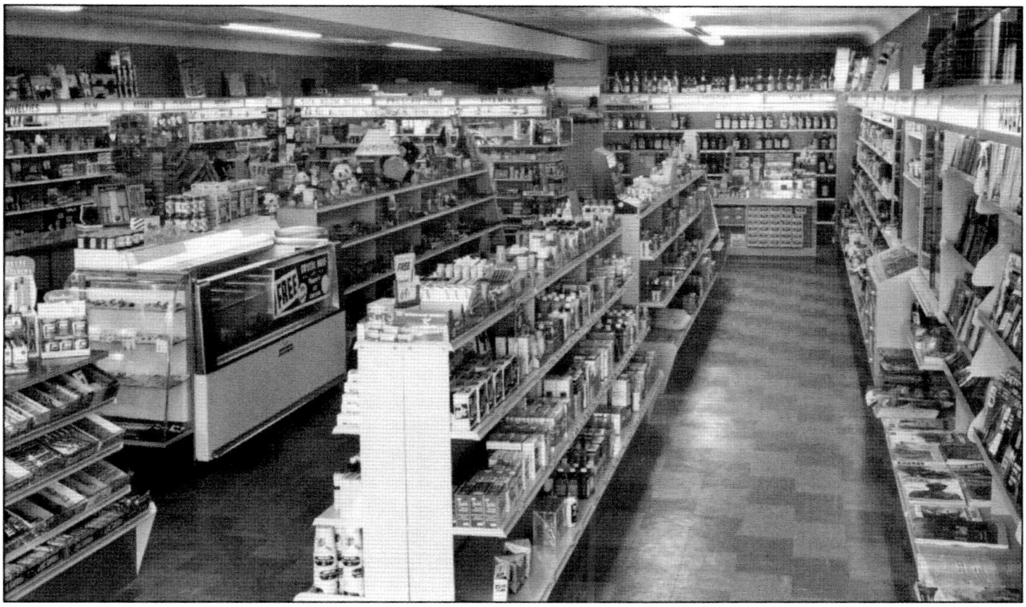

Kronner Drugs had a large variety of items. It sold candy, magazines, and gifts, as well as pharmaceutical products. A liquor department was located in the back of the store, next to the drug counter, where prescriptions were filled. The new store had a soda fountain on the west side. In the photograph below, Frank Kronner, the owner, is serving Helen McDonald a Coca-Cola. (Both courtesy of Judy and Casey Kronner.)

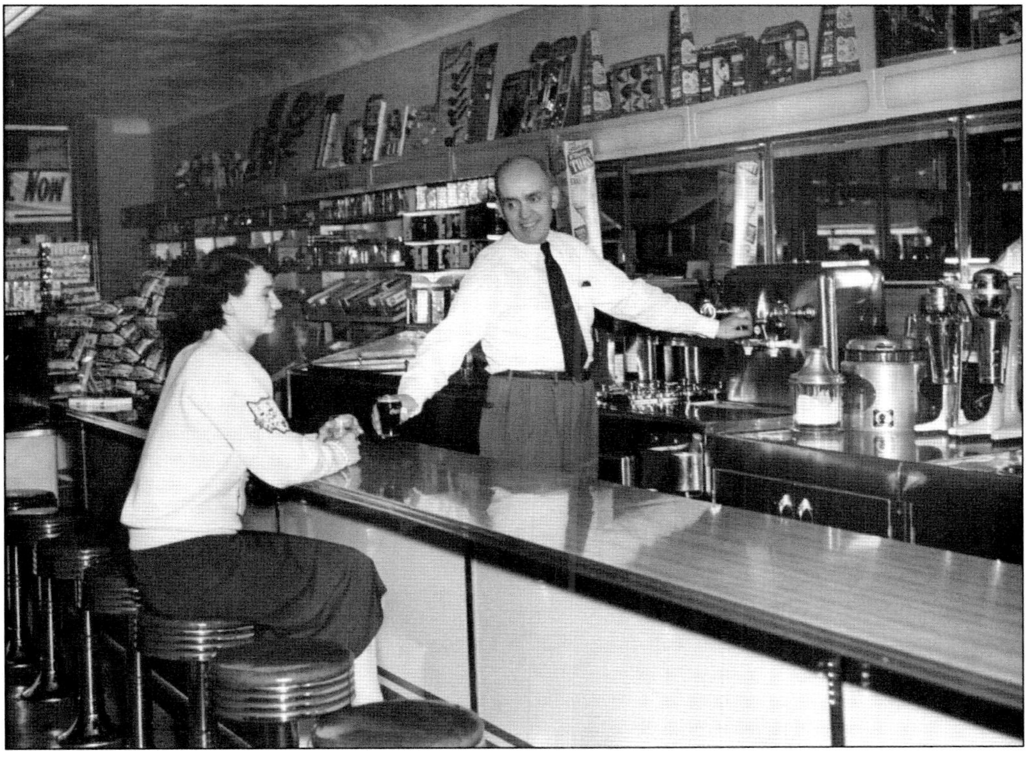

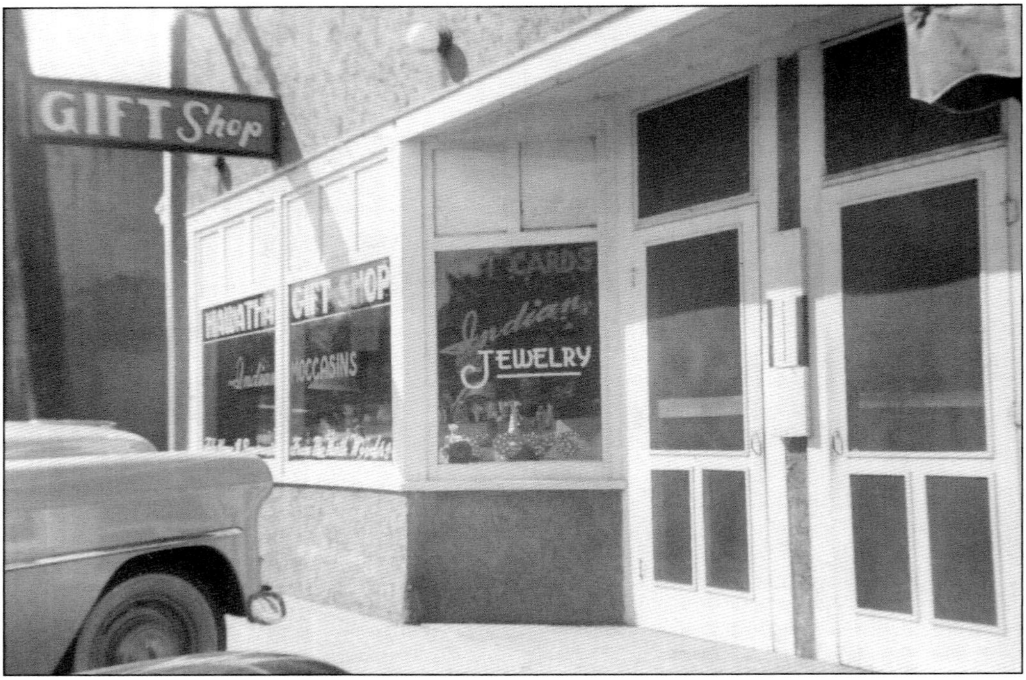

Frank Kronner also operated the Hiawatha Gift Shop, located a few doors west of the drugstore. The small store carried jewelry, souvenirs, and moccasins. It operated from 1955 until 1975, when the Kronners opened Shoppers Korner. (Both courtesy of Judy and Casey Kronner.)

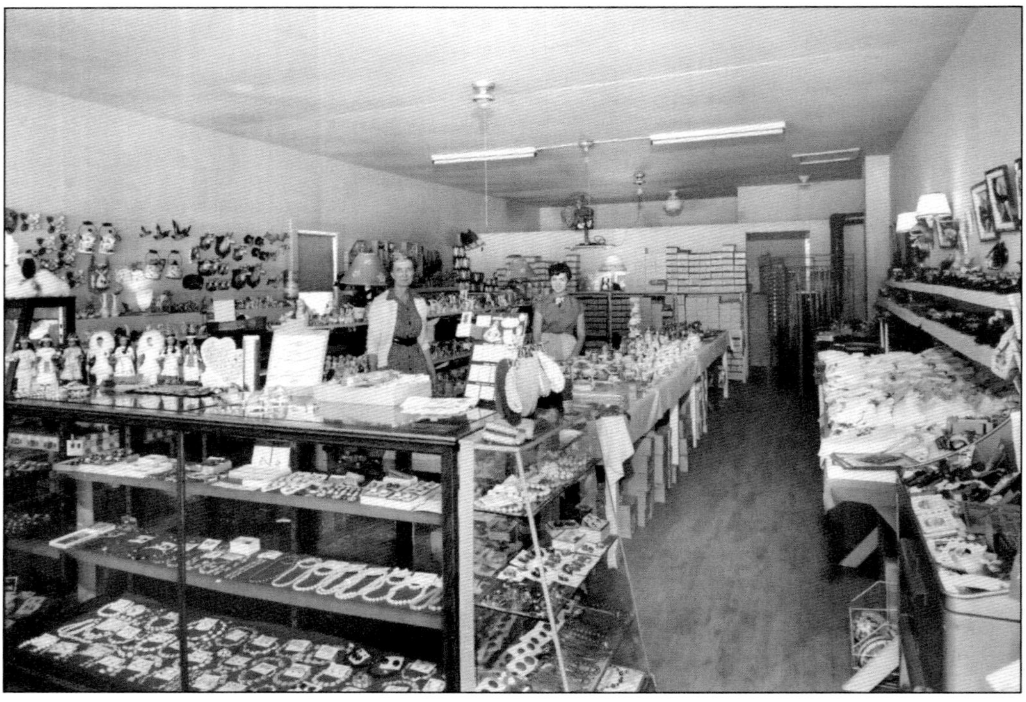

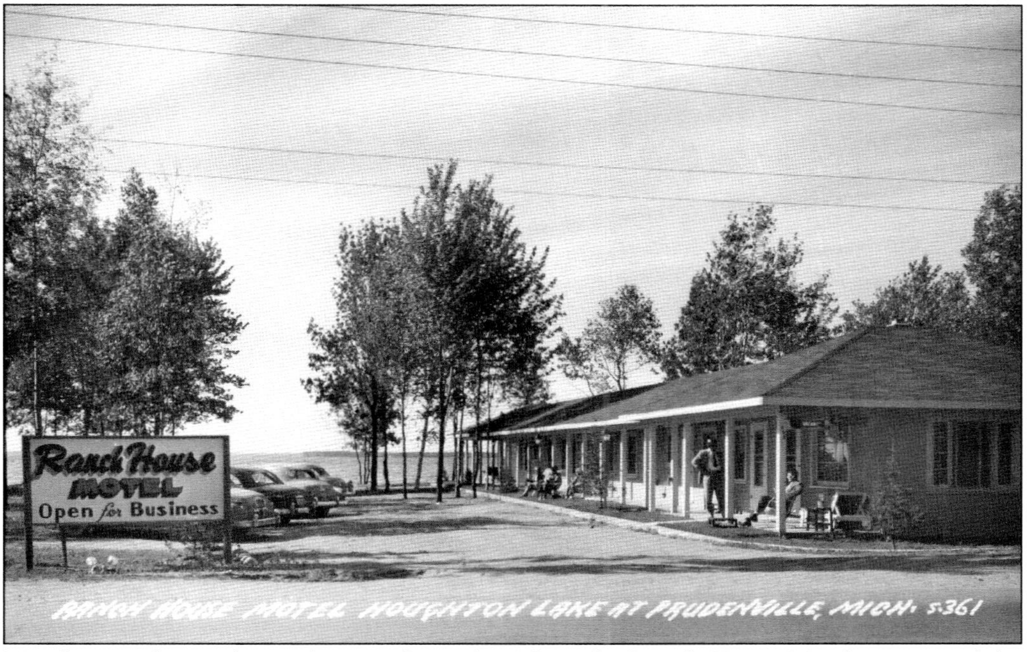

Motels started to replace cabins in the early 1950s. The Ranch House Motel was one of the popular motels on the East Bay. It was just east of Prudenville, on M-55. Today, it is privately owned condos.

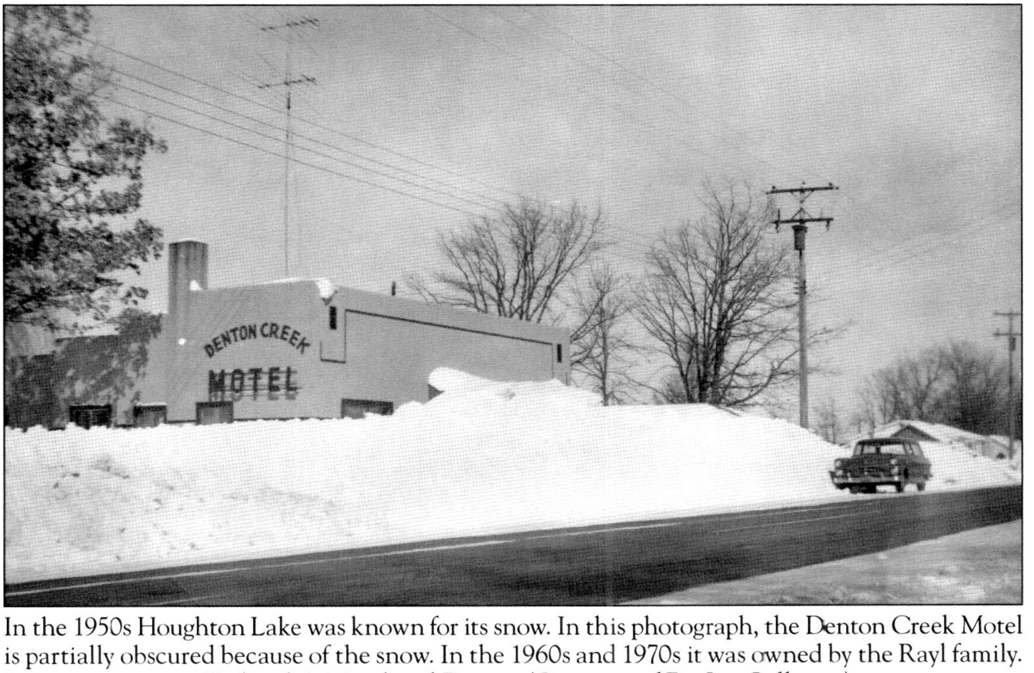

In the 1950s Houghton Lake was known for its snow. In this photograph, the Denton Creek Motel is partially obscured because of the snow. In the 1960s and 1970s it was owned by the Rayl family. It now operates as Korbinski's Motel and Resort. (Courtesy of Dr. Jim Sullivan.)

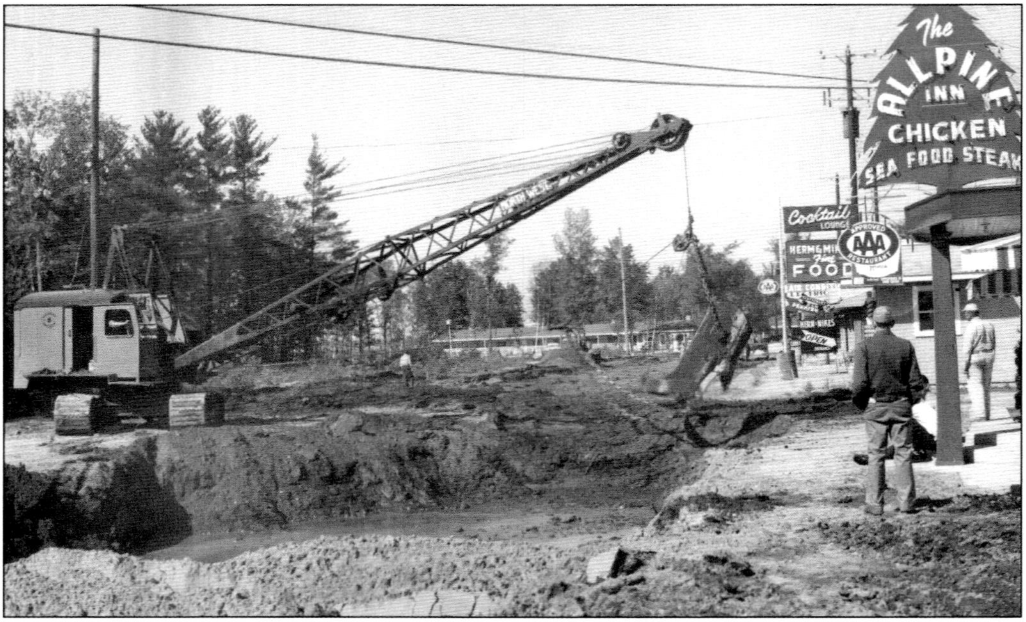

The State of Michigan made a major change to Houghton Lake in the late 1950s: the widening of M-55. This was a large road project, because M-55 is the main road on the south side of the lake. As the corner in Prudenville had expanded, traffic became very limited. During the roadwork, Herm & Mike's stayed open for business. (Both courtesy of Judy and Casey Kronner.)

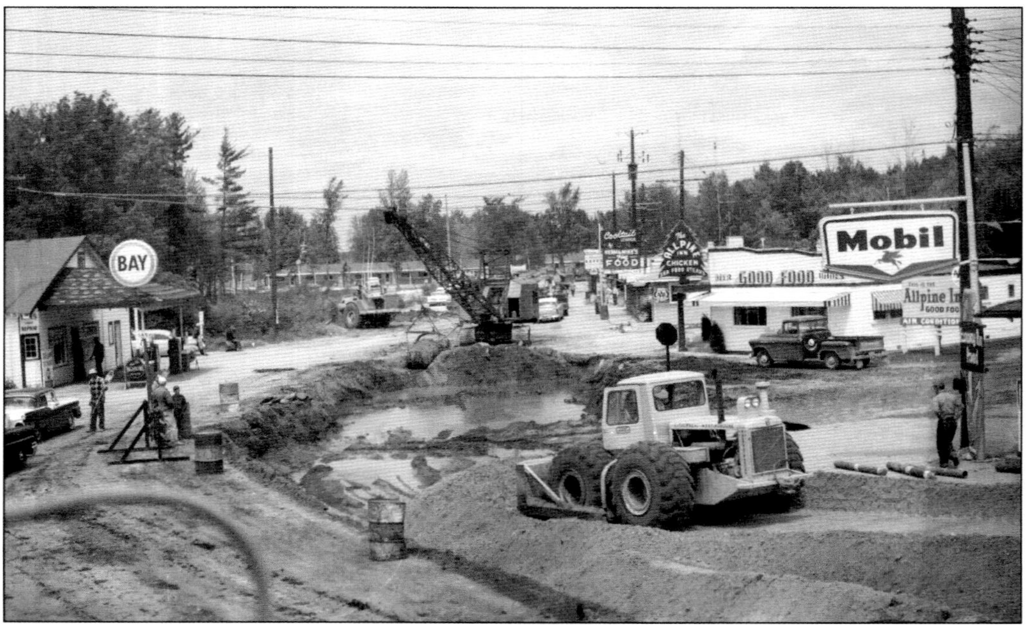

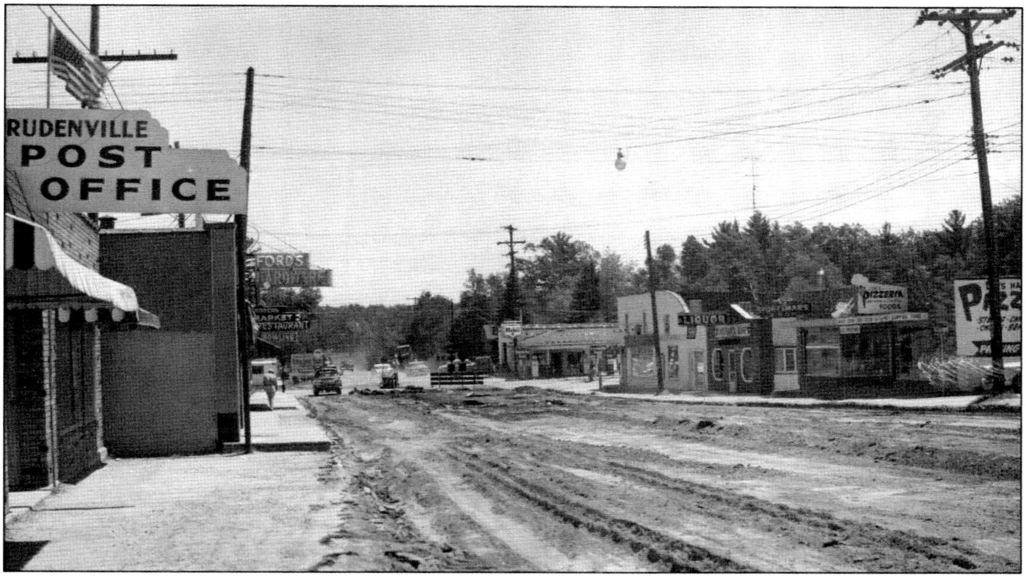

Looking east on M-55, Emmett and Bob Sullivan's store, called the Sportsman's Shop, and Geni's Pizzeria are at right, on the south side of M-55. These were very popular spots in Prudenville. The Sportsman's Shop carried the best brands of clothing at the time: White Stag and Jansen. Sporting equipment, from archery supplies to skis and more, were found at the store. At this time, the post office (left) was on the north side of the road. Later, a post office was built on the corner of M-55 and Sullivan Street. (Courtesy of Judy and Casey Kronner.)

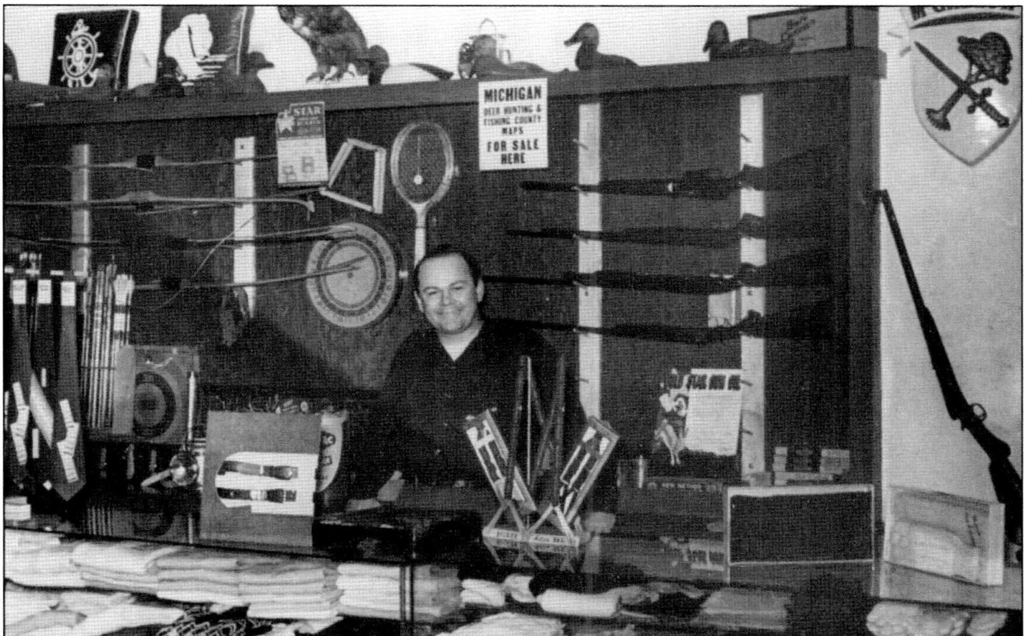

Daniel Robert "Bob" Sullivan stands behind the counter of the Sportsman's Shop. Clothing and guns and bows surround him. The shop also carried snow-skiing equipment. In the late 1950s, Bob Sullivan ran the pro shop at the local ski park. (Courtesy of Dr. Jim Sullivan.)

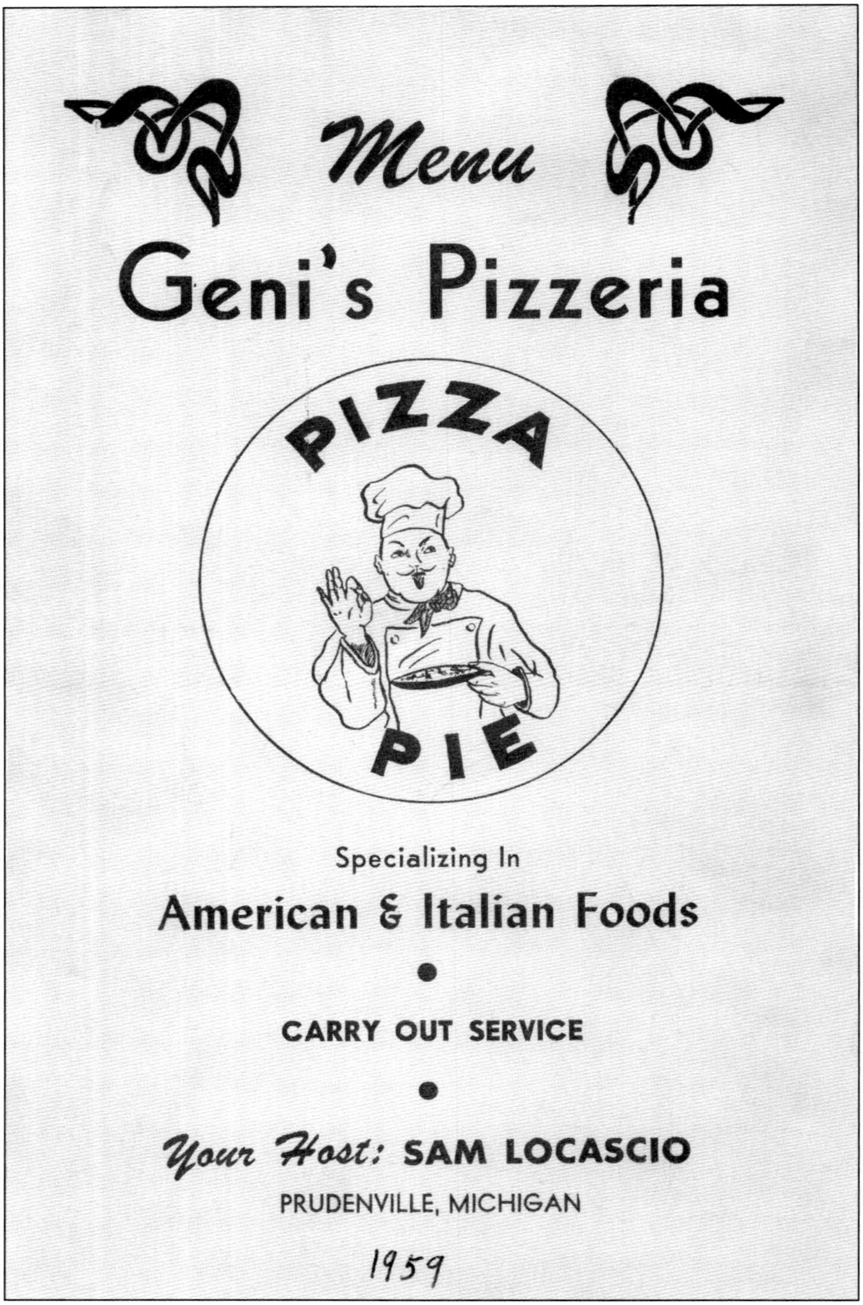

Emmett and Bob Sullivan were good businessmen; when they built their store, they also created a space to lease. Sam Locascio leased the space for his pizzeria, Geni's, which was open from 6:00 a.m. to 4:00 a.m. daily. It served the best pizza, and its carryout service was very popular. The pizzeria had a drive-up window on the side; pizzas were handed out on a cardboard round in a paper bag. This was a favorite place for young people to go after the Music Box closed for the night. In the early 1970s, the pizzeria continued, but it was called Dominic's. It was St. Vincent DePaul's in the 1990s, and then it became a storage for the surplus store. (Courtesy of Mark Barnhart Sr.)

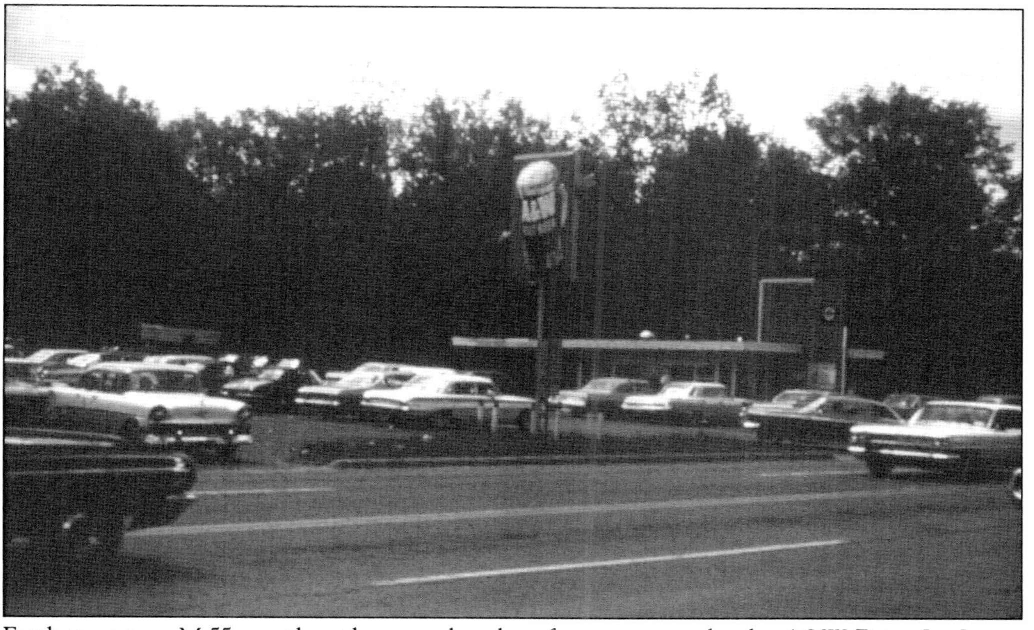

Farther west on M-55 was the other popular place for young people, the A&W Drive-In. It was the first drive-in restaurant in Houghton Lake. On weekends in the summer, it was hard to find a place to park. This 1964 photograph of a full parking lot speaks to the restaurant's popularity. It remained open through the 1960s. The site is now occupied by Shaker's Restaurant. (Courtesy of Mark Barnhart Sr.)

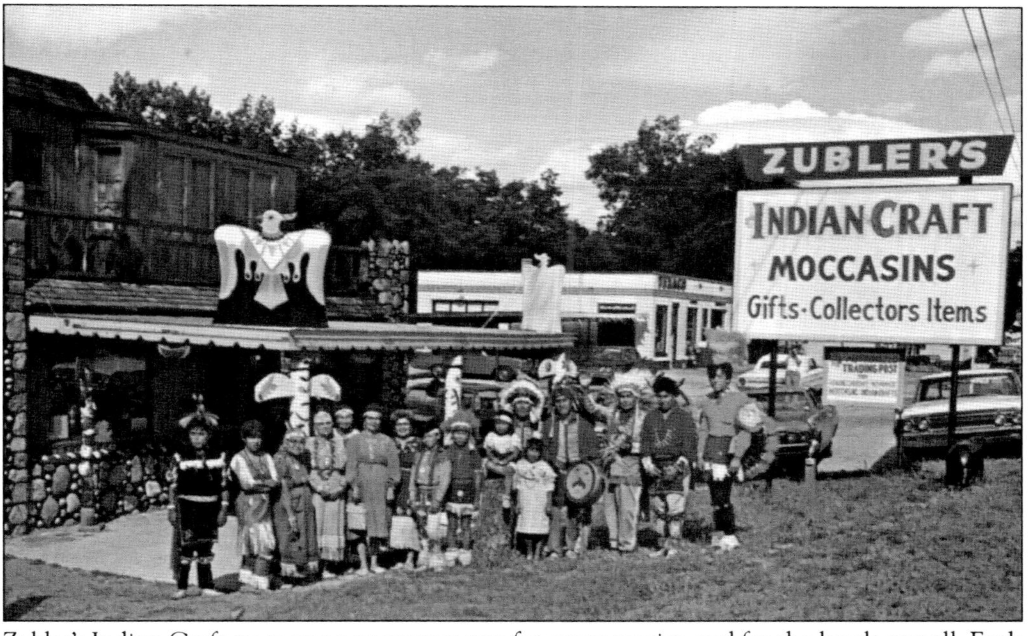

Zubler's Indian Craft store was a necessary stop for every tourist, and for the locals as well. Each Thursday, a group of Native Americans perform a powwow. The event includes native dancing, recitation of folklore, and photo opportunities. The powwow is free of charge. The event is still a favorite today.

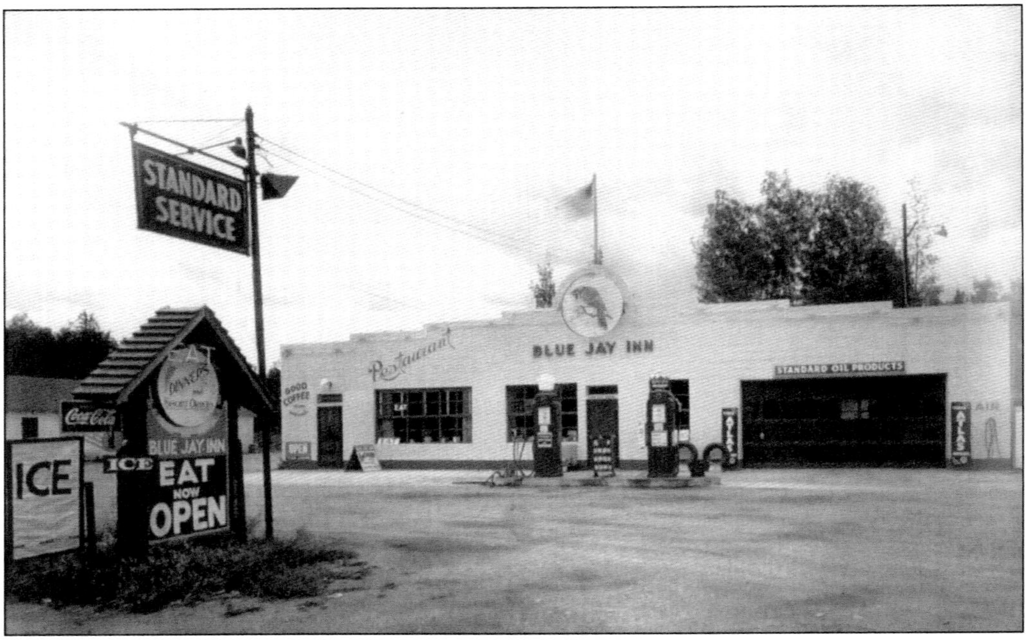

The Blue Jay Inn and Standard Oil service station were halfway between Prudenville and the Heights. Eventually, the restaurant was enlarged and the gas station closed. The site became home to the Pick-Wick, which was in business until the 1990s. It was razed, and Auto Value is now on the site.

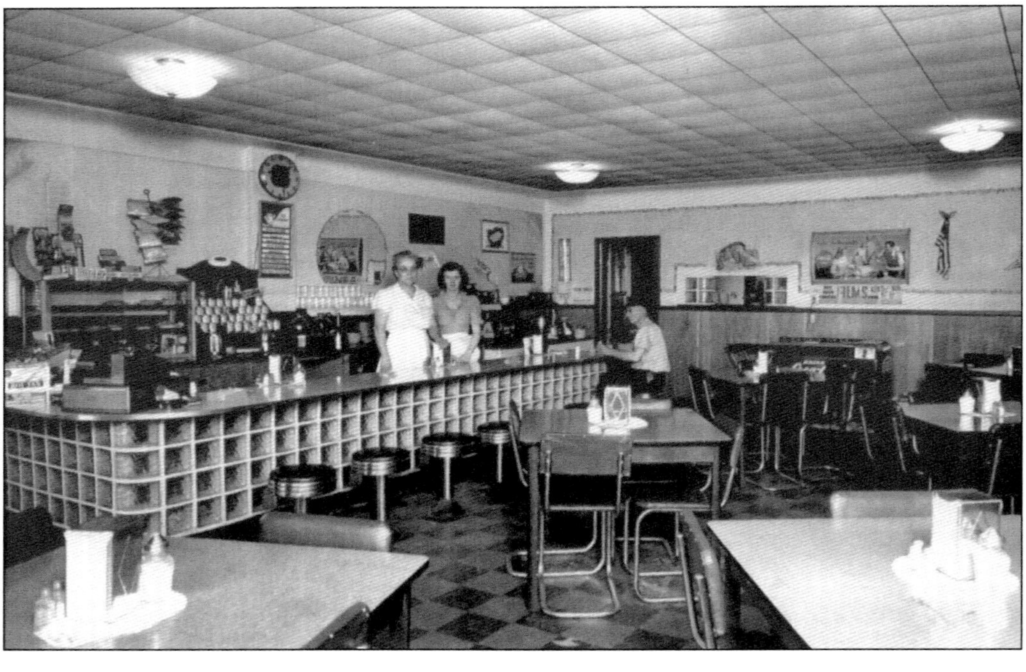

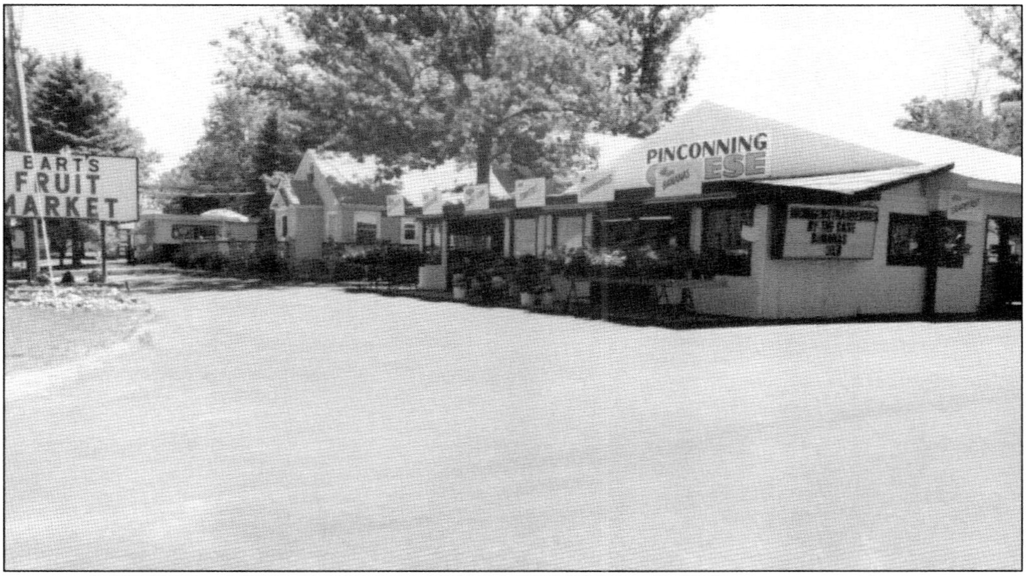

Bart's Fruit Market started out as just a shed and crates of produce, as well as Pinconning Cheese. Bart Bartholomew and his family bought the market from Bill Walraven in the early 1970s. Bart's wife, Ilene, and six of his seven children ran the market. Over the years, the Bartholomews expanded the store and put a log exterior on the building. Bart's is still in business and attracts visitors and locals with its beautiful flowers and produce, as well as the pumpkin patch in the fall. (Courtesy of Bart's Market.)

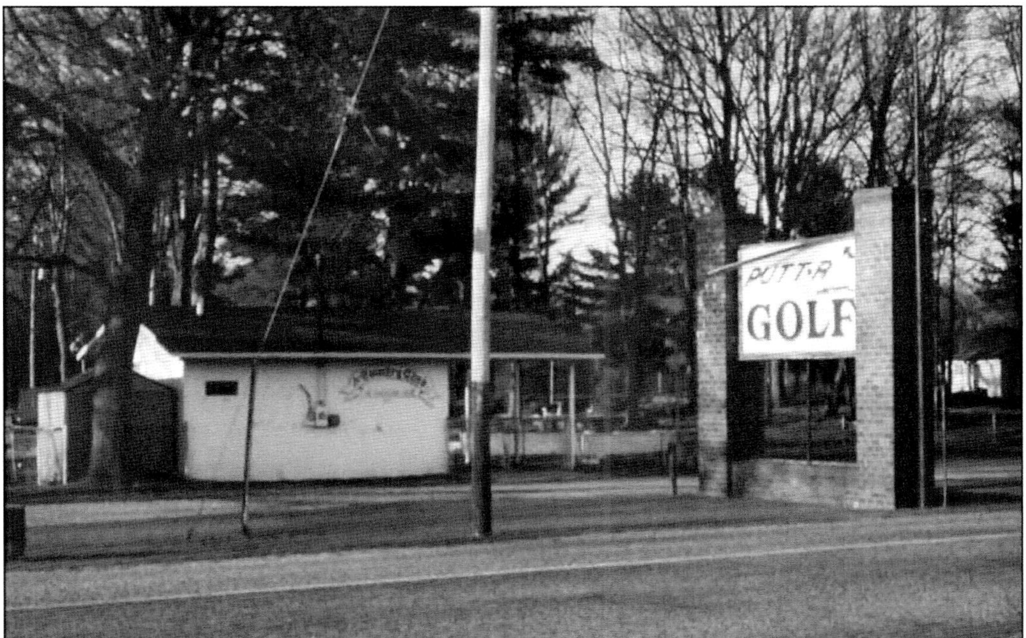

The Putt-R golf course was the original miniature golf course in Houghton Lake. It is just east of where the Music Box stood. This area also had a go-cart track and trampolines in the 1960s. The only thing that remains is this golf course. (Courtesy of Mark Barnhart Sr.)

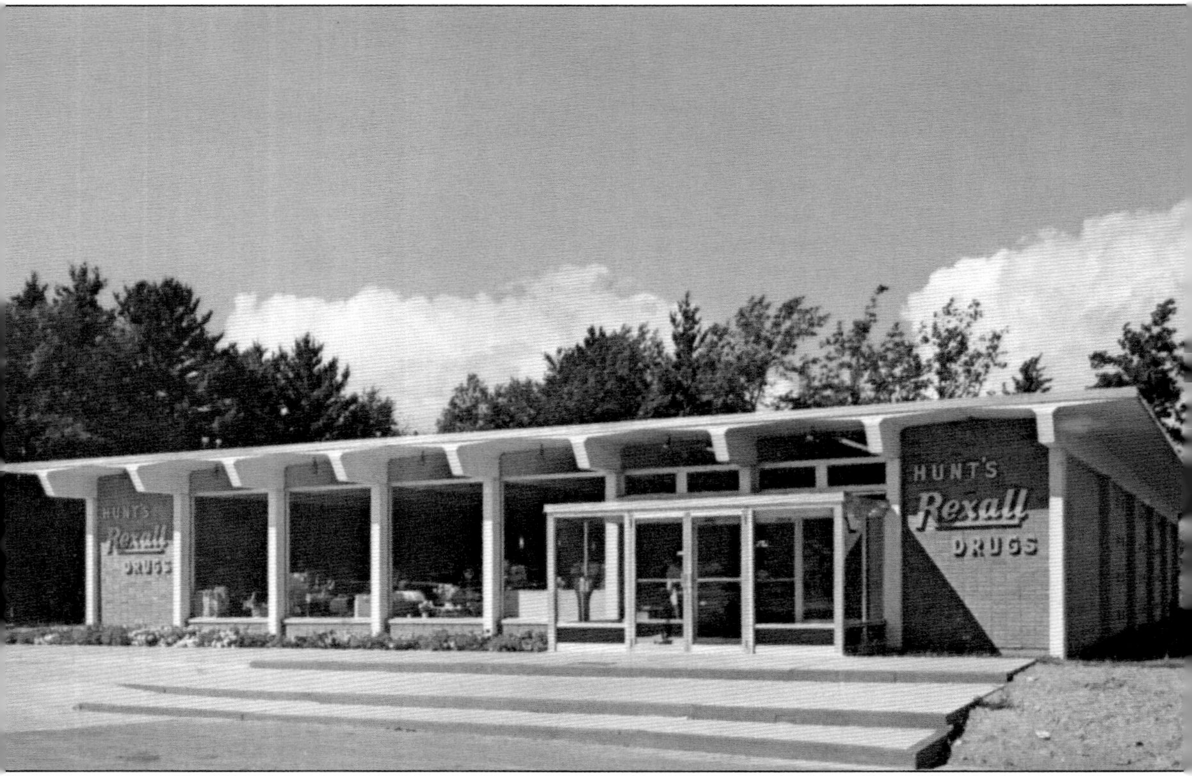

Hunt's Drugs removed its original log building in 1967 and opened its new store in 1968. Hunt's, which had a soda fountain, was popular with the high school crowd. The original log building had a stone fireplace in the soda fountain area. Pat Marra was the pharmacist. Hunt's had a large photography department, specializing in 35-millimeter cameras. The business was sold to the Rite-Aid Corporation, which razed this building and erected a new store.

Four

JOHNSON'S

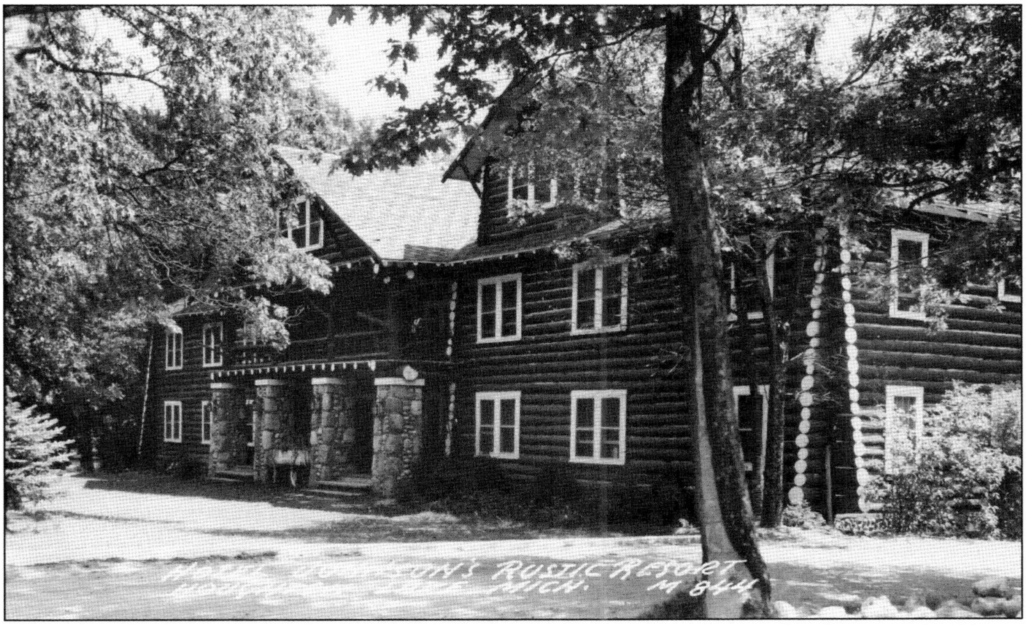

Frank R. Johnson came to Houghton Lake from Chicago in 1924. He was the director of publicity and sales manager for the Grennan Bakeries, which operated in Chicago and New York. Johnson came to Houghton Lake for rest and relaxation and fell in love with the area. Before his first stay ended, he bought 1,500 acres of land, including two miles of shoreline in the Prudenville area. Johnson's Rustic Tavern Resort lodge was the first to open, in 1925. Johnson built it initially to accommodate visitors that came to see him and his family.

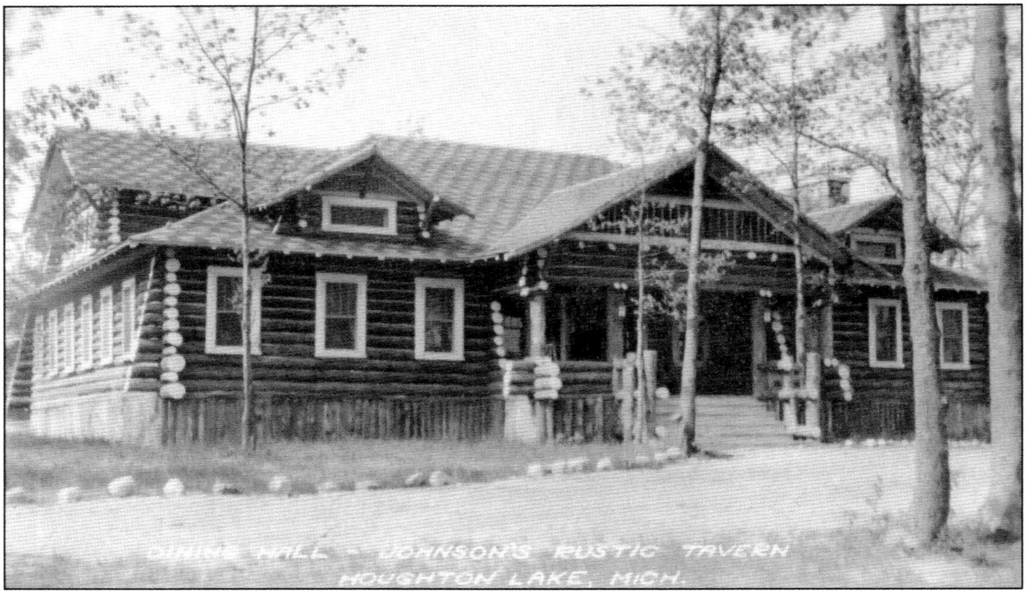

By 1926, Johnson began to expand his business. Vacationers in the cabins at the resort had kitchen facilities, but the lodge guests needed a place to take meals, so the dining hall opened. The hall offered breakfast, lunch, and dinner at reasonable prices for the guests. Dancing was also part of the dinner hour, and guests could dance at no charge to the dance band.

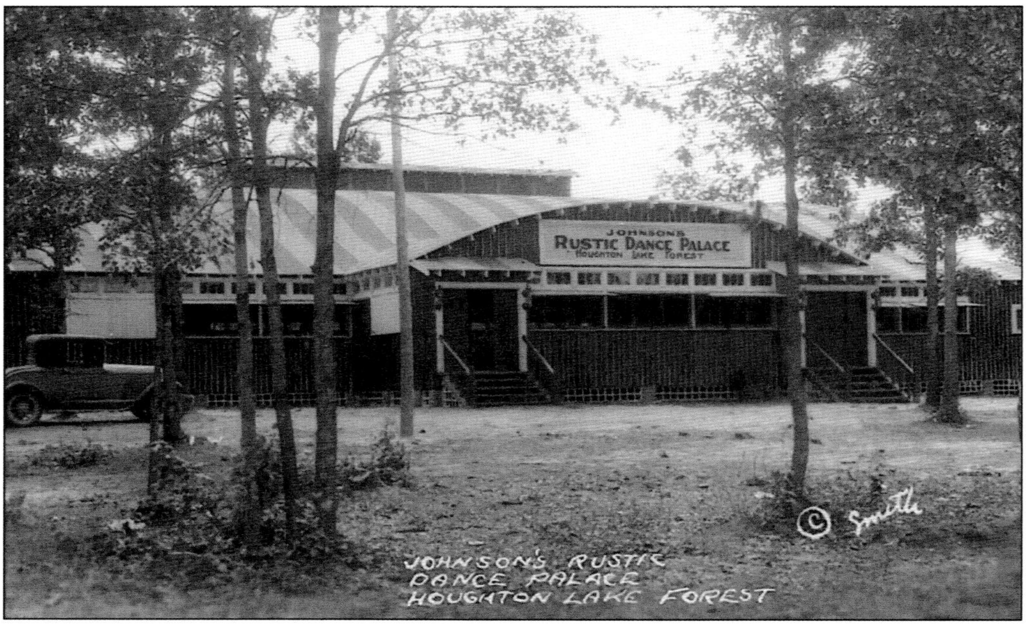

The big attraction in the early 20th century was dance halls. Johnson opened his, Johnson's Rustic Dance Palace, in 1926. It became a popular place during these years. The dance palace featured a large wooden dance floor and a stage on which 10-piece bands preformed. Prohibition was the law of the land when the dance palace opened for business, making dancing and socializing the main attractions. The dance hall was the beginning of the nightlife for which Houghton Lake became famous.

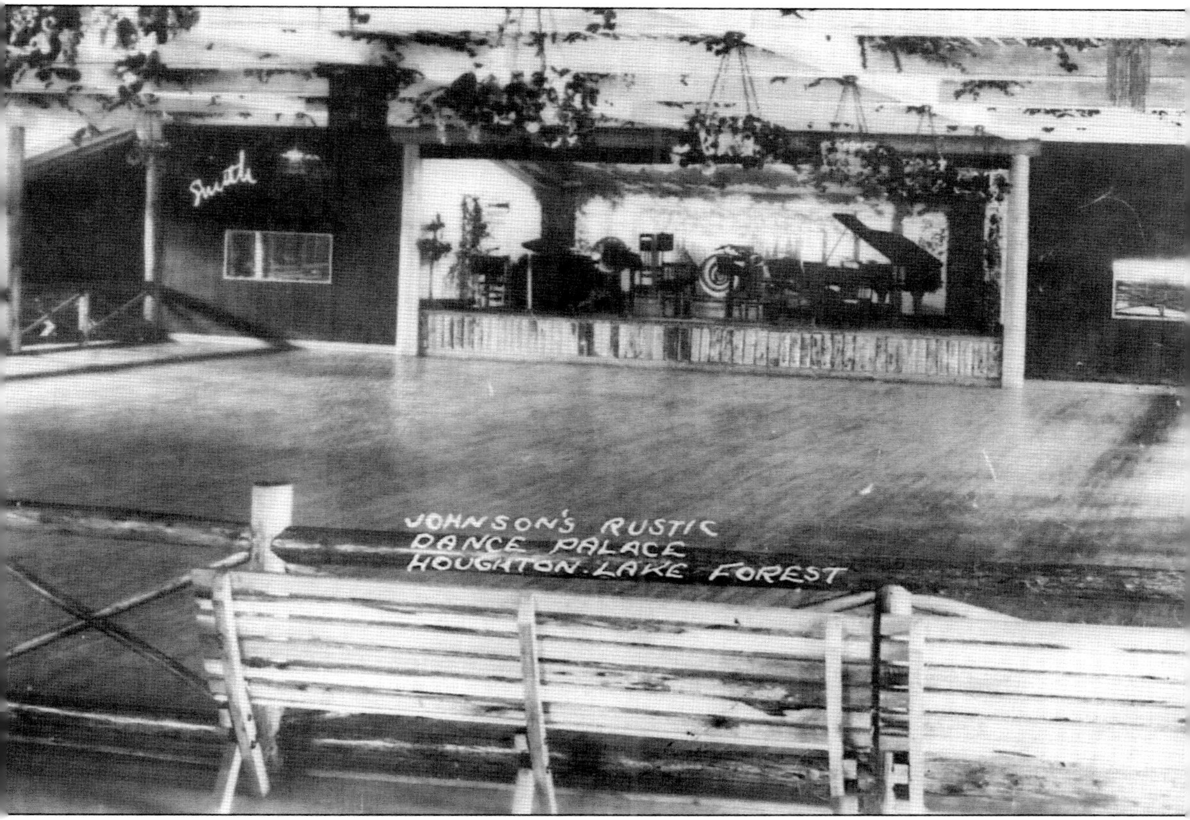

In 1942, the Rustic Dance Palace closed, as most men were fighting in World War II. It reopened after the war, and, by the 1950s, the palace was being run by John Donahue. From 1957 to 1961, Mary Louise Chandler operated the dance palace. John Donahue regained control on April 27, 1961. The following year, the dance palace became the Houghton Lake Playhouse. It hosted summer stock theater featuring television and movie stars. The dance floor became the stage for theater-in-the-round performances. A major attraction for a decade, the venue closed in 1969. The chamber of commerce bought the building when the playhouse went dark, using it for various community events. As it was becoming too costly to maintain, the chamber sold the building to the Houghton Lake Historical Society in 2001. This is one of the few original buildings remaining in Houghton Lake.

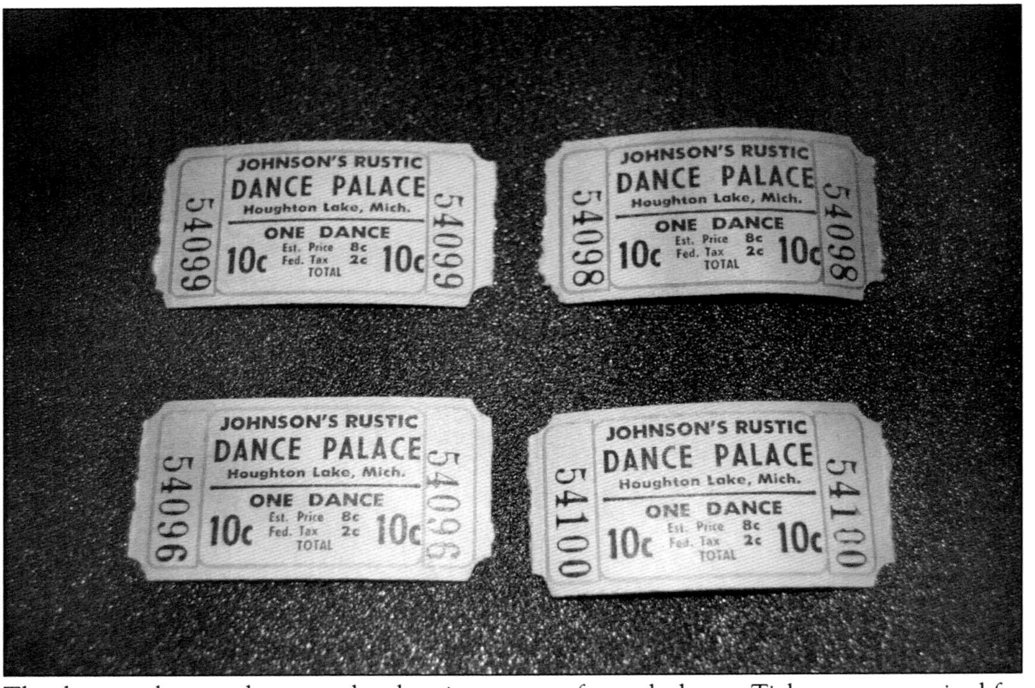

The dance palace made money by charging patrons for each dance. Tickets were required for each couple to enter the dance floor. The fee for each dance was 10¢; 8¢ for the dance, and 2¢ for the federal tax that was charged at the time. A couple rolls of tickets still survive, and they are on display at the Houghton Lake Historical Society's museum.

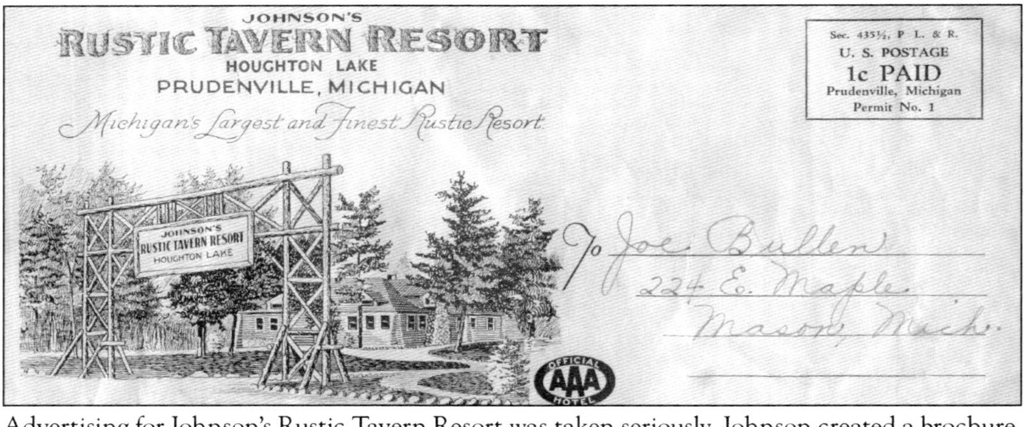

Advertising for Johnson's Rustic Tavern Resort was taken seriously. Johnson created a brochure, one side of which was used for the address. These were sent out to potential guests to urge them to book a vacation at the resort. (Courtesy of Lorrie and Randy Krause.)

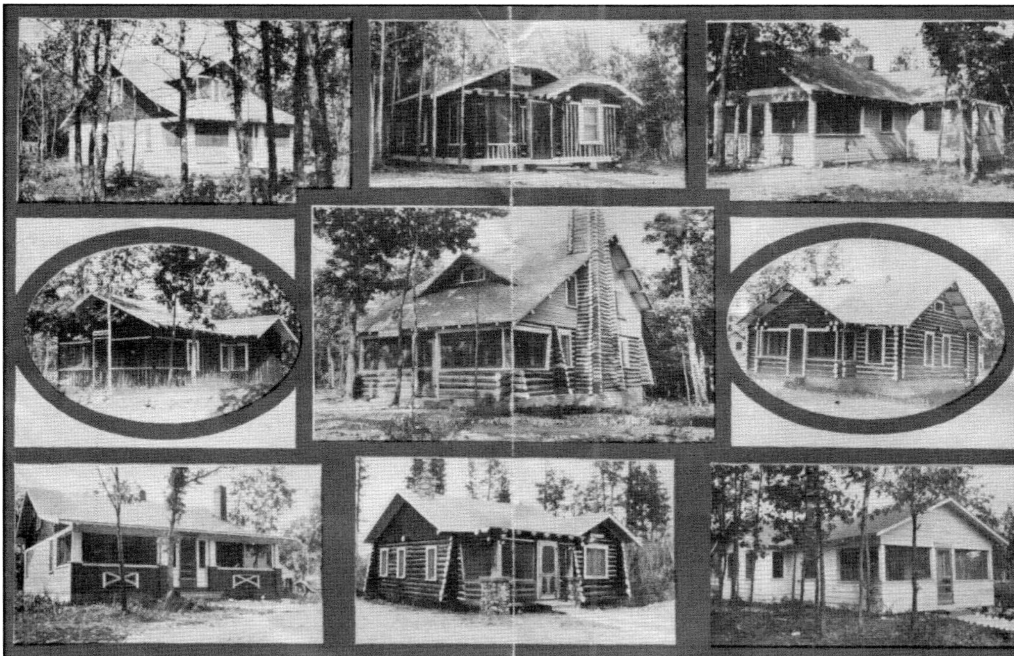

Twenty Finely Furnished Log Cabins, Bungalows and Cottages For Rent

Offer privacy and all the "comforts of home" with every convenience and pleasure of Michigan's Largest and finest RUSTIC Resort, at a minimum of expense.

All of the high class well furnished summer and winter homes illustrated upon this page, and many others, were built and are owned by us — built and furnished for you, your family and your friends—all ready to move into; with a log fire in the grate, ice in the refrigerator, electric lights and service, a boat at the dock ready for you, on the shore of a lake famous for its great number of big fish. You furnish the table linen, towels and groceries, we do the rest, or you can take as many meals as you like at our RUSTIC Tavern, located in the heart of the resort, at popular prices—dinner dance every evening.

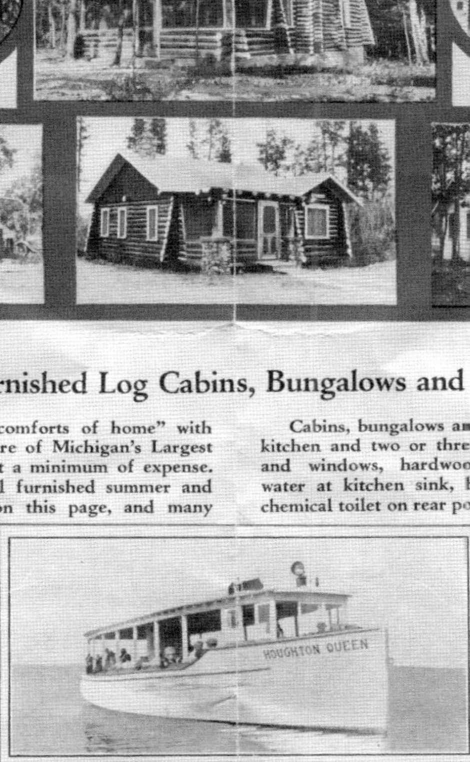

Cabins, bungalows and cottages have a living room, kitchen and two or three bedrooms, screened porches and windows, hardwood floors, excellent drinking water at kitchen sink, have latest improved odorless chemical toilet on rear porch with a 150 gallon iron tank underground, vented to the roof—no out-door toilets are permitted at Johnson's RUSTIC Tavern Resort. Beds and bedding are of the best; a double day-bed is a part of the living room equipment; a cot is provided when requested.

Most of our cabins, bungalows and cottages contain fieldstone or brick fireplaces. A cheerful wood fire is a comfort and a pleasure when required.

Milk, cream, vegetables and groceries are delivered to guests daily if desired. Stores and garages near-by.

The brochure had several pages, each telling of the wonderful amenities to be found at Johnson's. There was much to advertise, as the resort included 20 cabins in addition to the main lodge and dining room. The cabins were of the highest quality and offered many features. Patrons could have food delivered to their cabin or take their meals in the dining room. The cabins had fireplaces inside and chemical toilets on the porches with iron holding tanks. This was a modern feature for the time, and Frank Johnson made sure those inquiring about the facility were informed of this. All of the activities were described, so that potential guests would have a full list of things to do, from swimming to horseback riding and golf to fishing. This information would assure the guests that a stay at Johnson's would be great fun. The *Houghton Queen*, a popular sightseeing boat, was featured in the brochure. (Courtesy of Lorrie and Randy Krause.)

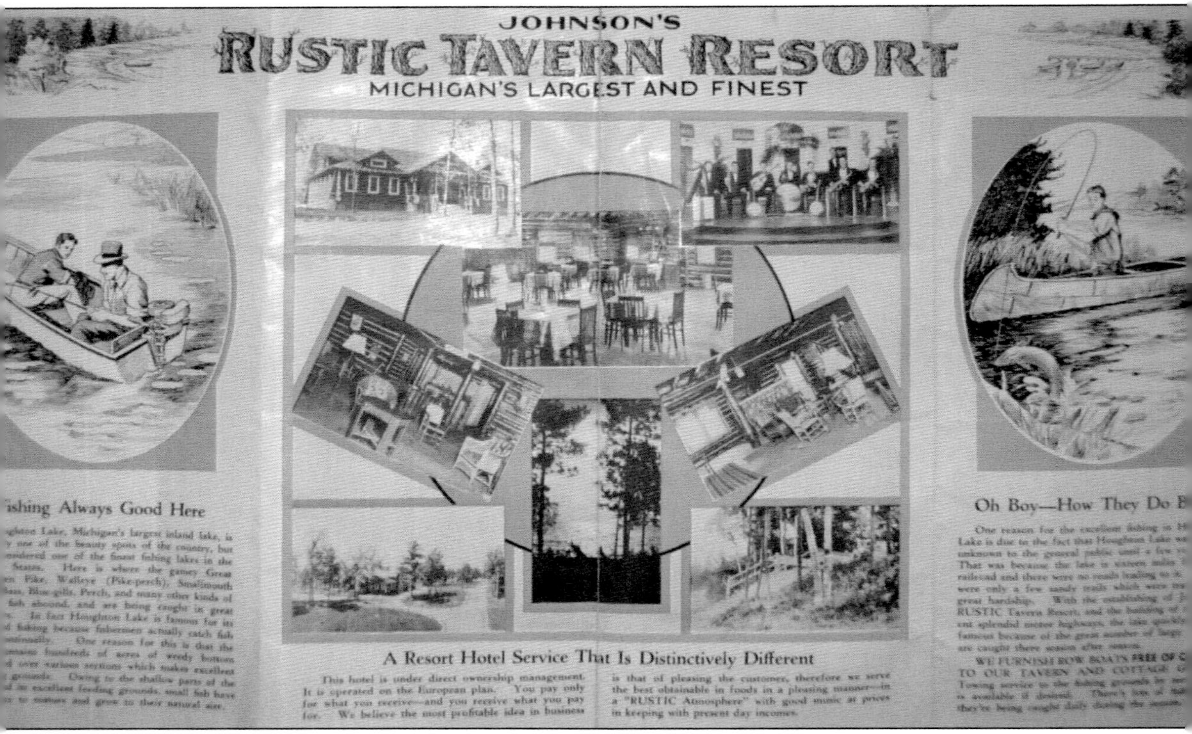

The Johnson's brochure opened up to a collage of photographs depicting the inside of the lodge, the dining hall, and the grounds. To heighten its appeal, beautiful sketches of peaceful fishing scenes gave the brochure the finishing touch. Other material could be enclosed with the brochure. During the Depression, Johnson included an additional piece that encouraged guests to take a needed vacation, promoting the stress-relieving benefits of leaving work behind. The brochure, complete with pricing information, was designed to sell the economic appeal of a stay at Johnson's Rustic Tavern Resort. At this time, a European plan was offered. Dinners cost between 75¢ and $1, and dancing was free in the dining hall. The brochure also included a darker note for which Johnson's Rustic Tavern Resort was known. The insert described how a reservation could be secured and also informed the reader that the management had the right to cancel or refuse a reservation for anyone that the management or other guests would find objectionable. It was widely known in town that Johnson's discriminated against people of color and Jews. (Courtesy of Lorrie and Randy Krause.)

In the lodge, this sign hung on the wall in the stairs leading to the guest rooms, reminding guests of the "zone of quiet." The guests' comfort was paramount at the resort. (Author's collection.)

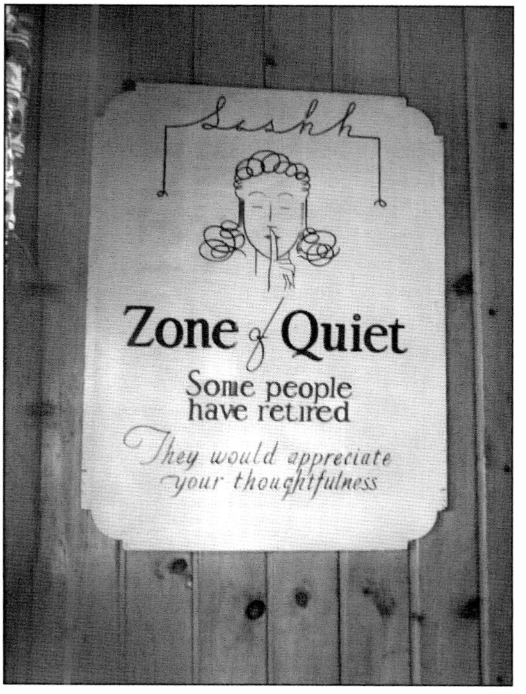

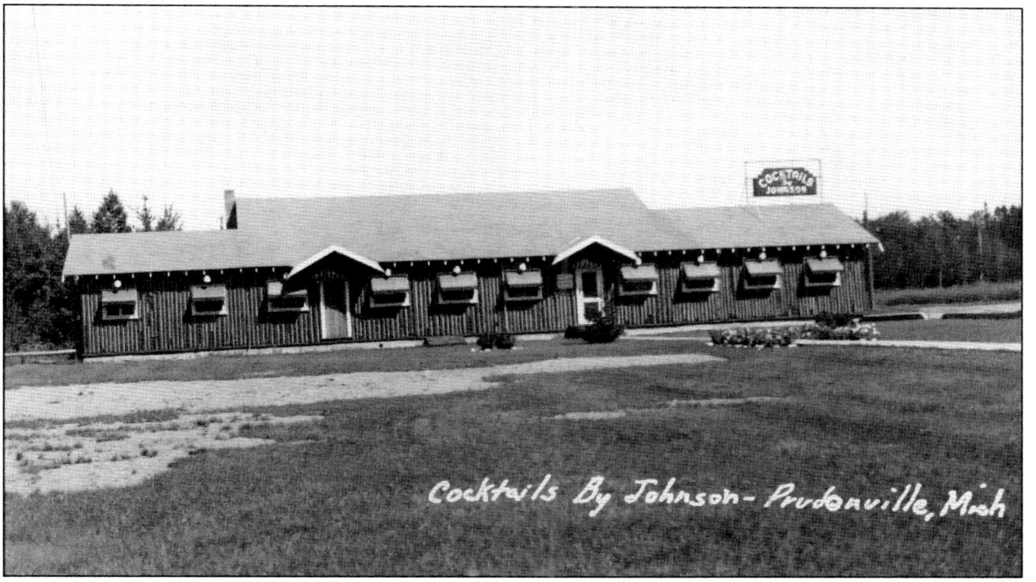

After World War II, Earl Johnson built the White Tail Cocktail Lounge. He had taken over the enterprise in 1936, after his father, Frank, passed away unexpectedly while on a cruise to the West Indies. The building's first location was in front of the Rustic Dance Palace. At some point, the building was moved to its present location, about a block from the former Johnson Realty office (now Coldwell Banker). It continued to operate as a cocktail lounge until the 1960s, when it became Traverse Bay Woolen Mills. Traverse Bay was a popular store in Prudenville, specializing in wool sweaters, blankets, and outdoor wear. It operated at the same location until it closed in the late 1990s.

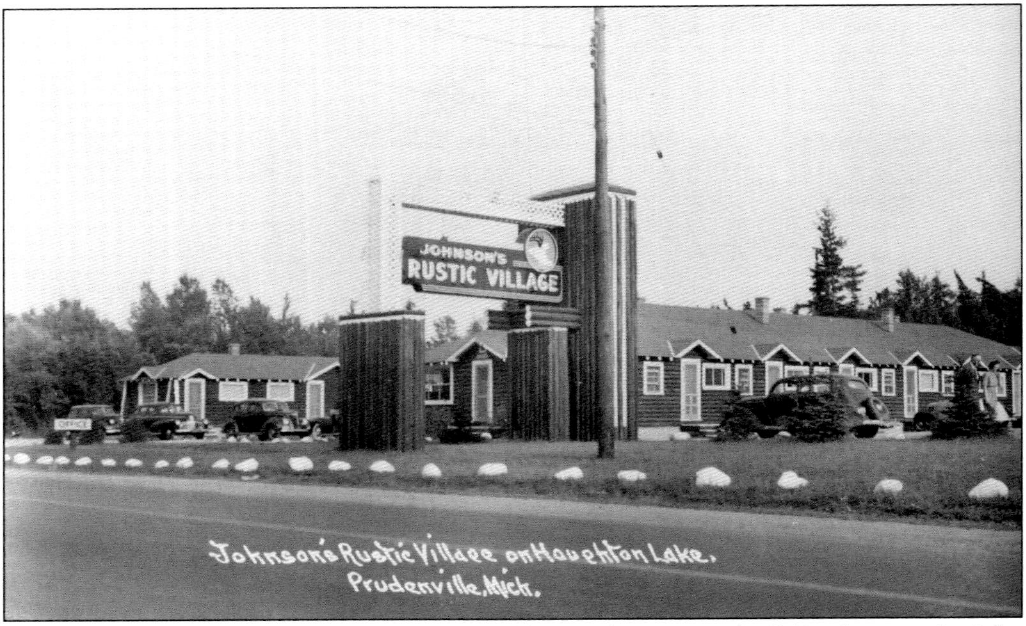

The Johnson enterprise encompassed many buildings. This is an early-1940s photograph of the log motel in Prudenville. Johnson's was so large that it was a village within itself. The company also began adopting the white deer logo. At the time it was built, Johnson's advertised that it was the largest motel east of the Mississippi River.

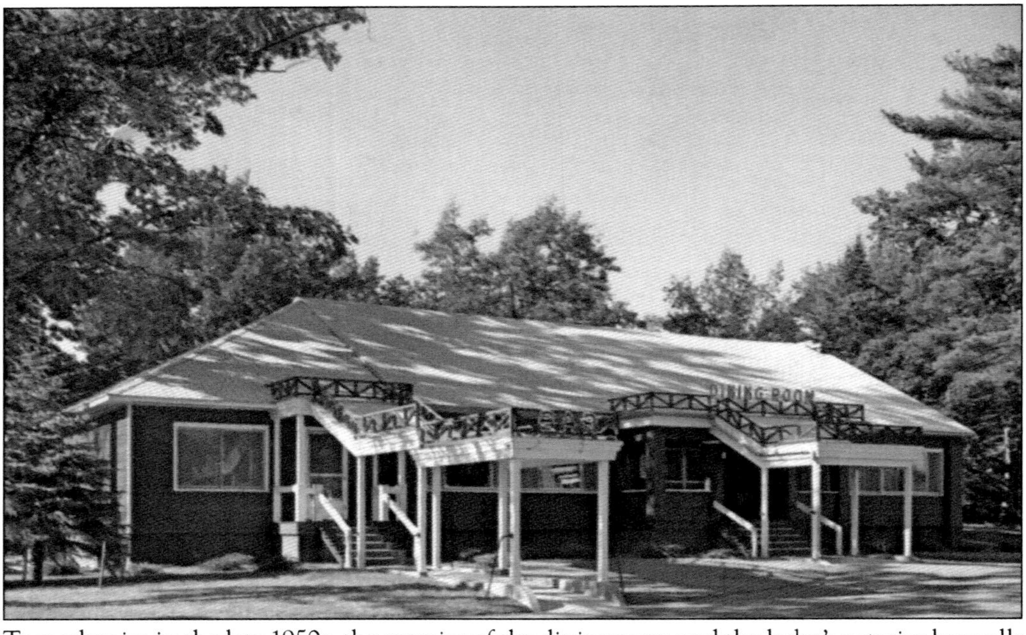

To modernize in the late 1950s, the exterior of the dining room and the lodge's exterior log walls were covered with wood siding and painted a redwood color. The third story of the lodge was removed because it was deemed a fire hazard. The exterior of the building remains the same in the present day.

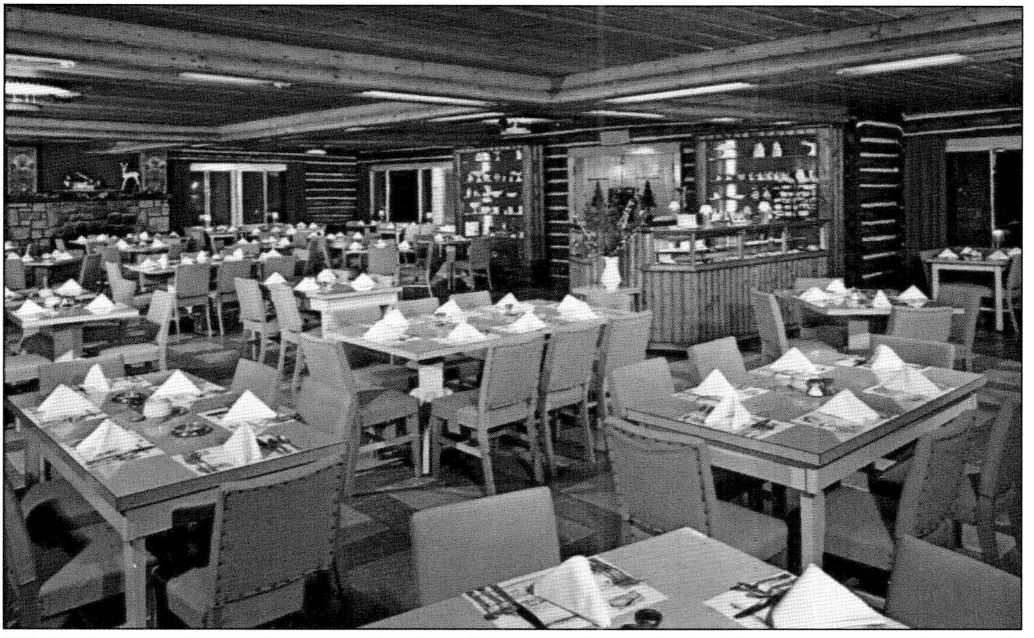

While the outside was dramatically altered from its former lodge-like appearance, the inside remained nearly unchanged, with its rustic log interior and stone fireplace. It was updated with modern furnishings of that era. The dining hall always retained its rustic charm.

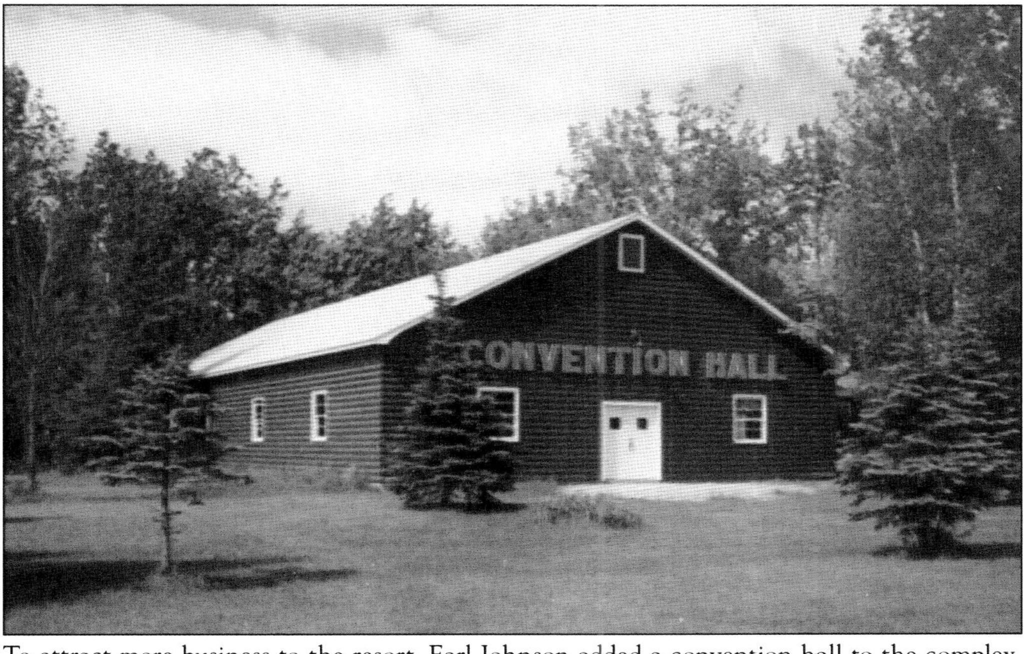

To attract more business to the resort, Earl Johnson added a convention hall to the complex. The hall would accommodate approximately 600 people. It was a very popular place, and it was used for wedding receptions and other events. The hall was eventually donated to the Knights of Columbus. It is now used as the framing department for Arnie's Arts and Crafts store.

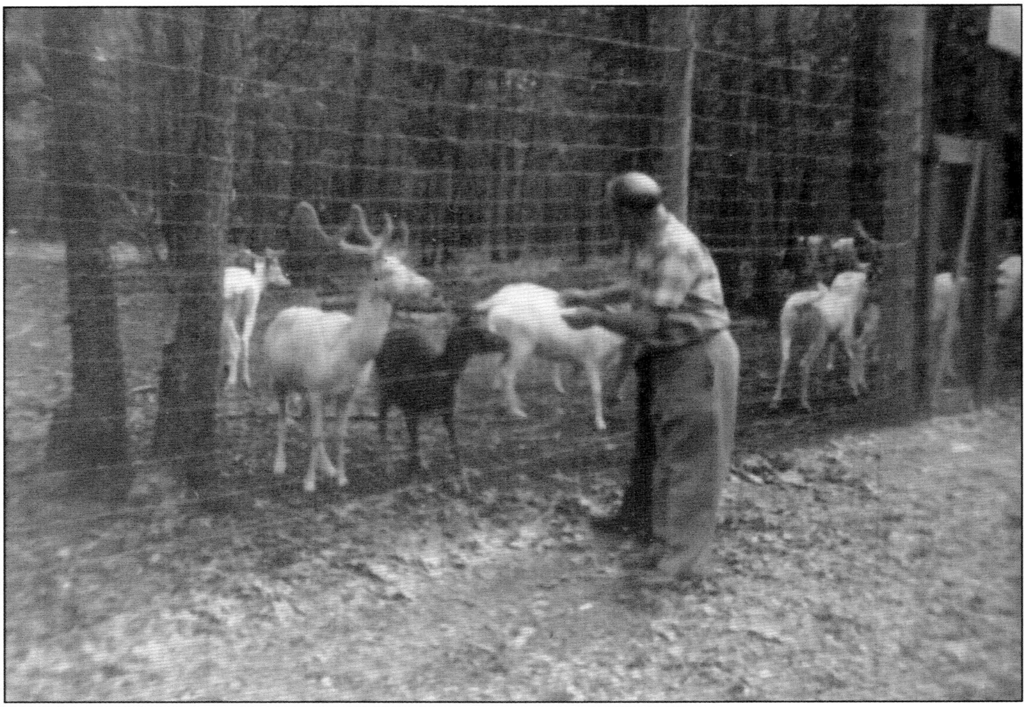

One attraction at Prudenville was Earl Johnson's herd of white deer. The deer came from the Randolph Hearst estate. They were kept in a couple of locations in Prudenville. Local residents as well as guests would stop by to see the deer and feed them.

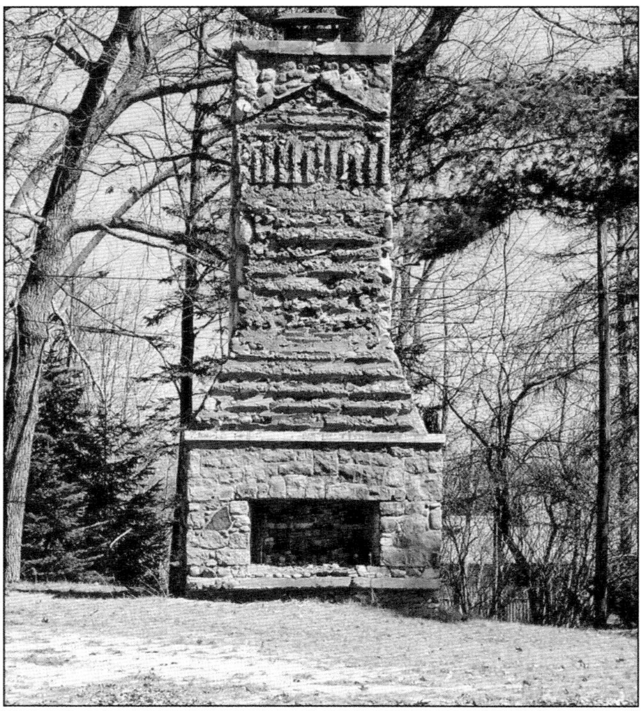

In 1968, Earl Johnson sold the lodge and dining hall to William Oliver Sr., who expanded the resort and kept both the lodge and dining hall open year-round. The dining hall was renamed the King's Table. It was a popular restaurant and nightclub in the 1970s. The King's Table was known to host great entertainment for the patrons' dancing pleasure. Tragically, it burned down in October 1979. All that remains today is the stone fireplace that graced the grand old dining room for 53 years. The Olivers sold the lodge to Bob and Laura Shea in 1980, and they operated it for about 20 years. It was sold again, in 2004, to Lorrie and Randy Krause. It remained open until May 2013, when it closed permanently. (Author's collection.)

Five

The Pines Theatre

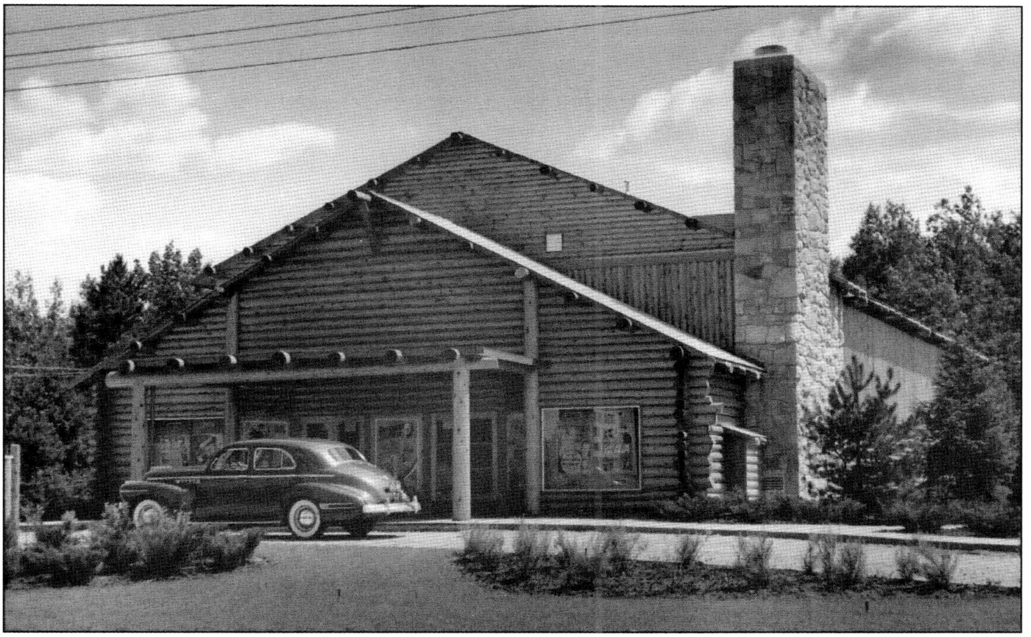

On May 30, 1941, the "showplace of the north" opened to the public. The Pines Theatre's opening movie was *Billy the Kid,* starring Robert Taylor. A Houghton Lake tradition of going to the Pines began. Over two million people have visited the Pines Theatre. It was constructed by two brothers, W. James and George Olsen. The Olsens wanted their Houghton Lake theater to be the gem in their theater holdings. To accomplish this, they hired C. Howard Crane, of the Kellogg & Crane design firm, to design their last theater. Crane was the designer of the Fox Theatre in Detroit, as well as the Detroit Opera House and many other theaters in Michigan. The Olsens wanted their Houghton Lake theater to be designed like a hunting chalet. No cost was spared in the design and construction of the Pines Theatre. The general contractor was Sieter Brothers Construction. (Courtesy of the Pines Theatre.)

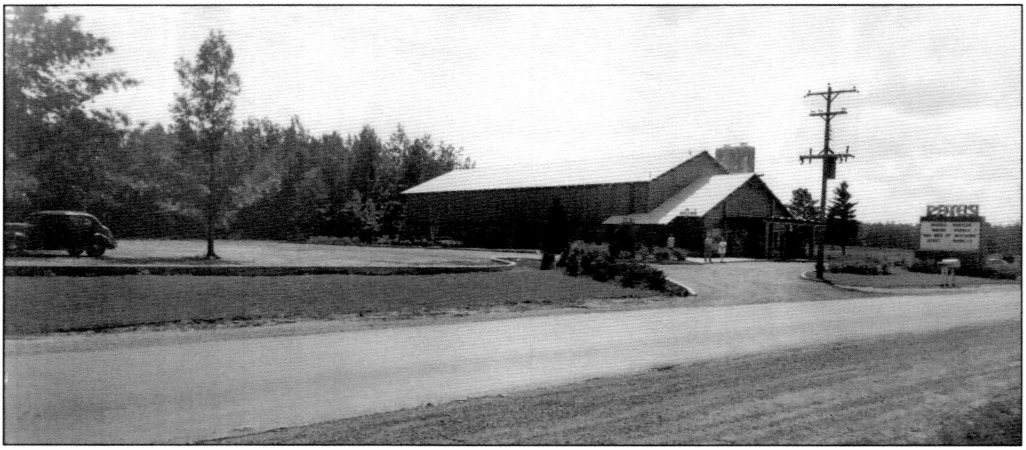

The Pines Theatre, constructed of pine and tamarack full logs, has a majestic presence on Houghton Lake's main road, M-55/US 27. Its log exterior blends into the wooded surroundings. The large parking area accommodated nightly moviegoers. Still standing in the parking lot is the parking tower, constructed like a fort lookout. The tower was used in the early days to watch over the parking lot to ensure the safety of the patrons. (Courtesy of the Pines Theatre.)

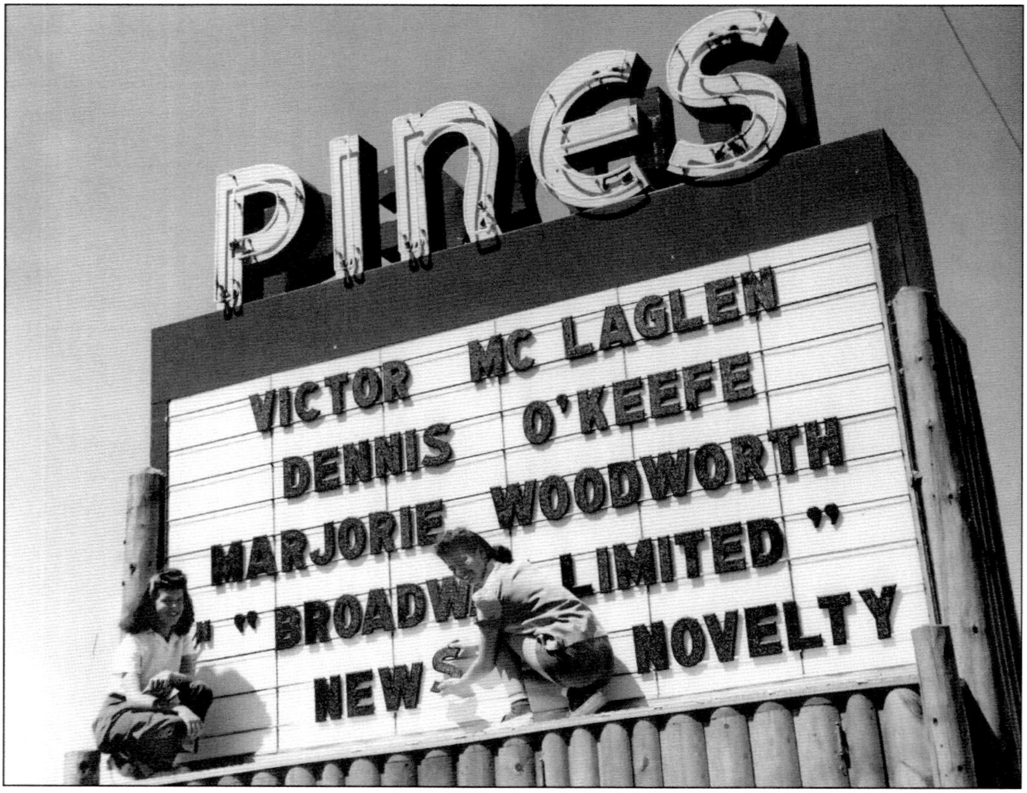

The large marquee alongside the highway was crowned with the word "Pines" lit up in neon. A ladder was required to make the weekly changes to the name of the movie playing at the Pines Theatre. The marquee was constructed of logs to maintain the hunting chalet theme. (Courtesy of the Pines Theatre.)

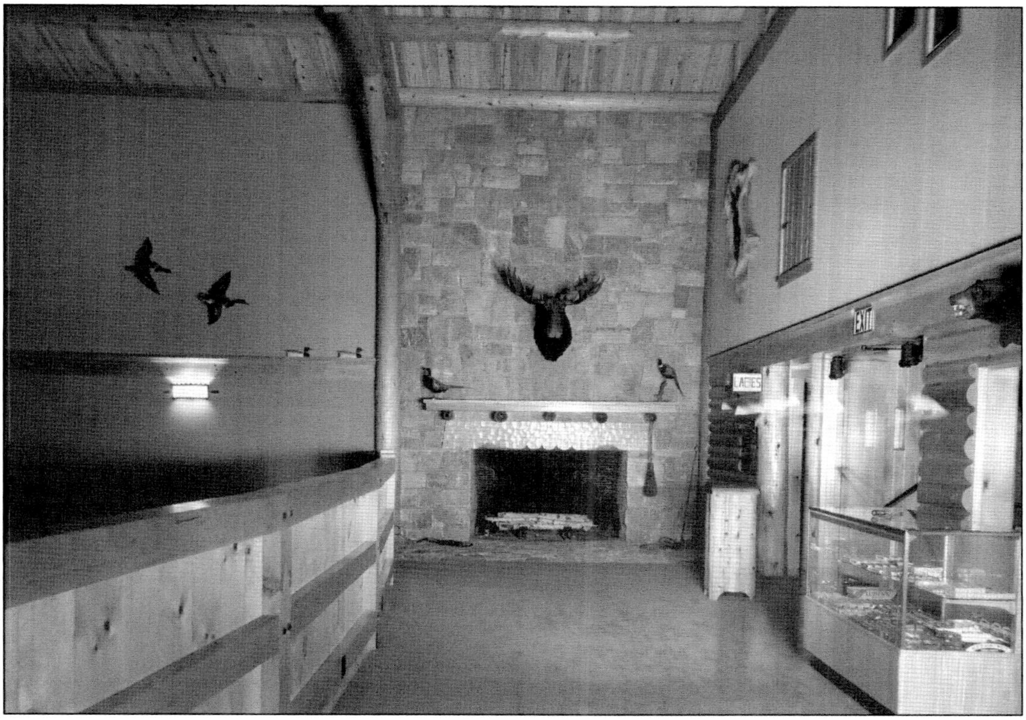

Once inside the large log edifice, moviegoers were in for a special experience. The hunting chalet theme continued throughout the building. The original lobby was designed with a floor-to-ceiling fieldstone fireplace. The interior was mostly log, with an open log ceiling. The most unusual feature of the Pines was the large collection of high-quality trophy mounts adorning the walls. The Olsens had between 20 and 30 mounts in the theater. (Courtesy of the Pines Theatre.)

Keeping with the hunting chalet motif, a painting of a bird hunter and his dog hung opposite the fieldstone fireplace. This is a rare photograph of that painting. When the trophy room addition was completed, this painting was lost. The candy counter at left in the photograph is still in use today. (Courtesy of the Pines Theatre.)

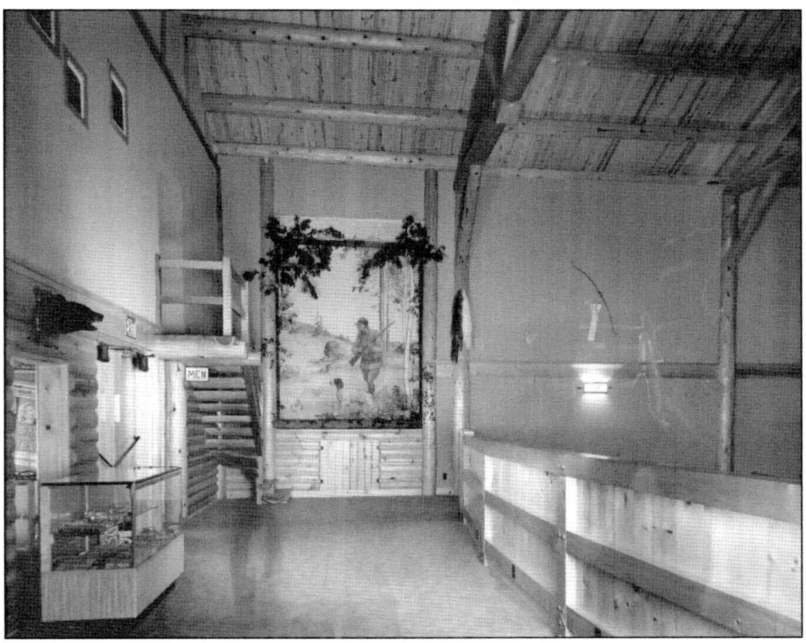

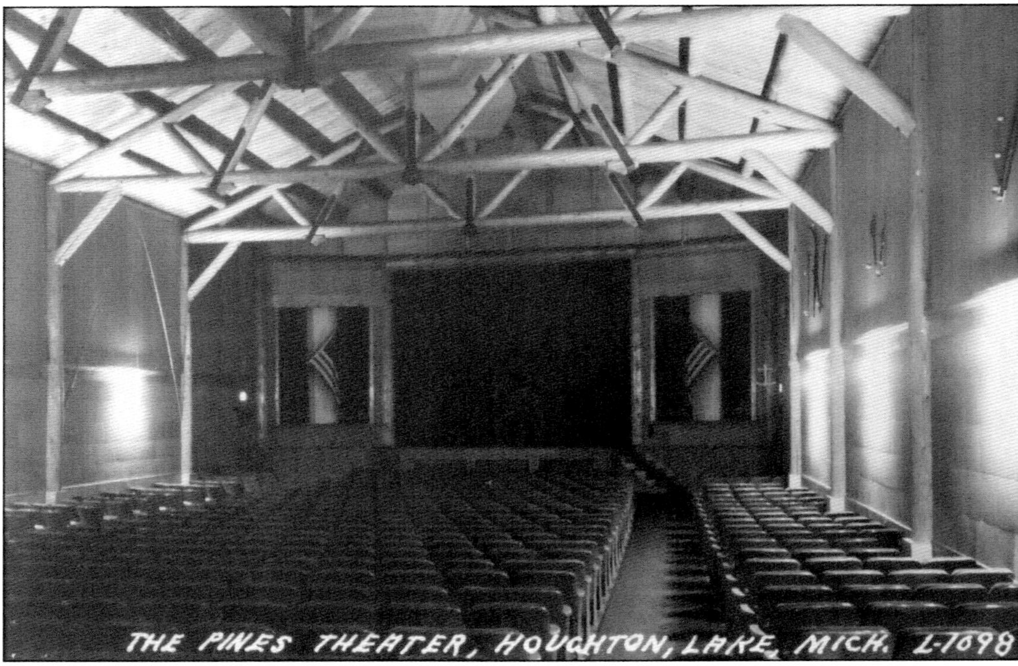

The viewing room of the Pines is massive. When the theater was built, the seating accommodated 500 patrons. The seating was installed by American Seating Company of Grand Rapids, Michigan. There are three sections of seating: the center stage and two side areas. The seating is still in use today, 72 years later. The original movie format was a square picture, so the screen was square. The sports equipment decorating the viewing room was part of the decor from the beginning. In the 1940s and 1950s, there were three showings per evening in the summer, requiring a staff of eight to ten people. (Courtesy of the Pines Theatre.)

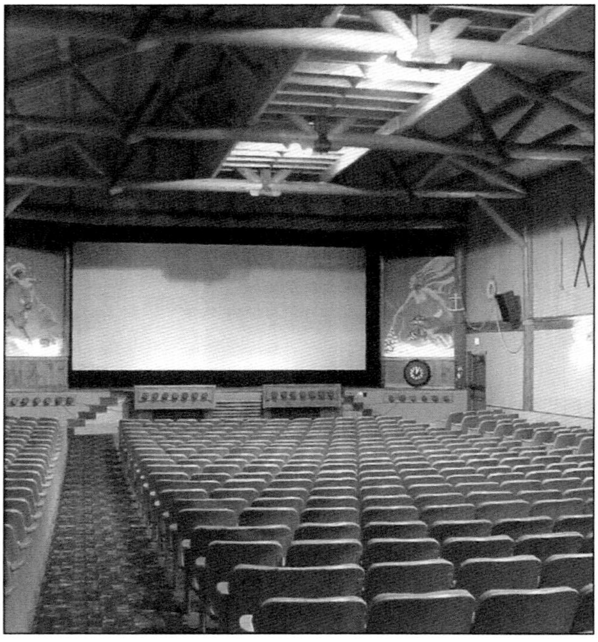

The development of CinemaScope in 1954 changed the format of movies. Keeping with the changes in Hollywood, the Olsen brothers remolded and updated the Pines Theatre. To accommodate the new screen, two logs had to be removed. The backstage area was added for the sound system. The new screen was 31 feet wide and 13 feet high. This screen layout is still used today. Admission in the 1950s was 55¢. (Courtesy of the Pines Theatre.)

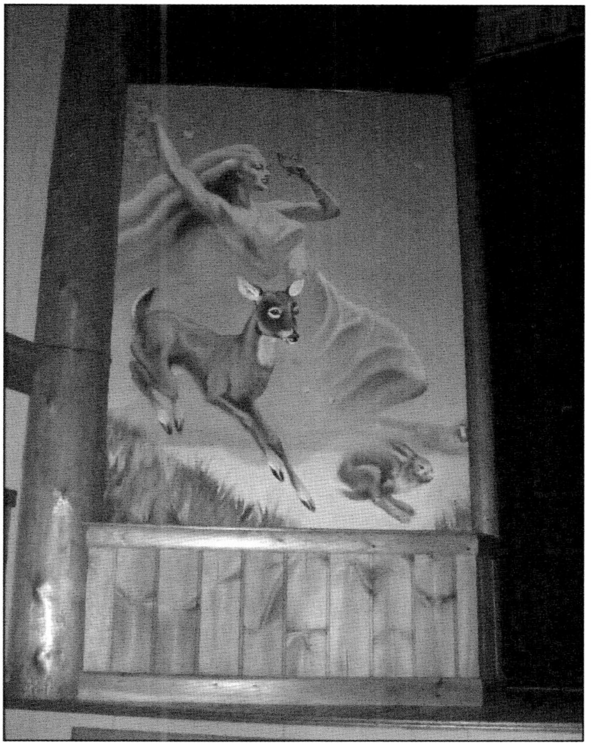

When the CinemaScope screen was installed, two paintings were mounted on each side of the screen. There is a debate about what the two paintings portray. Is it the goddess of summer and the goddess of winter? Or, is it the good wind and the bad wind? Little is known about the paintings and their artist. An Olsen family member told the Frasers that a woman from Detroit painted them. Regardless, they are a unique part of the Pines Theatre, and they have been there since the 1950s. (Both courtesy of the Pines Theatre.)

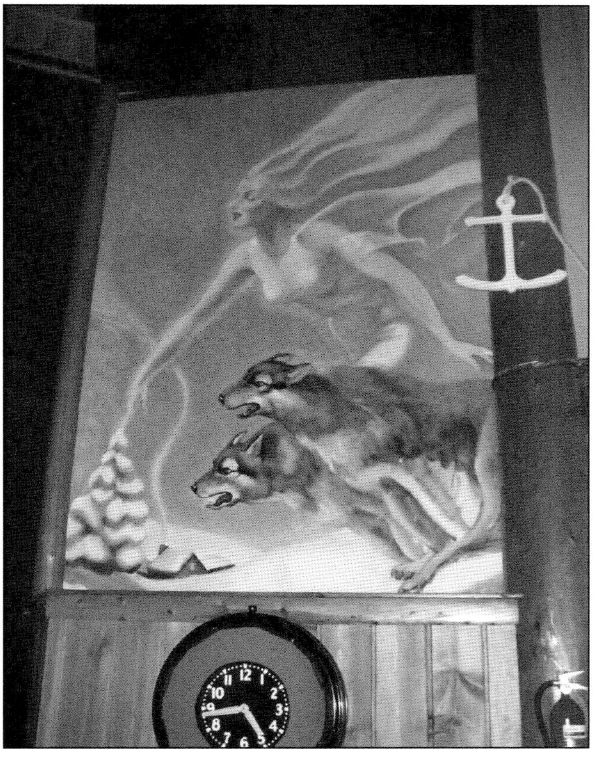

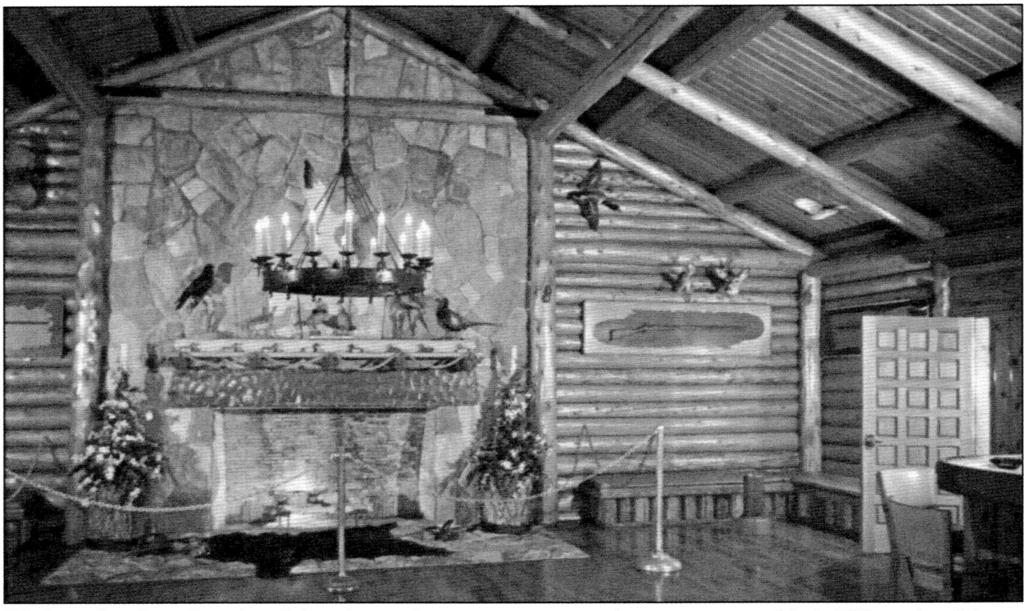

Within the first decade of the theater's existence, a trophy room was added. What the Olsens intended for this room has not been discovered. For many years, it was used as a waiting room for intermissions and between showings. Smoking was allowed in this room for many years. (Courtesy of the Pines Theatre.)

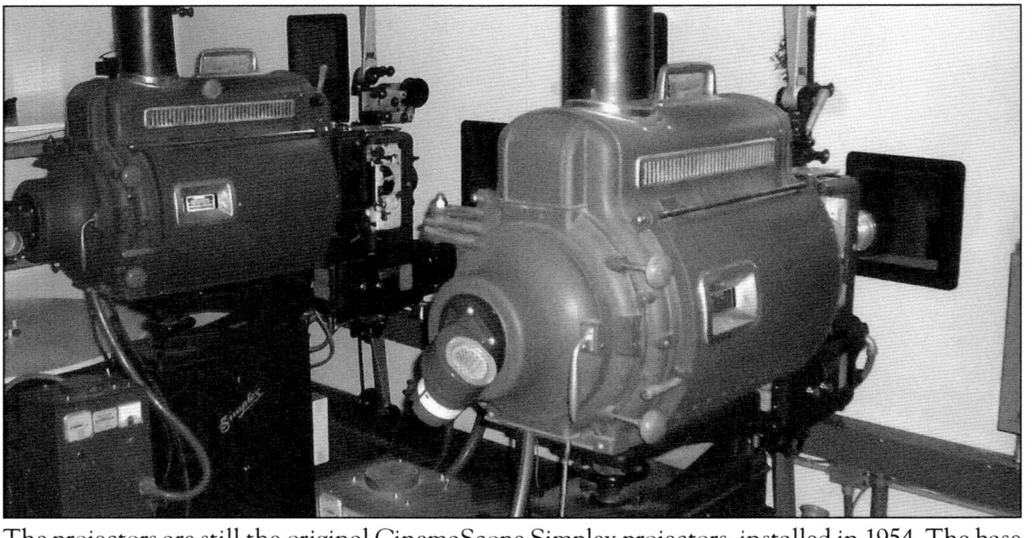

The projectors are still the original CinemaScope Simplex projectors, installed in 1954. The base and the sound heads are original. The light source and film-changing features have been updated. Only the highest-quality equipment was and still is used at the Pines Theatre. Before the mid-1970s, movie projection was a union job. Only the projectionist was allowed in the booth. Every 20 minutes, the reels had to be changed, alternating between projectors. The booth, constructed of concrete, was fitted with fireproof shutters over the light source and a fireproof door. This was necessary, as the original film was made out of nitrate and was highly flammable. In 1973, the film changer was updated to a platter, which saved labor and allowed a movie to run from beginning to end. (Courtesy of the Pines Theatre.)

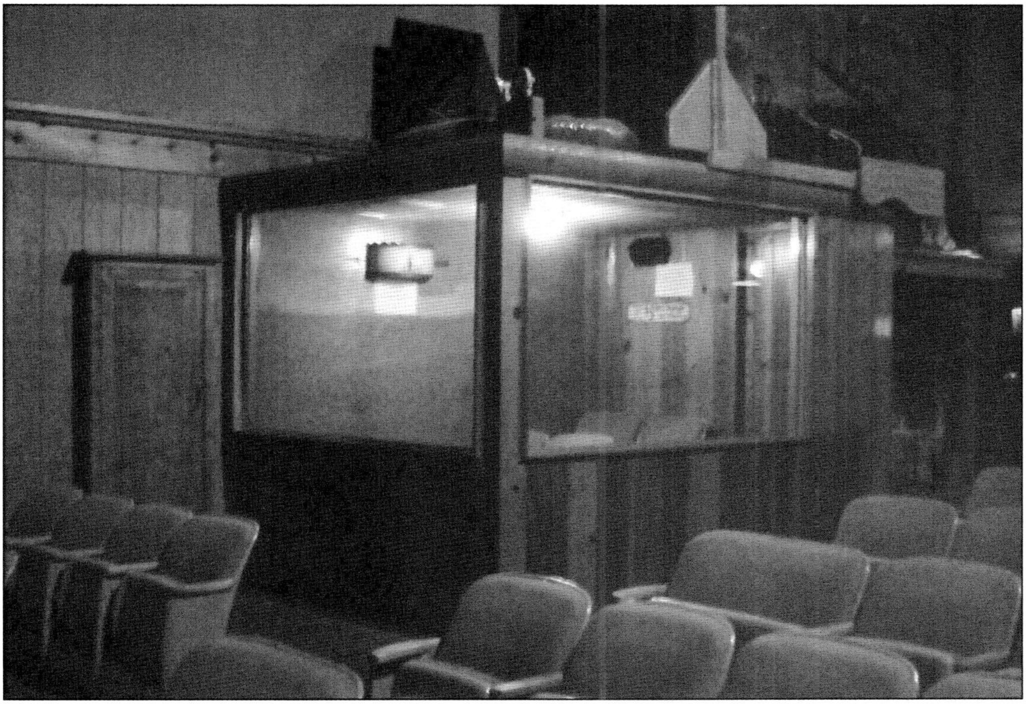

Unique to the Pines Theatre is a cry room. It is a soundproof room to provide families with young children a place to view the film. The rest of the viewing room's occupants are able to enjoy the movie without the disruption of babies and small children. (Courtesy of the Pines Theatre.)

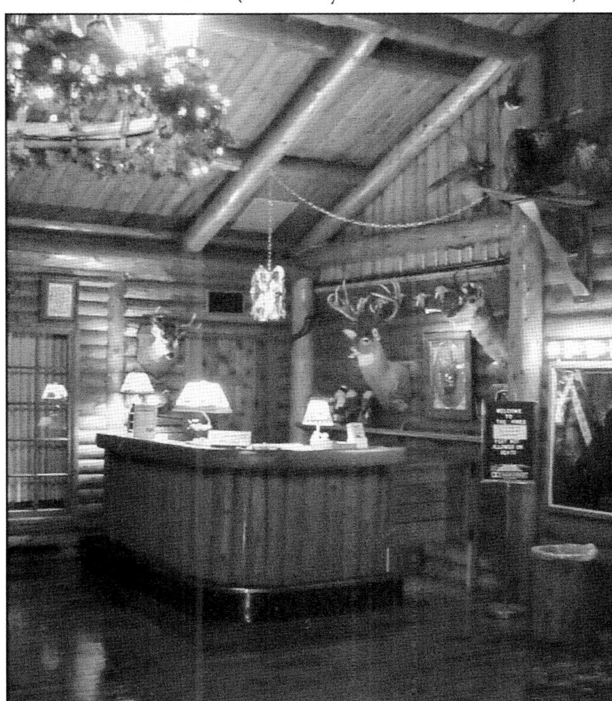

With the passing of the Olsen brothers, their movie houses were sold to Triangle Enterprise. Unfortunately, Triangle managed all the theaters as a movie chain, without much regard for the uniqueness of the Pines Theatre. By 1973, the building was in serious disrepair. C. Floyd and Ruby Huddy bought the Pines Theatre from Triangle. The Huddys set to work, spending hundreds of thousands of dollars to restore the Pines to its glory. They hired Sieter Brothers Construction to oversee the restoration of the building. If the Huddys had not bought the theater, it would be only a memory of the "good old days" at the lake. (Courtesy of the Pines Theatre.)

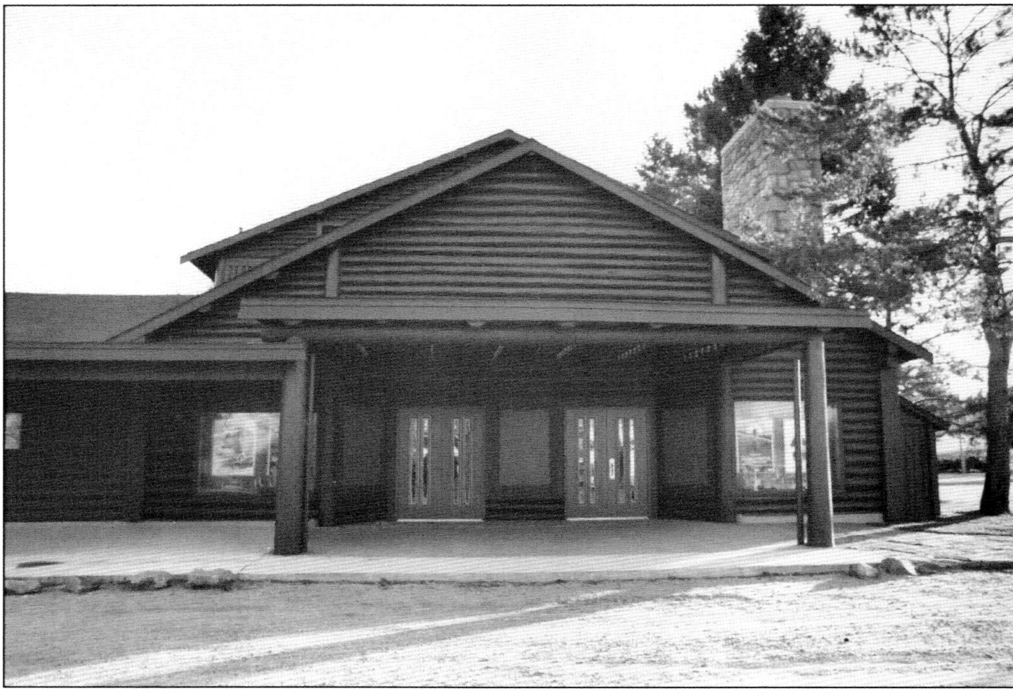

The major change that Mr. and Mrs. Huddy made to the Pines was the addition to the trophy room. They moved the concession stand and the ticket booth to the trophy room. This kept the lobby behind the viewing room quiet for the patrons. It also routed the exiting patrons through the old lobby, while patrons for the second showing could wait in the trophy room between movies. (Courtesy of the Pines Theatre.)

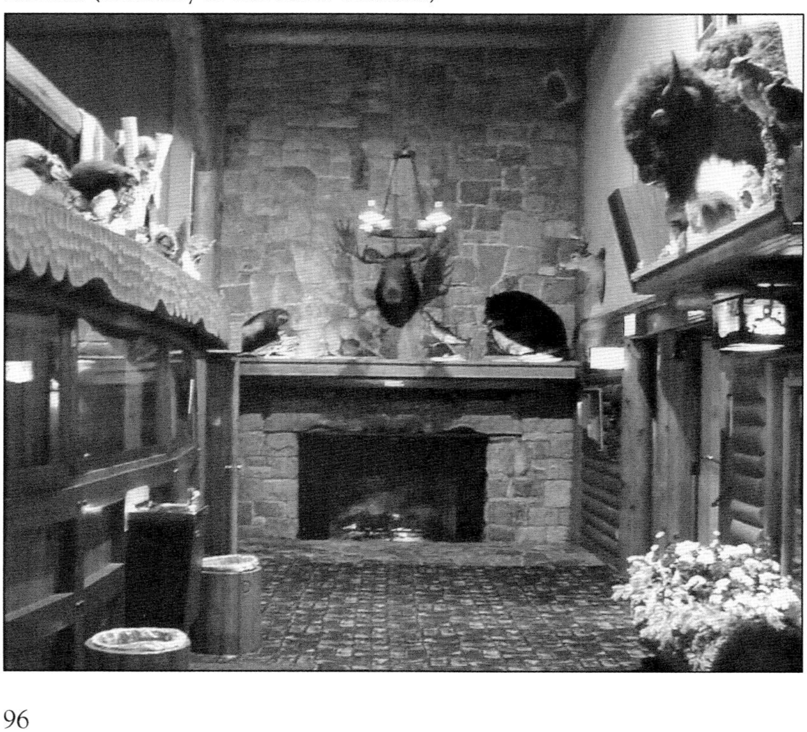

The Huddys expanded the trophy mount collection to 75 quality mounts. To display the mounts, they enlarged the mantles of both fieldstone fireplaces. They also raised the half wall behind the viewing room to accommodate the new mounts. Finally, a display area was added above where the concession stand once stood. (Courtesy of the Pines Theatre.)

To complete the changes, French doors were installed between the lobby and the trophy room. The bear rug, which had always hung over the banister to the projection room, was placed above the doors. (Courtesy of the Pines Theatre.)

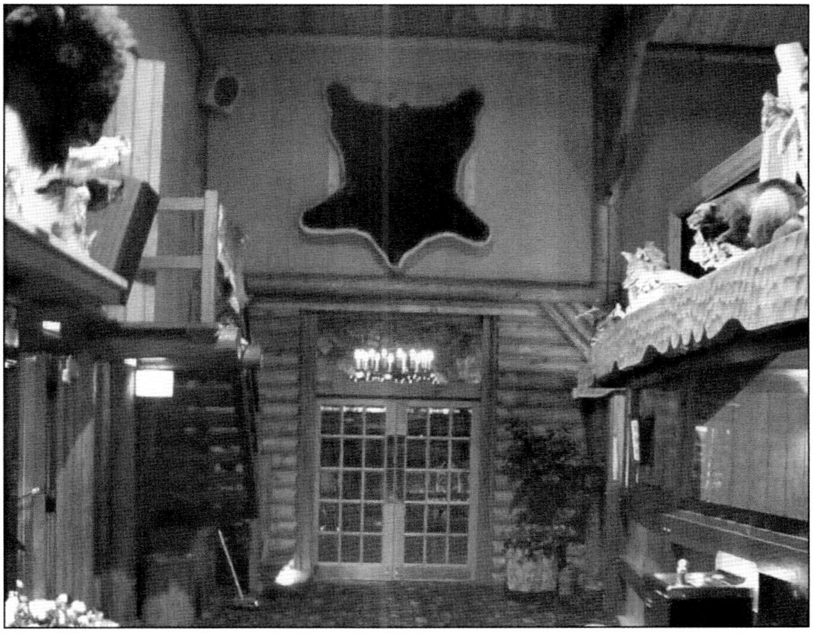

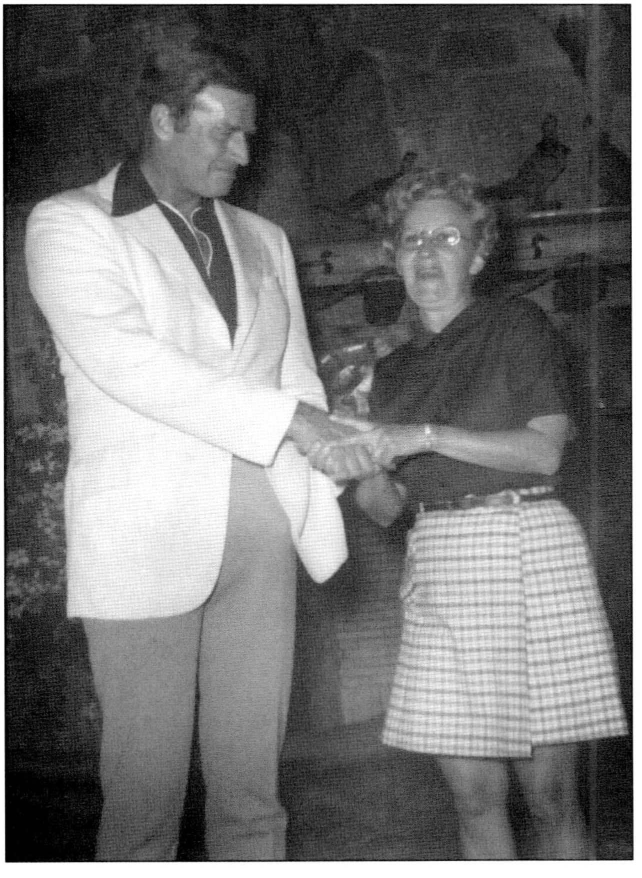

The Pines Theatre hosted Charlton Heston (left) in the mid-1980s. Heston was from the neighboring town of St. Helen. He came to the Pines for a private viewing of one of his movies. Ruby (right) and Floyd Huddy were happy to accommodate this local star. (Courtesy of the Pines Theatre.)

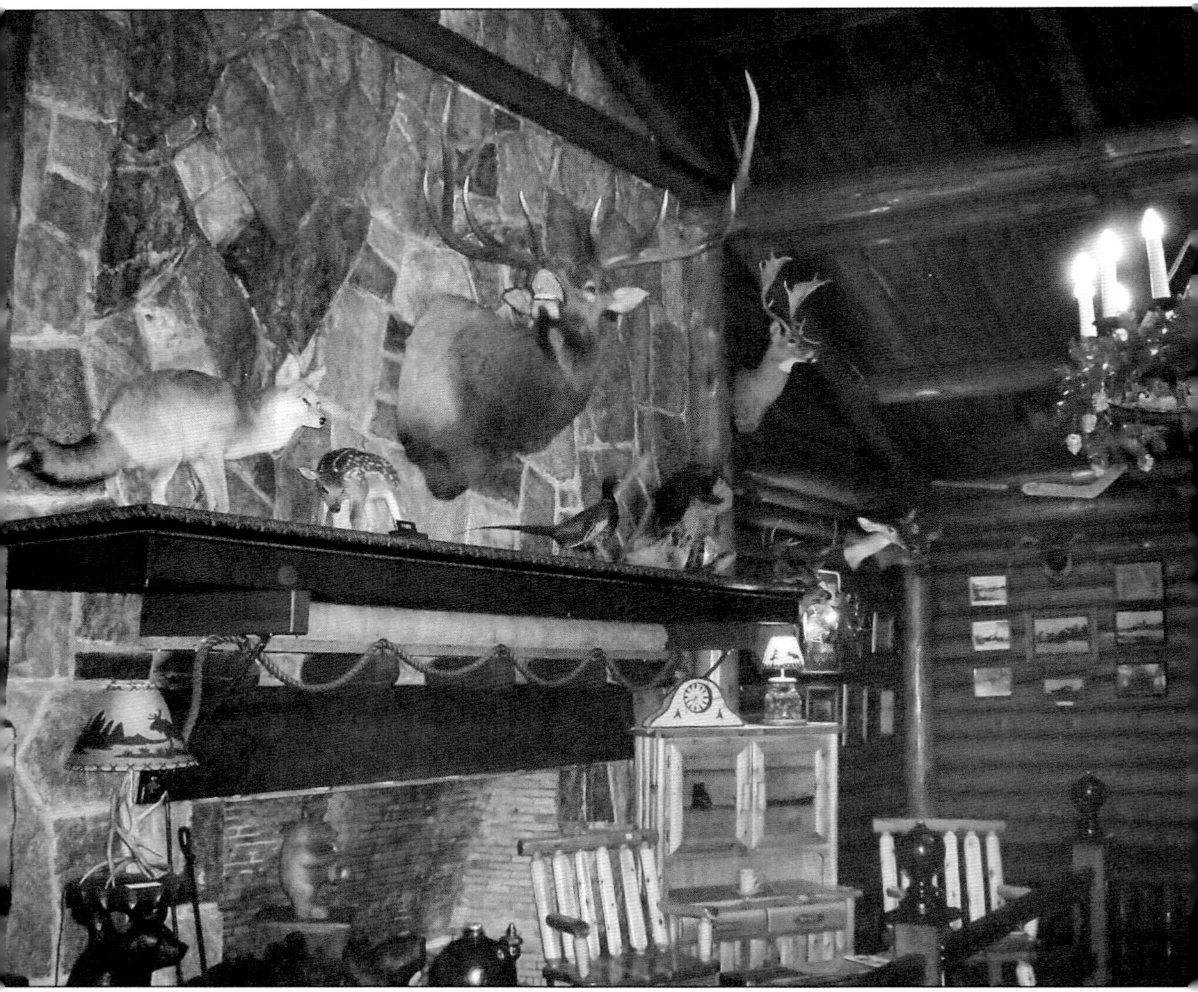

The Huddys owned the Pines for 24 years. During that time, they upgraded the sound system twice, in 1990 (to Dolby Stereo) and in 1996 (to Dolby Digital). In 1997, the Huddys sold the Pines Theatre to Les Newton and Louise Fraser, who currently own it. They have a true love for this iconic theater. They work very hard to preserve the history the Pines Theatre holds while also keeping up with the advances in the movie industry. In 2012, the Pines installed a digital projection system. The first movie shown in digital at the Pines was Steven Spielberg's *War Horse*. In 2013, the Cretors popcorn machine was replaced. The machine had been in use since the late 1940s. It was still in good working condition, but it could not meet the demands of the larger popcorn containers. The Pines only sells Zastrow popcorn, grown in Hemlock, Michigan. The new popcorn machine is a Cretors, made in Chicago. The Pines Theatre is not only a wonderful movie venue, it is a museum experience as well. (Courtesy of the Pines Theatre.)

Six

The Music Box

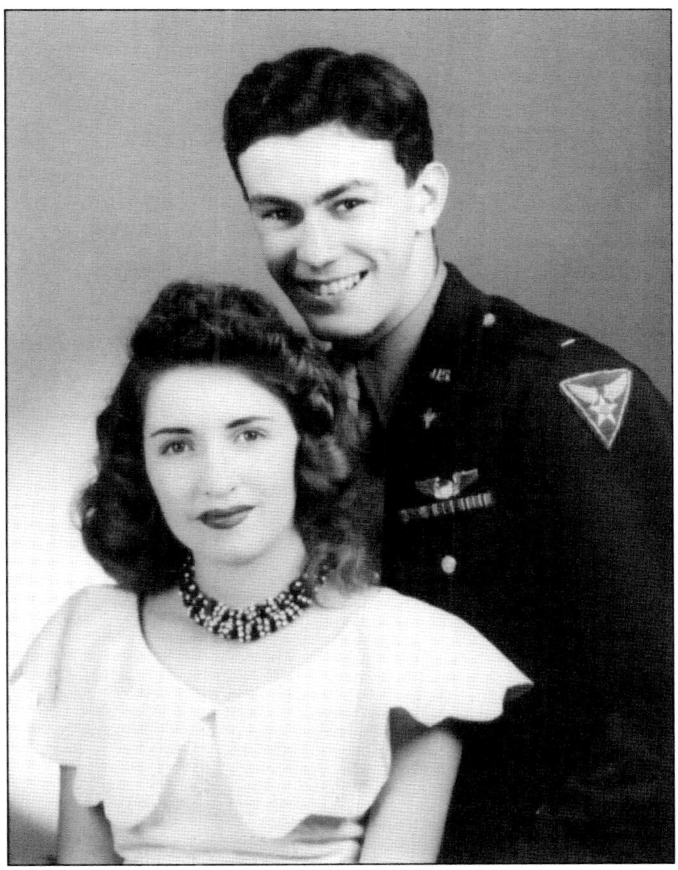

At the close of World War II, a young Army Air Corps pilot, Leland "Lee" Kelly, was tasked with a mission to fly a couple of general officers from France to Manila for a meeting. While he was waiting for the return flight, the generals told Lee to do some sightseeing. Touring the town, he saw some teenagers playing records and dancing on the street corner. He asked why they danced on the corner, and he was told that it was the only thing they had to do. Kelly wrote home to his bride, Shirley (née Verinder) Kelly, and told her about his encounter. Shirley had grown up in Houghton Lake and knew what it was like to have little entertainment in town. They both agreed that they had to create a place for teens to dance. (Courtesy of Mark Barnhart Sr.)

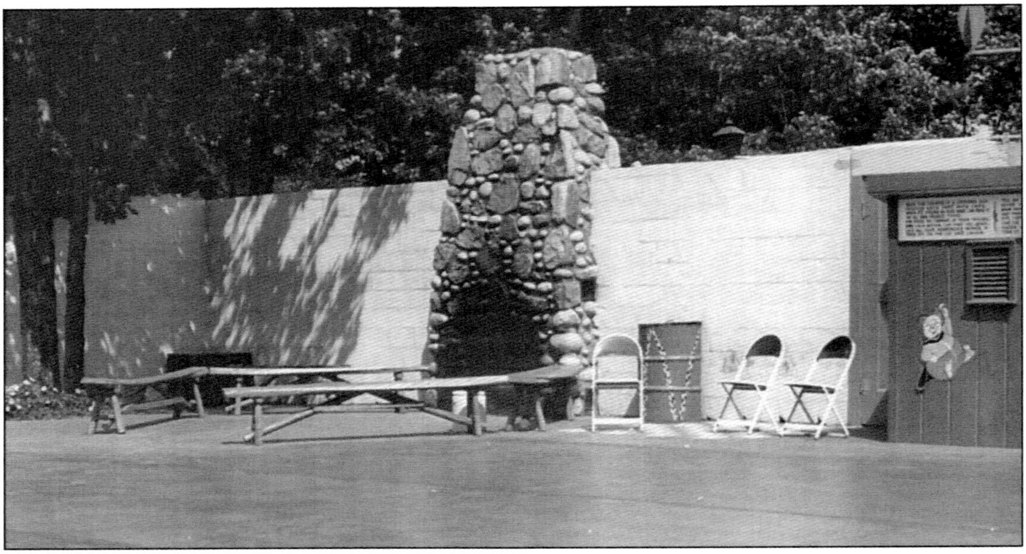

Shirley and Lee Kelly opened the doors to their teen dance hall on July 6, 1946. They named it the Music Box. That first summer, it was open every Saturday night. The venue had a small concrete dance floor, with a jukebox in the corner where the teens could play their favorite records. The dance floor was enclosed with a four-foot cinder block wall. The facility lacked electricity to power the jukebox, so an electrical cord was strung across to Bill Elwell's Sinclair station and campground. Admission was 5¢. It was a small but important start for a fine establishment that would touch the lives of teens for three and a half decades. (Courtesy of Mark Barnhart Sr.)

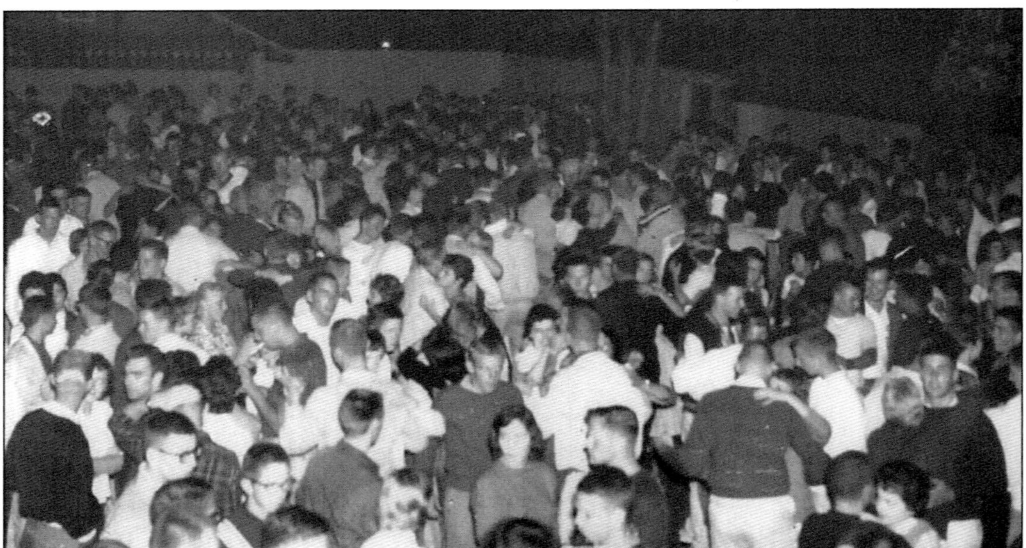

As time passed, word spread all over the state and to neighboring states about the Music Box. Some teens drove up just to dance under the stars on Friday or Saturday night, while others talked their parents into vacationing in Houghton Lake so they could go to the famous Music Box. Photographs were rarely taken in "the Box," as it was a place just for teens. This photograph was permitted by Shirley Kelly to document the sea of teenagers on the dance floor in the mid-1960s. The largest crowd was 7,200 teens on July 1, 1967. (Courtesy of Mark Barnhart Sr.)

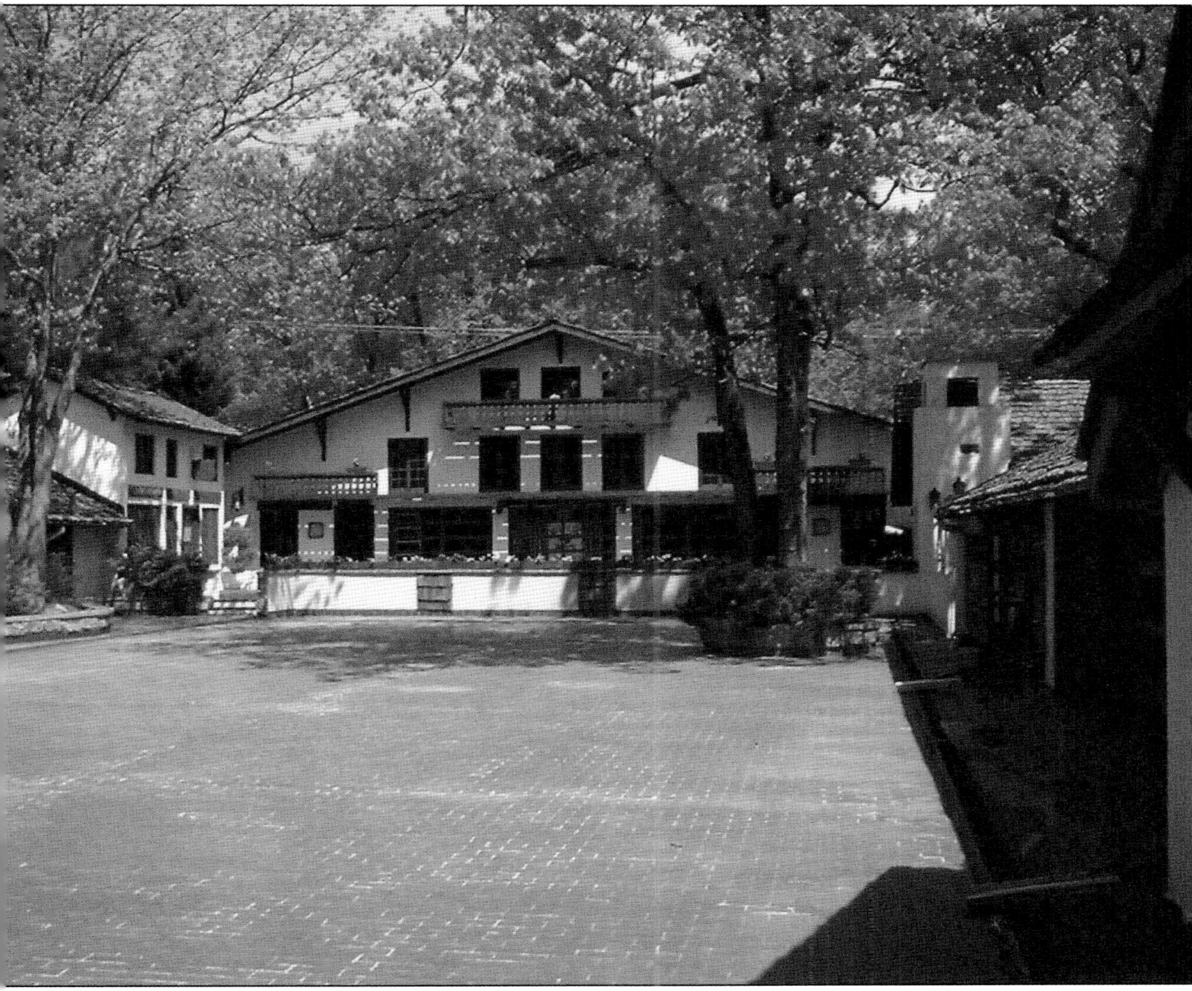

The Music Box expanded over the years to accommodate all the teens who showed up each night. By the early 1950s, the venue was open every night during the summer. In the 1960s and 1970s, Lee Kelly worked days at Camp Nokomis, and, every night, he greeted his patrons at the door. Shirley played the music and kept the kids dancing all evening. Known as "Queenie," she sat in the record tower, spinning records and watching out for any misconduct. By the 1960s, the Music Box took on an Alpine motif. The winter room was remodeled, and it was open every Saturday night during the winter. The room was equipped with its own sound system. The dance floor was expanded, and the walls were raised to protect the dancers from sightseers. A replica of the old post office and school added to the charm of the Box. Off to the far side of the main dance floor was the Verinder Chapel, named for Shirley's maiden name. Besides the famous outside dance floor, there were two rooms where patrons could dance if it rained. In addition, the winter room was opened on major holiday weekends to accommodate the larger crowds. (Courtesy of Mark Barnhart Sr.)

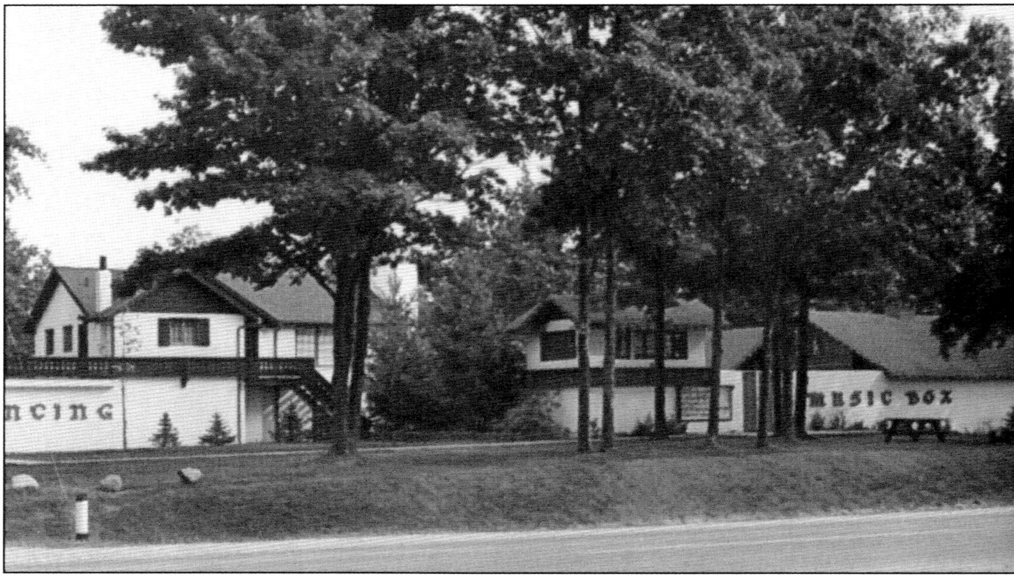

The exterior of the Music Box featured the same Swiss motif as the inside. It gave the place an enchanted feel. Certain songs became traditional favorites over the years. In the 1940s, it was "Auf Wiedersehen." During the Korean War, Kate Smith's "God Bless America" was played often. From the Vietnam War until the Music Box closed, two songs signaled the end of an evening: Skeeter Davis's 1962 hit "The Little Music Box" and Connie Frances's 1964 version of "God Bless America." (Courtesy of Mark Barnhart Sr.)

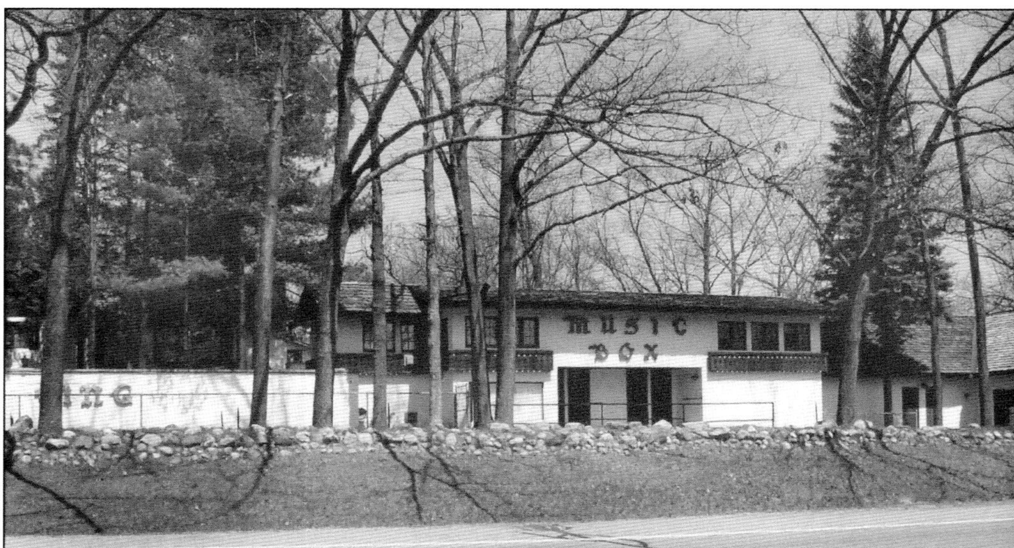

In 1965, the Music Box was remodeled. The record library was extended over the main entrance, and the patio, chapel, and restaurant were added. In 1965, the Music Box had brief competition from Daniel's Den, part of a chain, located in the Houghton Lake village. Sonny and Cher preformed there in July 1965. After the act, the teens left Daniel's Den to go to the Music Box. Sonny and Cher inquired about where they were headed, and then followed the crowd. The famous duo went dancing at the Music Box. (Courtesy of Mark Barnhart Sr.)

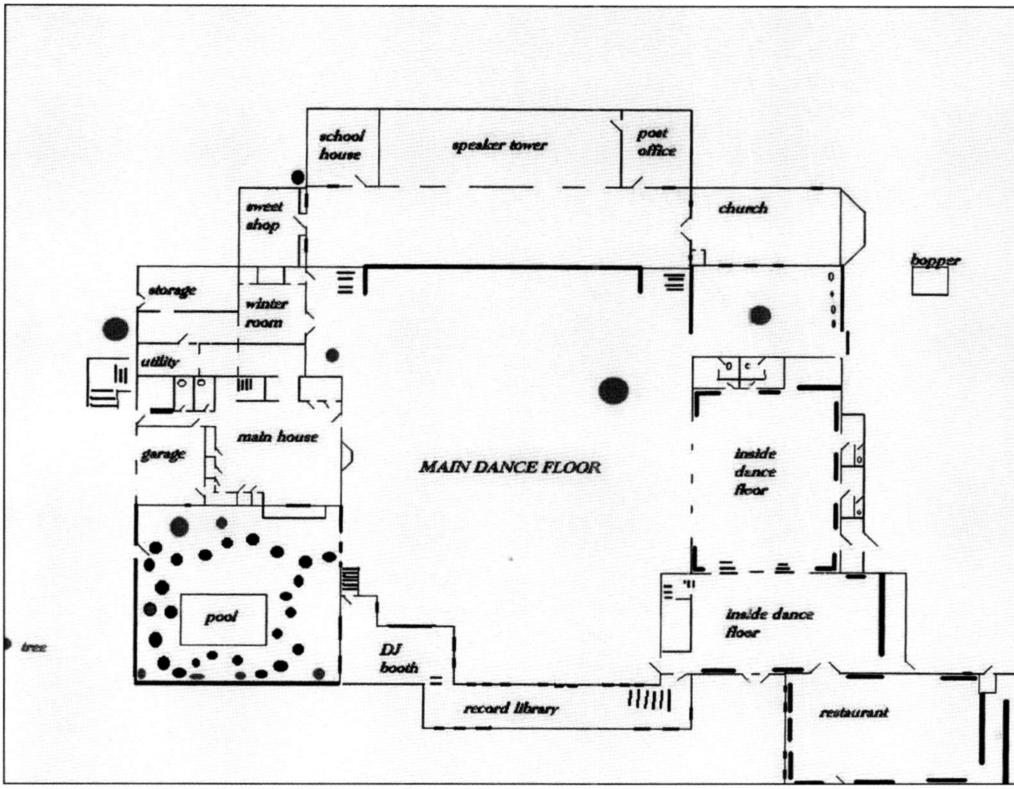

The Music Box was not just a place for teens to dance, it was also Shirley and Lee Kelly's home. The complex included their residence, a swimming pool, a sweet shop, a restaurant, a record library, and a Coca-Cola bar. The Music Box's collection of records included 78-rpm discs, totaling about 1,000, from the years 1946 to 1948. In 1948, 45s were the new medium for records. The Box's collection of 45-rpm records, spanning from 1948 to 2002, contains more than 5,000 records. The record collection is still intact and is held in a private collection. (Courtesy of Mark Barnhart Sr.)

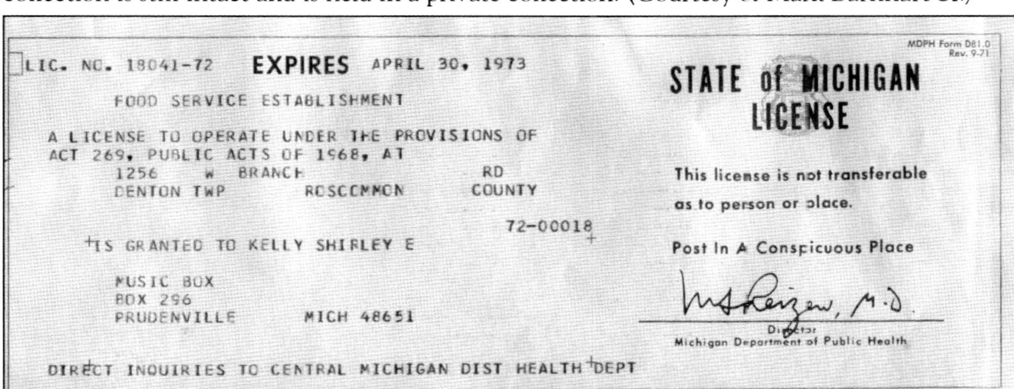

MDPH Form D81.0
Rev. 9-71

LIC. NO. 18041-72 EXPIRES APRIL 30, 1973

FOOD SERVICE ESTABLISHMENT

STATE of MICHIGAN
LICENSE

A LICENSE TO OPERATE UNDER THE PROVISIONS OF
ACT 269, PUBLIC ACTS OF 1968, AT
1256 W BRANCH RD
DENTON TWP ROSCOMMON COUNTY

This license is not transferable as to person or place.

72-00018

IS GRANTED TO KELLY SHIRLEY E

Post In A Conspicuous Place

MUSIC BOX
BOX 296
PRUDENVILLE MICH 48651

Director
Michigan Department of Public Health

DIRECT INQUIRIES TO CENTRAL MICHIGAN DIST HEALTH DEPT

The Music Box was a Coca-Cola establishment. Cokes could be bought at the bar in the inside dance room or at the restaurant, which was always a great place to get to know a new friend. Cokes were affordable in the 1950s and 1960s—just 10¢. By the 1970s, the price had increased to 25¢. Teens who worked up an appetite could snack on hot dogs and chips. (Courtesy of Mark Barnhart Sr.)

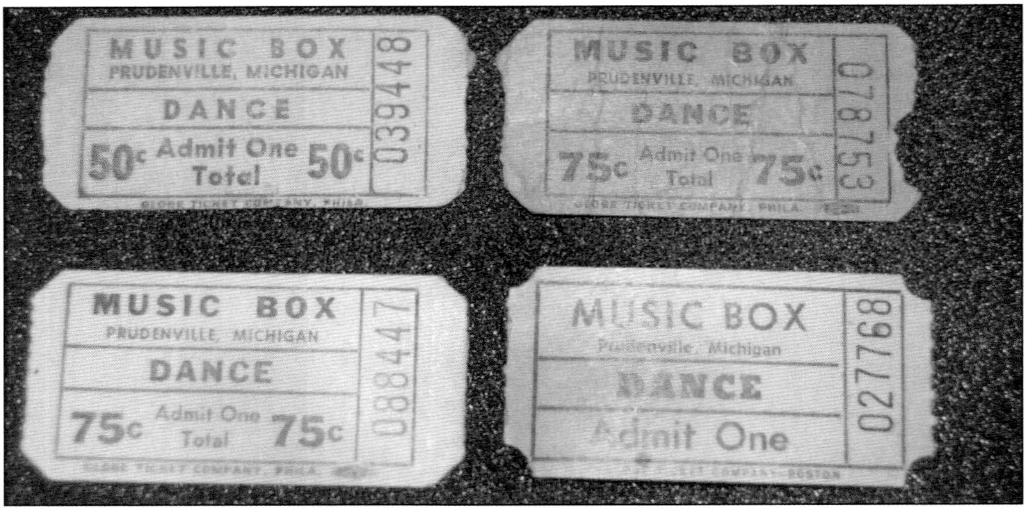

Admission to the Music Box was affordable. When it first opened, it cost 5¢ to enter. Over the years, the cost saw modest increases. In 1957, the admission increased to 50¢, and, in 1965, it went to 75¢. For $1, teens could dance from 9:00 p.m. to 1:00 a.m. and have change left for a Coke. When the Music Box closed its doors for the final time, admission was $4. (Courtesy of Mark Barnhart Sr.)

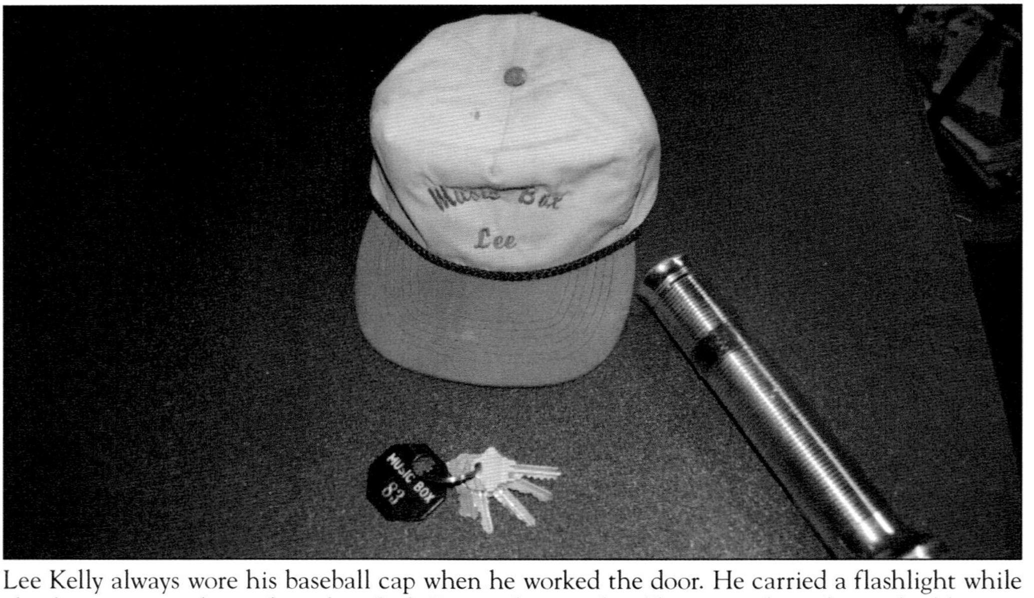

Lee Kelly always wore his baseball cap when he worked the door. He carried a flashlight while checking cars in the parking lot. Only Lee and a couple of his trusted employees had keys to the entire building. Because the tickets only changed when the price changed, upon entering the Music Box, patrons received a ticket, and their hands were stamped to allow reentry during the evening. The stamp changed every evening, but the rules did not. Lee made sure that those who had been drinking alcohol were not allowed in. He also checked to see that the dress code was being followed. Pants or skirts above the knee and midriff tops were not allowed. Lee and Shirley Kelly were very strict about the rules, which assured parents that it was a safe place to allow their teens to frequent. The patrons were expected to conduct themselves as young adults. (Courtesy of Mark Barnhart Sr.)

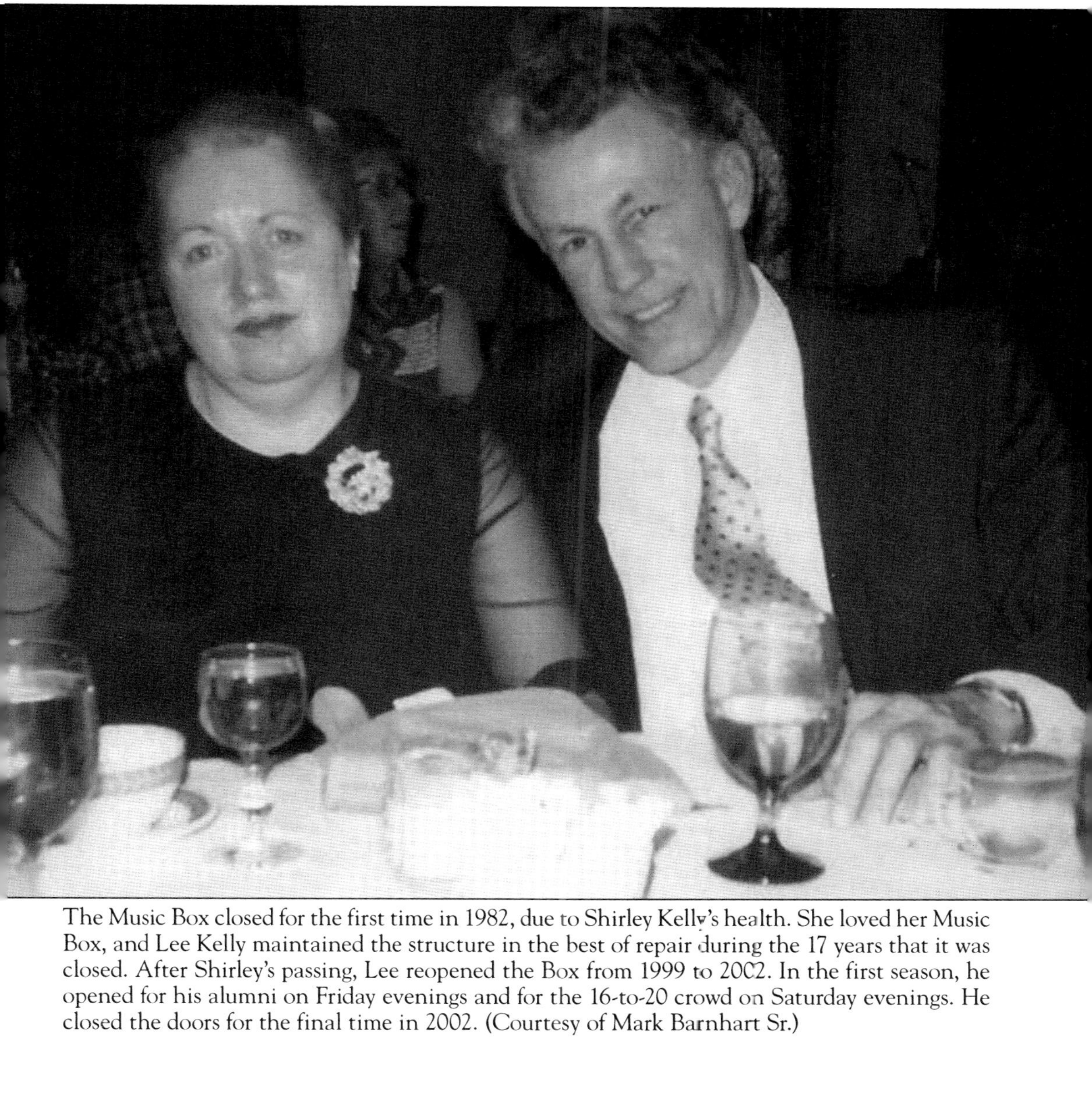

The Music Box closed for the first time in 1982, due to Shirley Kelly's health. She loved her Music Box, and Lee Kelly maintained the structure in the best of repair during the 17 years that it was closed. After Shirley's passing, Lee reopened the Box from 1999 to 2002. In the first season, he opened for his alumni on Friday evenings and for the 16-to-20 crowd on Saturday evenings. He closed the doors for the final time in 2002. (Courtesy of Mark Barnhart Sr.)

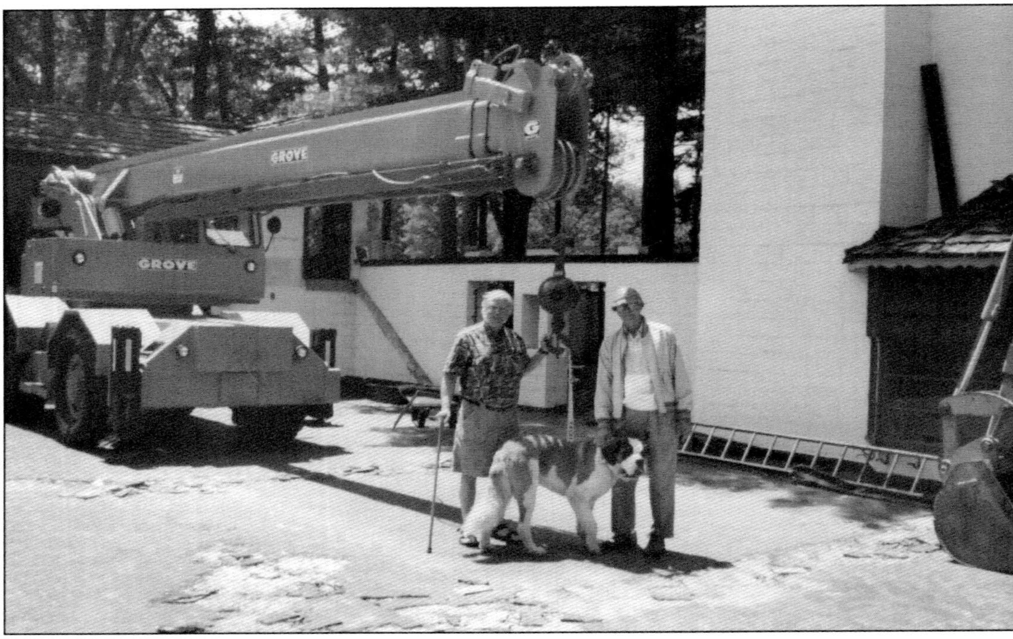

Lee Kelly had the beloved teen nightspot razed in July 2004. He could not be sure that a new owner would run it according to his and Shirley's high standards, which included no alcohol. So, to ensure that its reputation remained, Lee had the structure torn down, with a few old friends watching. (Courtesy of Dr. Jim Sullivan.)

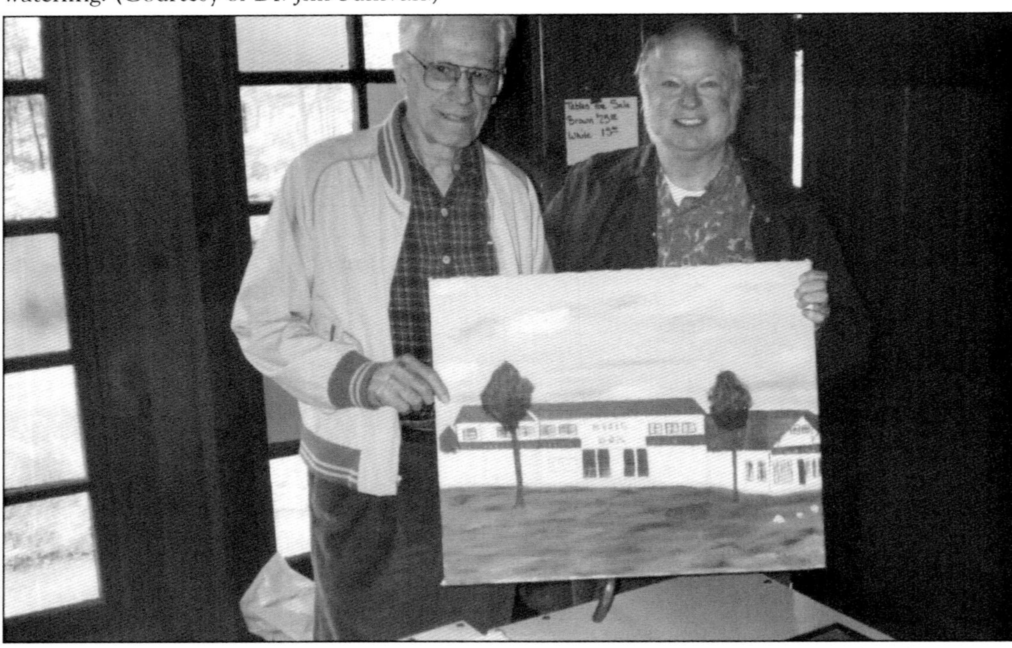

All that remains are the treasured memories of those who danced as teens under the stars, as well as some memorabilia. One beloved piece is the painting of the Music Box that Jim Sullivan (right) made for his bosses, Lee and Shirley Kelly, in 1969. Lee (left) returned it to Jim during the demolition. (Courtesy of Dr. Jim Sullivan.)

Seven

Tip-Up Town

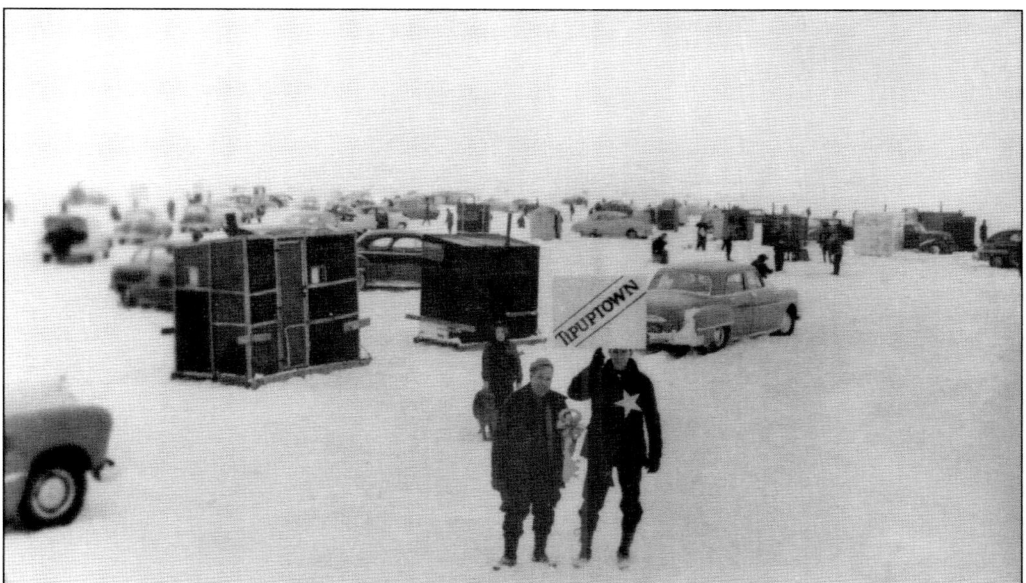

In 1951, Bob Sweet and Bob Carman, two locals, devised a diversion to combat the doldrums of winter: a fishing festival on the frozen lake. The idea was to boost tourism and bring the locals out onto the ice for fun and tomfoolery. A contest was held to name the newly planned festival, and Tip-Up Town USA won. The name is a registered trademark. The newly devised "town" needed elected officials; the first mayor was Ralph Wenig (left), and the marshal was Tom Botsford (right). The first Tip-Up Town was held on February 17, 1951.

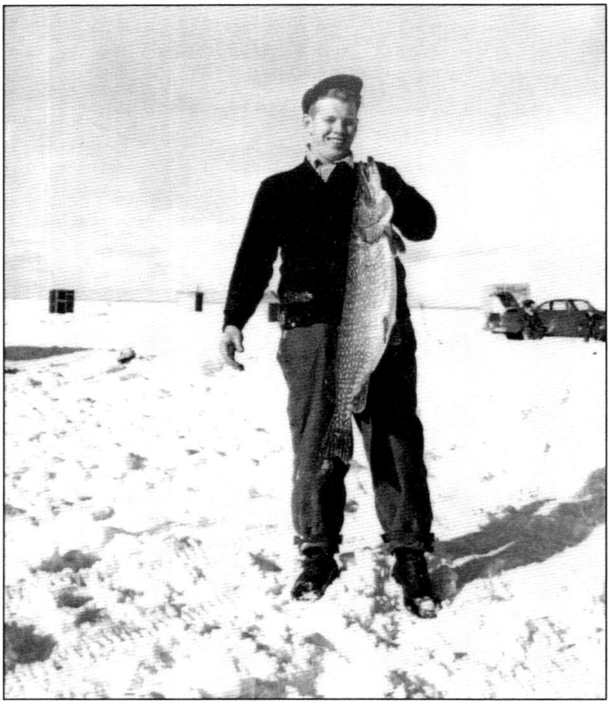

Ice-fishing contests were one of the main attractions at Tip-Up Town. Prizes were awarded to the largest fish. While fishing was taken seriously, fun was the main objective. Section three of the Tip-Up Town bylaws states: "The purpose of the village on the ice is to promote bigger lies, hilarity, tom foolery and good will."

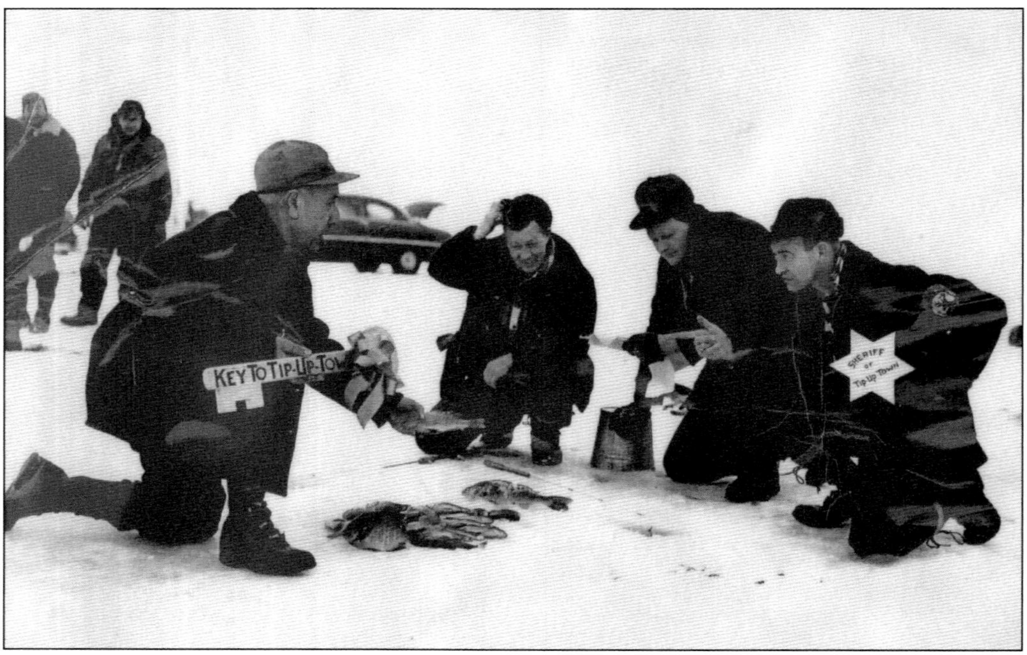

The mayor and marshal had much responsibility in the temporary village on the ice. They inspected fish that were caught and enforced the laws of the ice. In 1953, a Tip-Up Town badge was required to take part in the fun. The badges, made of wood and cut in the shape of fish, cost 50¢. If a visitor to the village entered without a badge, the marshal took them into custody. They were locked in the jail until they bought a badge or bribed the marshal.

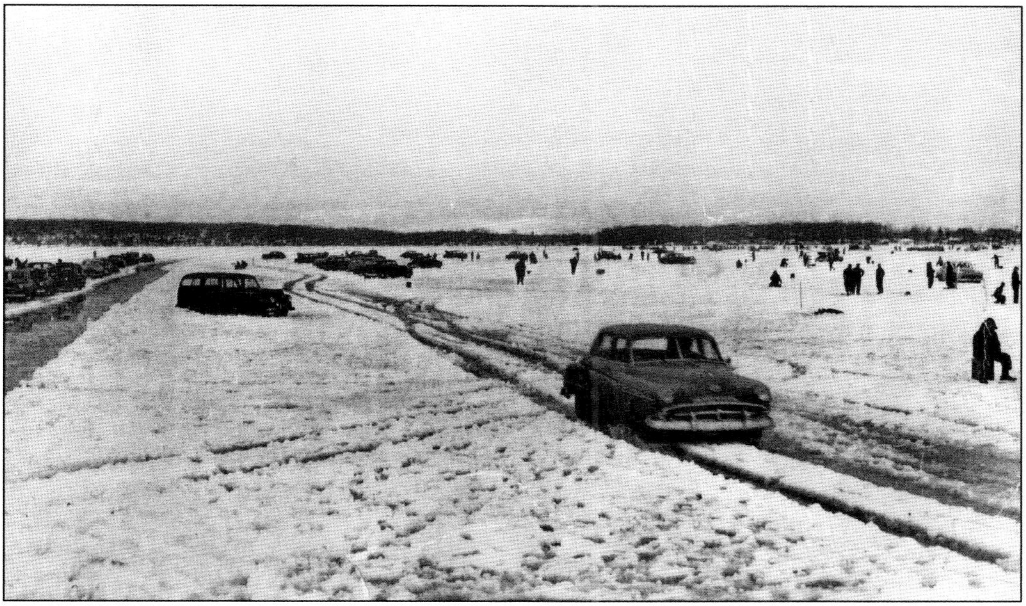

A common sight in the early years of Tip-Up Town were cars driving on the ice to the town's site. Many serious fishermen had ice shanties on the frozen surface. Others just fished by their car. To direct visitors to the site, wooden pennant signs were placed along the route for visitors to follow.

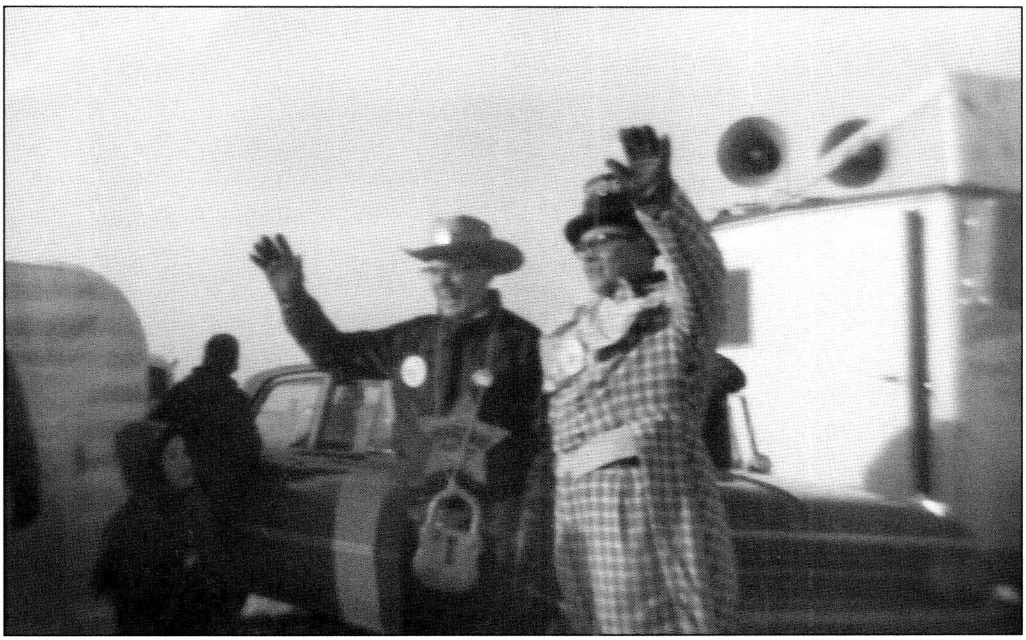

Selecting the mayor and marshal for Tip-Up Town is a community event. In the past, a potluck dinner was held, initially at the stone school and then at the high school. Speeches are still given by the candidates, and big promises are made. Then, the town votes for its favorites. In 1964, Bob Detmer (right) was elected mayor and Pinky Randall (left) was marshal. By this time, the mayor and marshal were designing elaborate costumes to enhance their visibility and improve the fun.

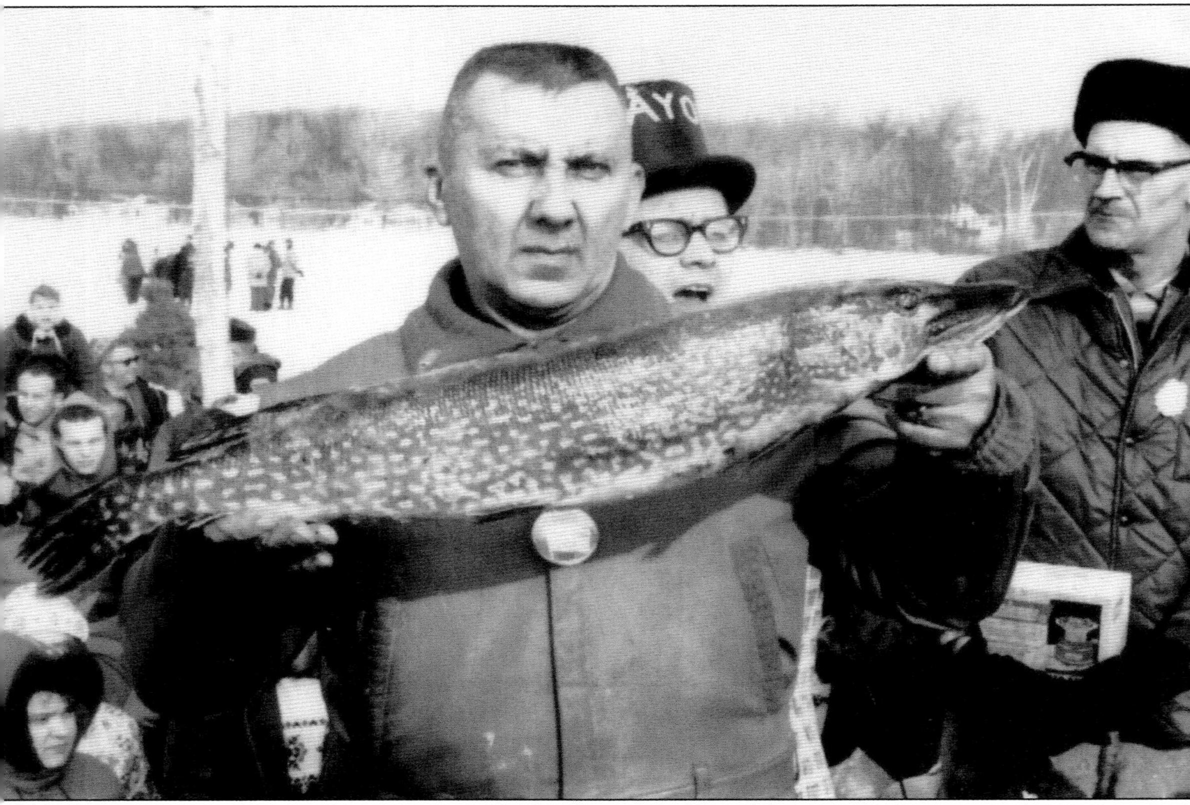

The fun and games drew many people during the first 14 years, but ice-fishing remained the big attraction. Shown here is an award-winning pike that this angler caught at Tip-Up Town USA 1964. (Courtesy of the *Houghton Lake Resorter.*)

Tip-Up Town USA's 1964 queen, Louanne DeBoer, displays her catch of two respectable northern pike. In the early years of the festival, the queen was chosen from women who were spotted taking part in the sport of ice-fishing at the ice village. They were then interviewed, and a panel of judges chose the winner for her sporting ability.

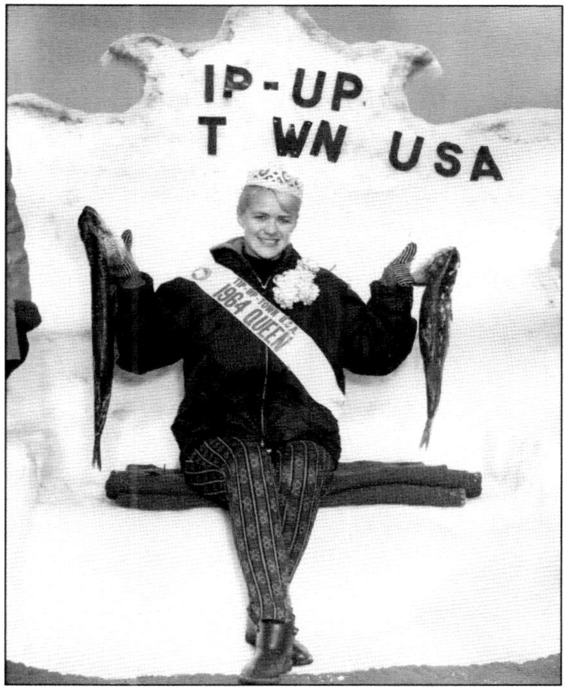

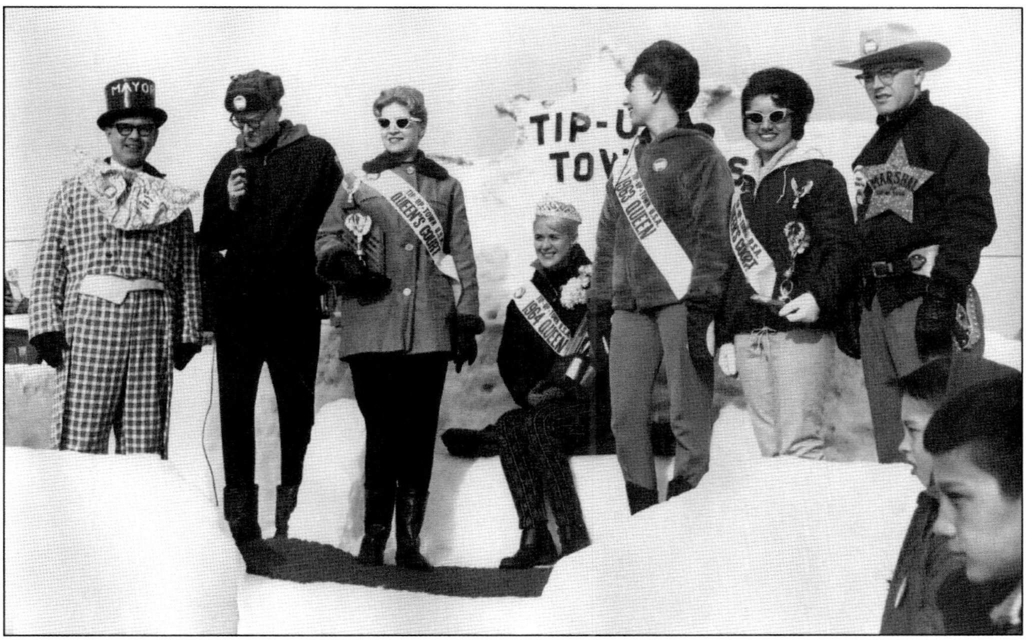

The crowning of the queen took place on Sunday afternoon. The queen was honored by a coronation ceremony while sitting on a thrown sculpted from snow. Tip-Up Town's very own snow artist and past town mayor Parker Seiler (second from left) designed and built the throne from snow. The court was made up of the runners-up to the queen. The past queen had the honor of crowning her successor. The 1963 queen was Louise Walma (third from right). (Courtesy of the *Houghton Lake Resorter*.)

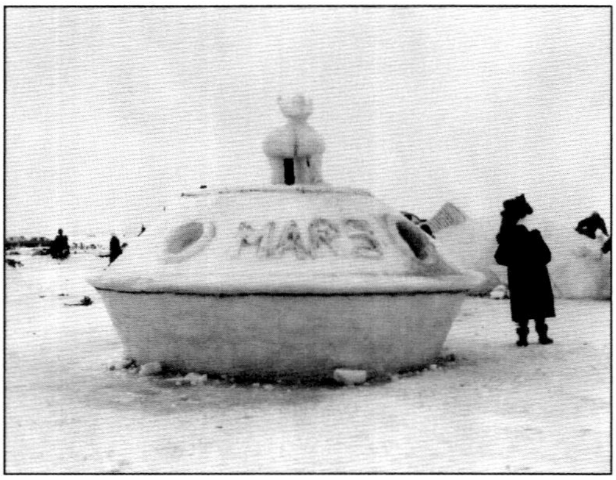

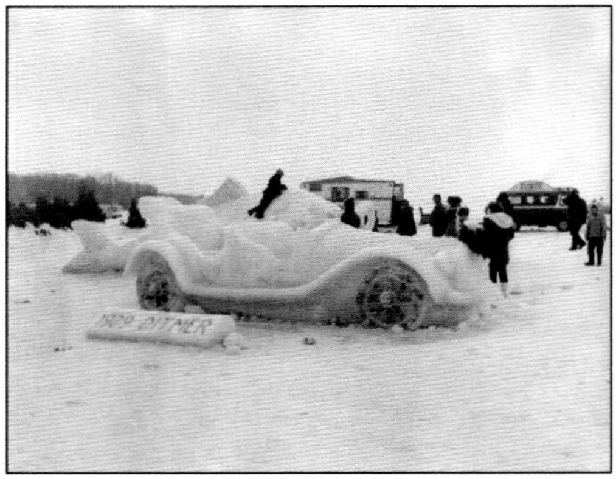

Parker Seiler had a wonderful imagination, and his works of art reflected it. Although they only lasted a few weeks, the sculptures brought joy to those who saw them, as well as to the youngsters, who had hours of fun climbing upon them. These two sculptures are in tribute to transportation, past and future. There were themes for the snow works, which delighted the crowds when they saw them for the first time.

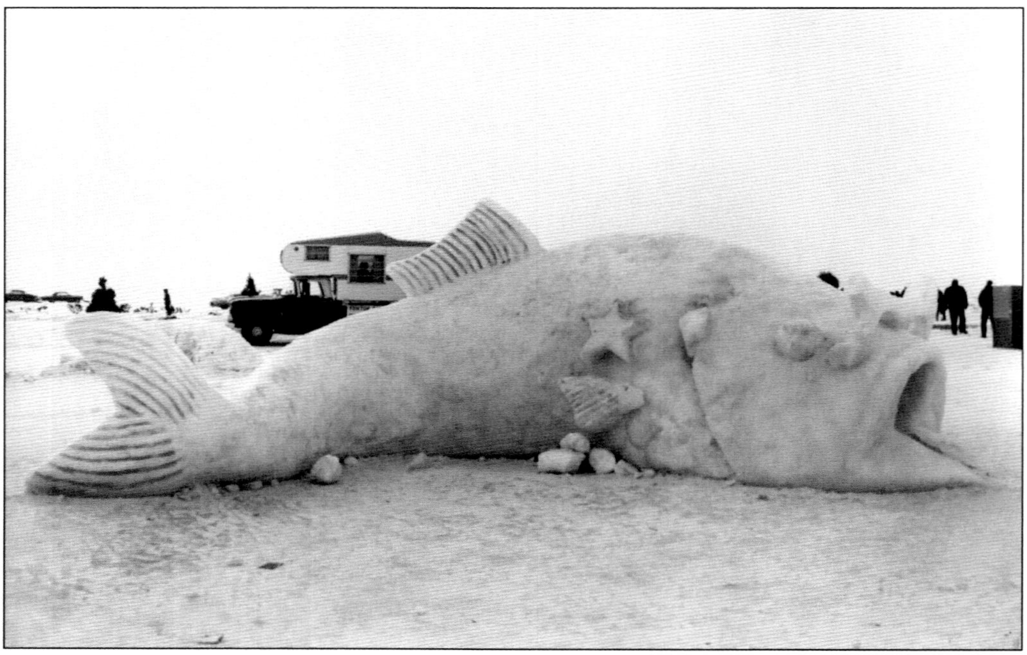

Regardless of the theme, there is always room for another fish. Parker Seiler landed the biggest catch of this festival, a whopper of a snow fish. Seiler shared his talent, teaching others the art of snow sculpting. A local elementary school teacher, he would hold a seminar for kids on Saturday to pass on his craft. Many kids who learned from Seiler went on to make wonderful snow sculptures for Tip-Up Town when they grew up.

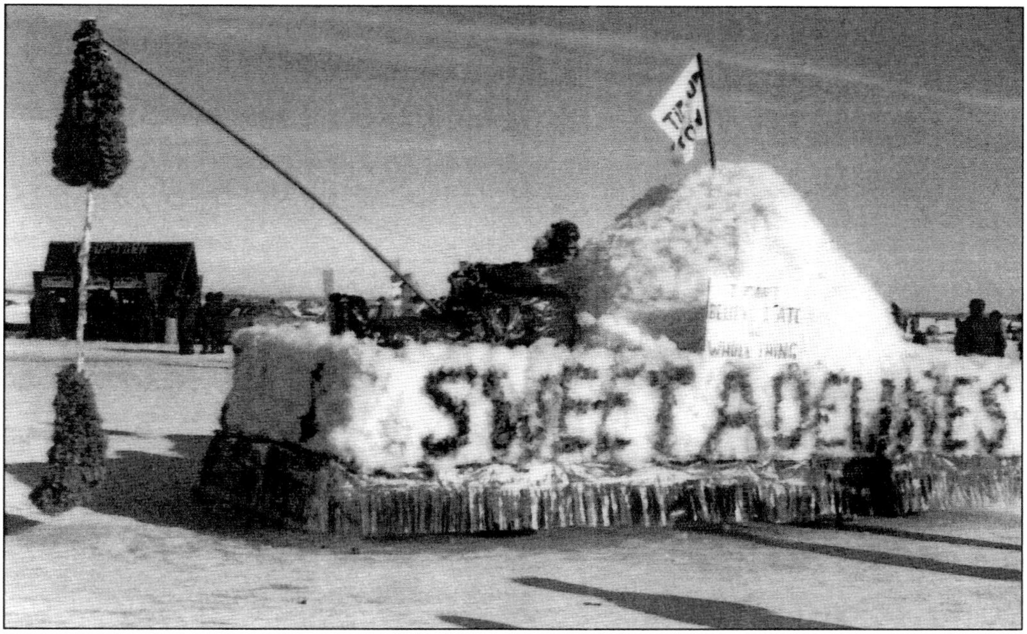

The first weekend of Tip-Up Town USA begins with a parade. In the early years, the parade was made up of cars that lined up to drive to the town. The drivers would go around the lake to the site. As time went on, floats were added to the parade. Local organizations would join in the fun and build floats in several different categories. The humorous category was very popular and always had great entries, as illustrated by the Sweet Adelines' float above. The Sweet Adelines were a women's vocal group. Cash prizes were awarded for first and second place finishers. (Both courtesy of *The Houghton Lake Resorter*.)

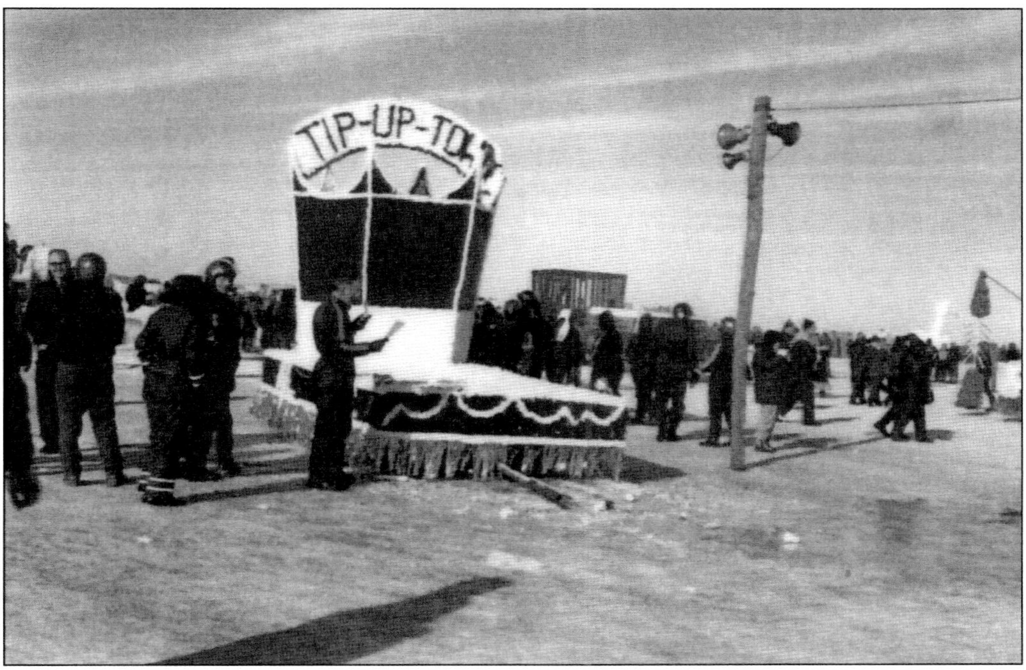

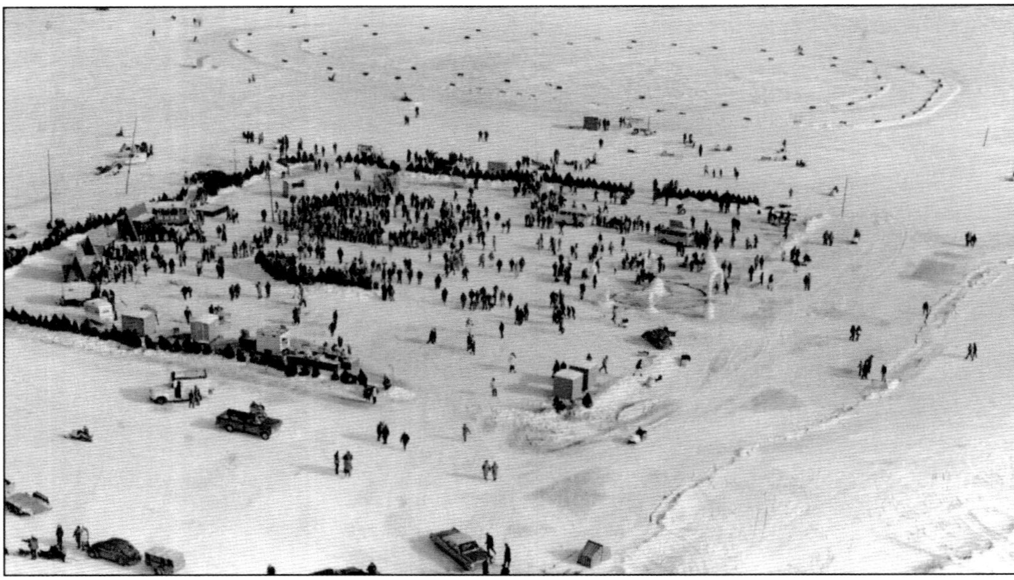

By 1966, snowmobiles were a big part of Tip-Up Town. The organizers decided to add a Grand Prix race to the events. The track for the race was on the ice adjacent to the Tip-Up Town village. That year, the race was held at the same time as the ice festival. In 1967, a second weekend was scheduled for the Grand Prix race. The race was moved off the ice to Emery and Tower Hill Road, to provide a safer track for the racers. Races were held until 1976. The second weekend remained, however, and Tip-Up Town became a two-weekend festival. (Courtesy of the *Houghton Lake Resorter.*)

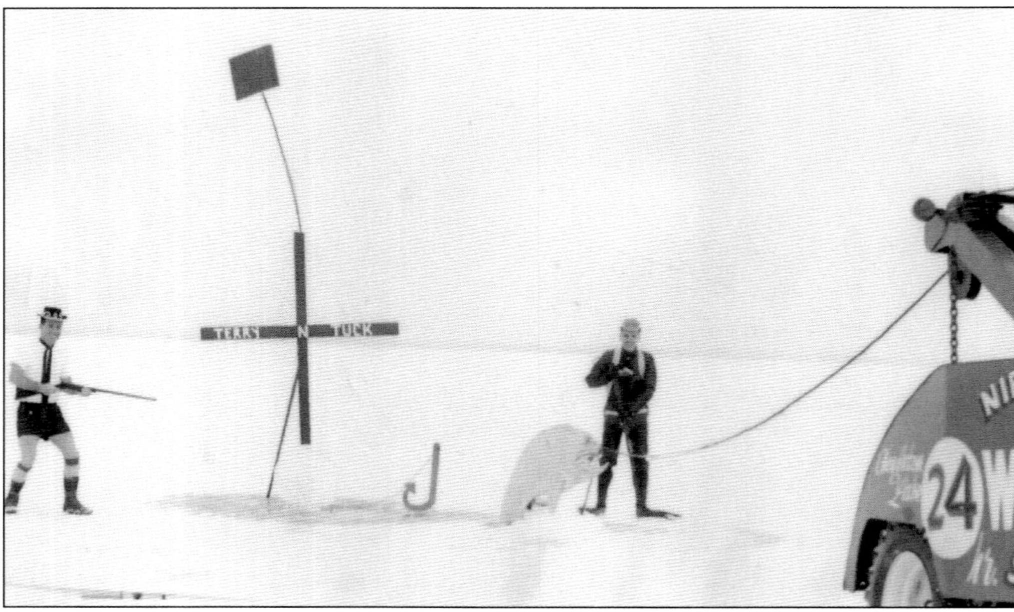

A tip-up is a device that is used to ice-fish. It is placed over a hole in the ice, and a red flag on the tip-up is bent over until a fish is hooked. The flag pops up, and the person fishing then checks the line. The 1966 mayor, Terry Elsholtz (left), and the marshal, Don Tuck, are having fun with an oversized tip-up and a wooden fish. All those who fish on Houghton Lake dream of a catch so big that they would have to hire a tow truck to land it.

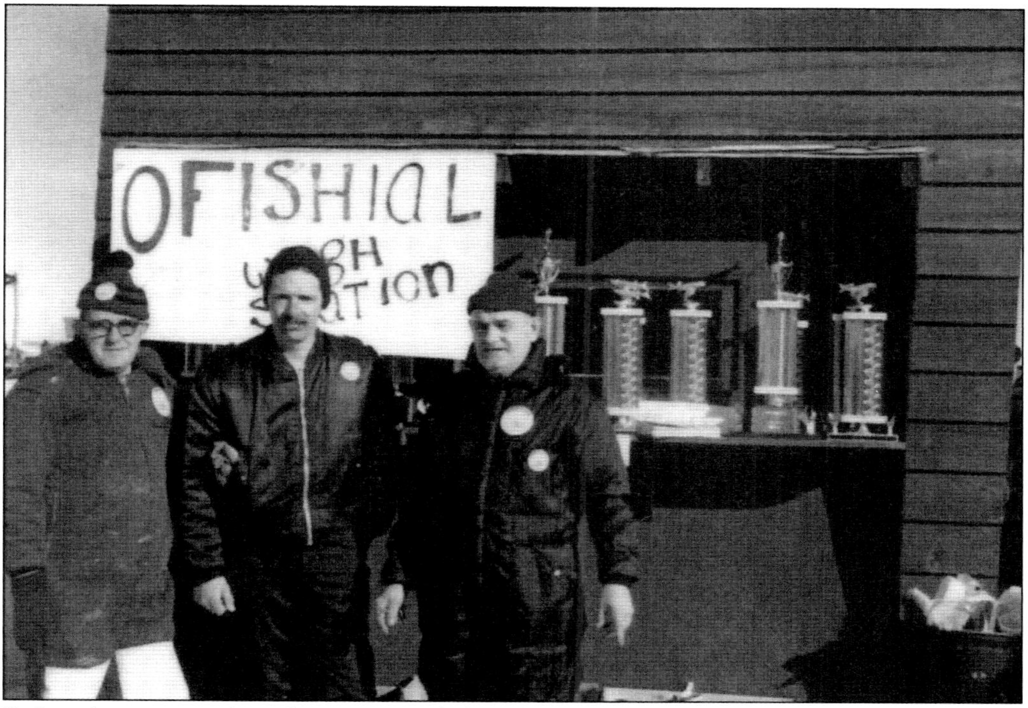

Before the prizes and trophies are awarded to those landing the big fish, the catches must be measured and weighed at the "Ofishial" Tip-Up Town weigh station (above). Fish are put on display so that visitors to Tip-Up Town USA can see and admire the great catches. Awards are given on Sunday afternoon. In the photograph below, anglers proudly display the trophies and prizes won for their superior ice-fishing skills. (Both courtesy of the *Houghton Lake Resorter*.)

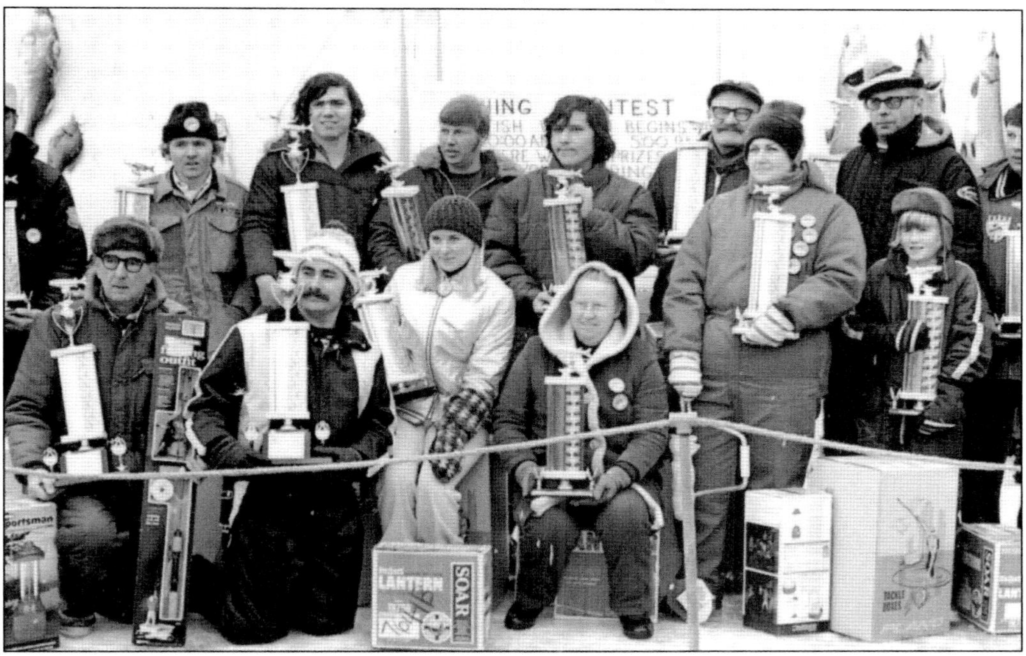

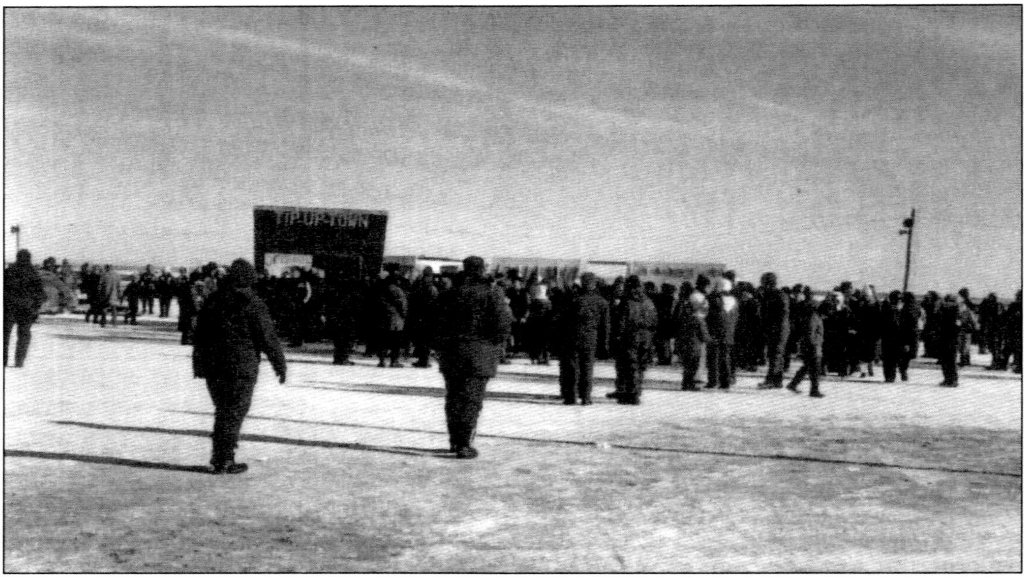

Crowds of visitors can participate in many activities. In the early days, these included dogsled rides and horse-drawn sleigh rides. Through the years, airboat, airplane, and helicopter rides became popular. The site includes games for both children and adults.

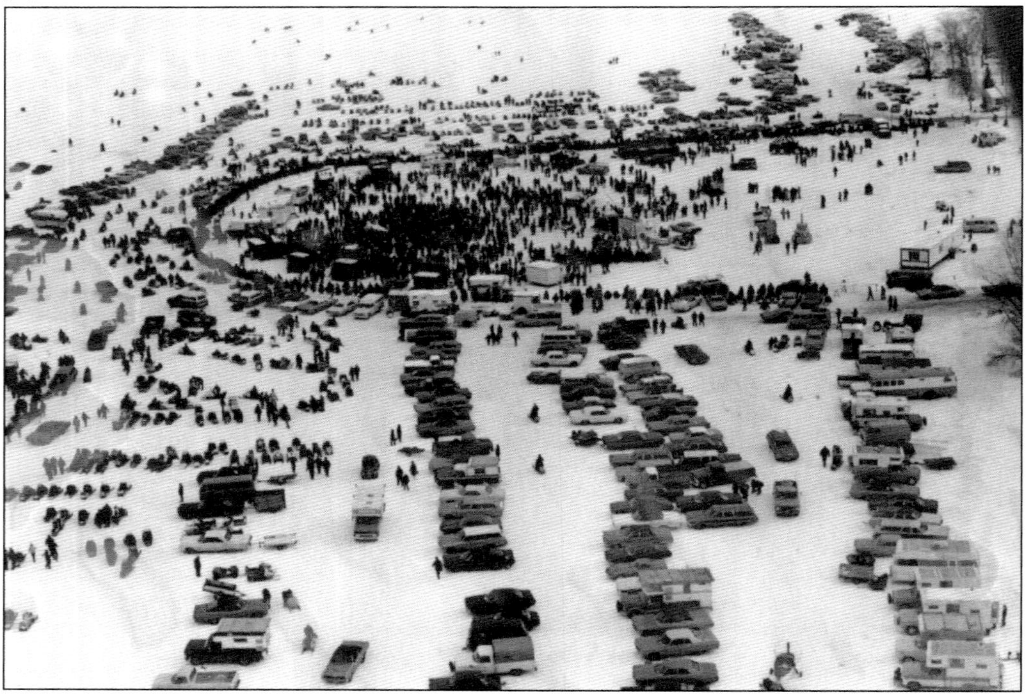

Tip-Up Town USA used discarded Christmas Trees to line the outer boundaries of the village. This 1971 aerial photograph of the festival site shows the tree-lined village surrounded by cars and visitors. This site is the permanent one, chosen in 1965 for the festival. It is held at the DNR boat launch, across from Houghton Lake Middle School. Visitors now park at the school and take the shuttle or walk to the site. (Courtesy of the *Houghton Lake Resorter.*)

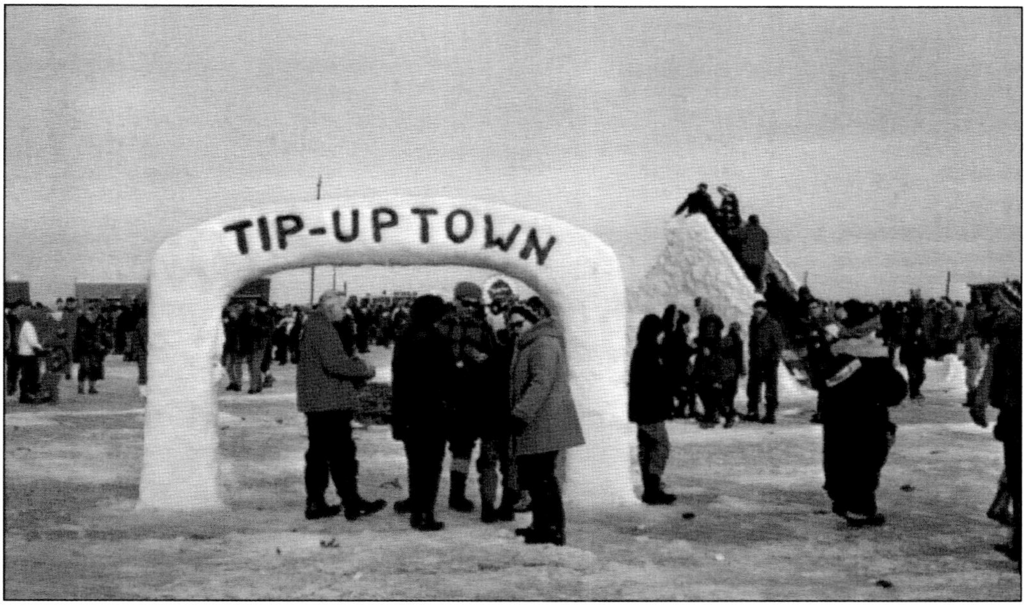

The archway into Tip-Up Town is a popular place for visitors to gather. Children and adults like the snow slide, which adds excitement to their day. As more people slide down, the slides become faster as the snow packs into an icy surface. People are lined up for their turn down the slide in the background of this photograph. (Courtesy of the *Houghton Lake Resorter*.)

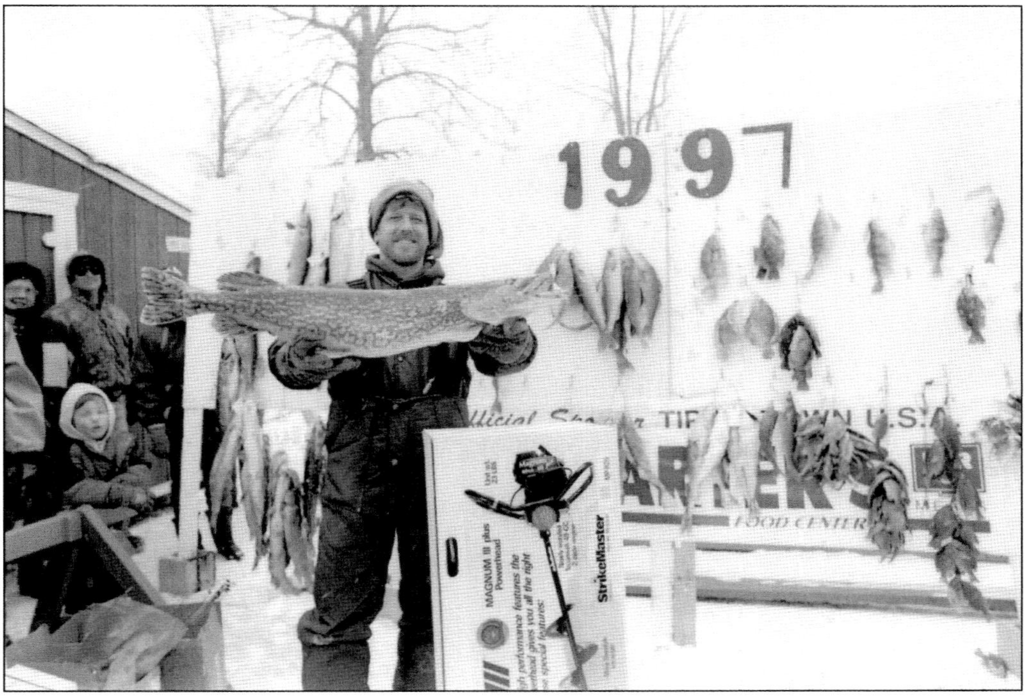

Anglers are still pulling the big ones out of Houghton Lake, 51 years after the first Tip-Up Town. This northern pike, caught at the 1997 festival, is a great example of the large fish that can be found in Houghton Lake. It just takes skill and time. (Courtesy of the *Houghton Lake Resorter*.)

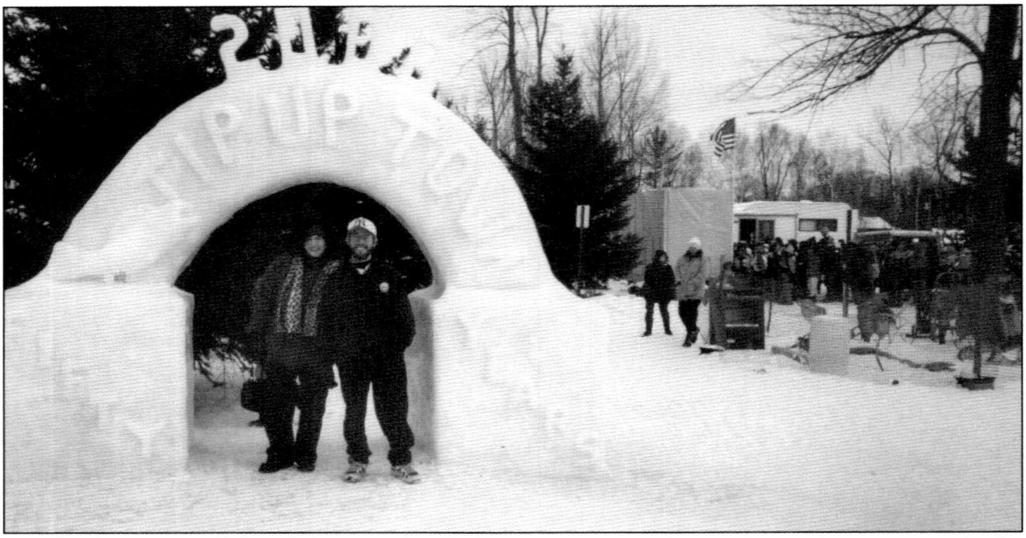

While some activities still take place on the ice, most are now held on the shoreline. With the warmer weather patterns, the festival is jeopardized if a mid-January thaw occurs. For the safety of the visitors, the carnival rides are now set on land. For the most part, drivers no longer take the risk of bringing their cars and parking on the ice. One thing that never changes is the arch, which welcomes visitors from near and far. Heather Harris, from Pennsylvania, and Jason Levinson, from New York, stopped under the arch to memorialize their visit to Tip-Up Town USA. (Author's collection.)

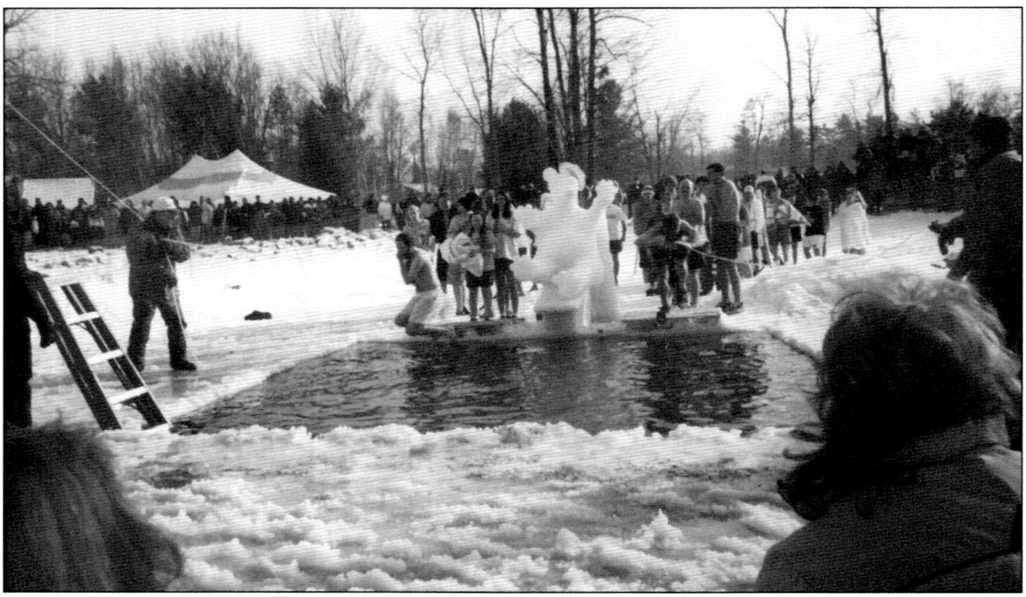

The polar bear dip was added many years after Tip-Up Town started, but it has become one of the most popular events of the festival. Locals and visitors line up to take their turn jumping into a large hole chopped into the ice. One jumper is allowed at a time, and safety ropes are used to quickly pull jumpers from the water. For their bravery, jumpers are awarded a tee shirt. Many people jump each year, but even more watch on the sides. After all, there is ice on that water. (Author's collection.)

Eight

Churches and Schools

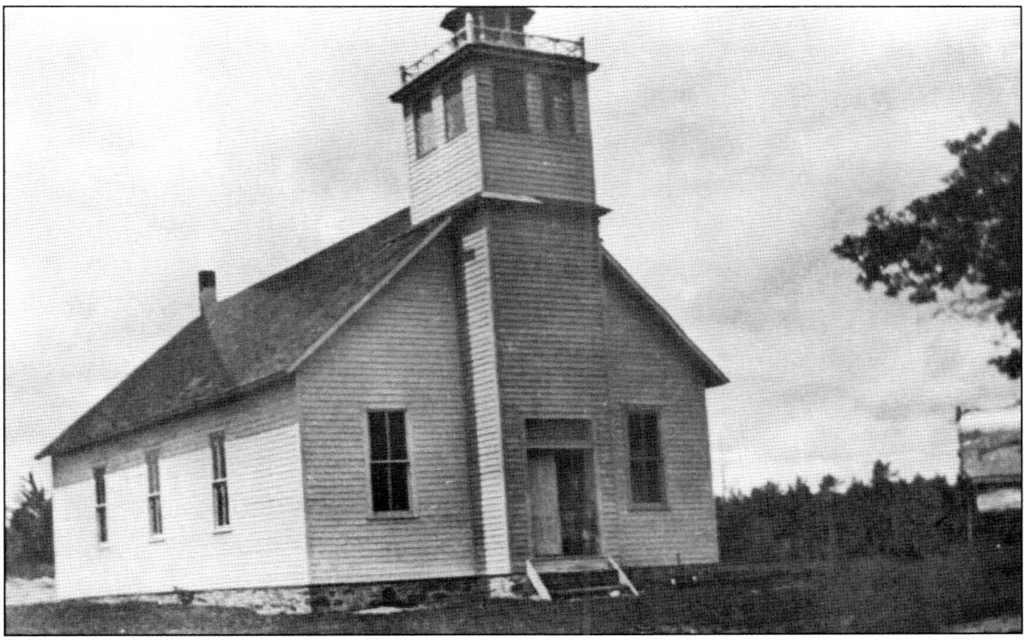

The Markey Baptist Church Ladies Aid Society met for the first time in 1906, and work was set in motion to build a church. In 1909, the church was built on Markey Road in Markey Township. The first pastor was Rev. Robert Stuck. It served the people until 1971, when it was decided that the congregation needed a new church. A new site for the church was chosen on Flint Road, and ground-breaking for the new church began in 1973. The cornerstone was laid on June 10 of that year. The first worship service was held in the new Markey Baptist Church on February 3, 1974. Rev. Robert Stuck was the pastor. This church continues to serve the people of the north shore of Houghton Lake today.

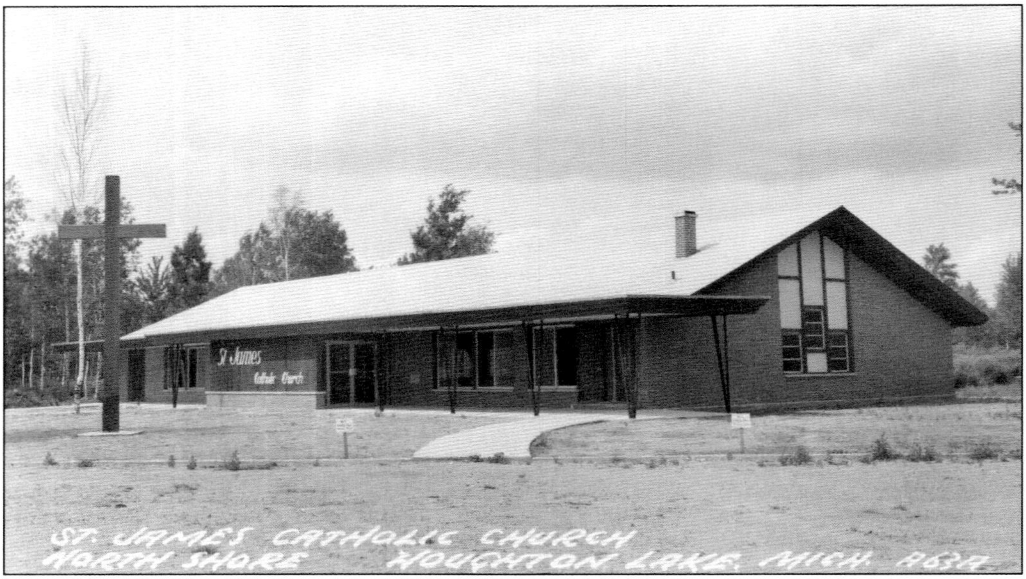

St. James the Greater Roman Catholic Church began as a mission church from St. Michael's Roscommon. Starting in February 1946, the priest from St. Michael's would use the Duck Inn Bar as a chapel to say Sunday mass. Then, two years later, a new temporary church on the lakeside, across from the church's present location, was used. In 1959, land was purchased to build the church. In 1961, it was given the name St. James the Greater. Rev. John Hoogterp was the pastor. In 1994, a new worship space was built, and the old church became the social hall.

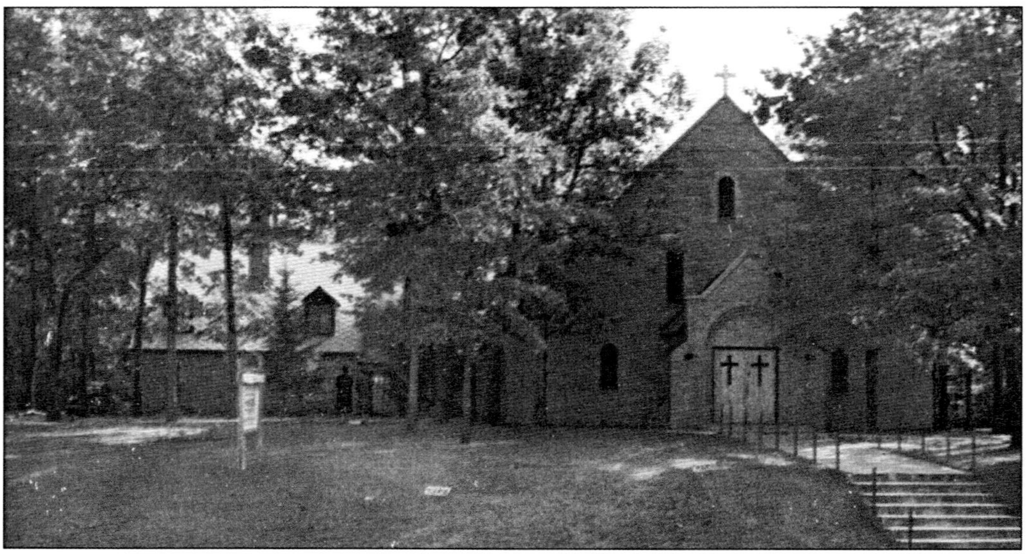

Our Lady of the Lake in Prudenville began holding mass on June 2, 1940. The church was dedicated in August 24, 1941, and was called the Church of the Assumption, Our Lady of the Lake. The original church accommodated 500 people. Local businessman Earl Johnson donated the land to the diocese of Grand Rapids, with the stipulation that Rev. Father Daniel Izzo would serve the parish as long as he liked. The rectory was built in 1946. In 1944, plans were made to build a school and convent, and these were completed and opened in October 1954. (Courtesy of Judy and Casey Kronner.)

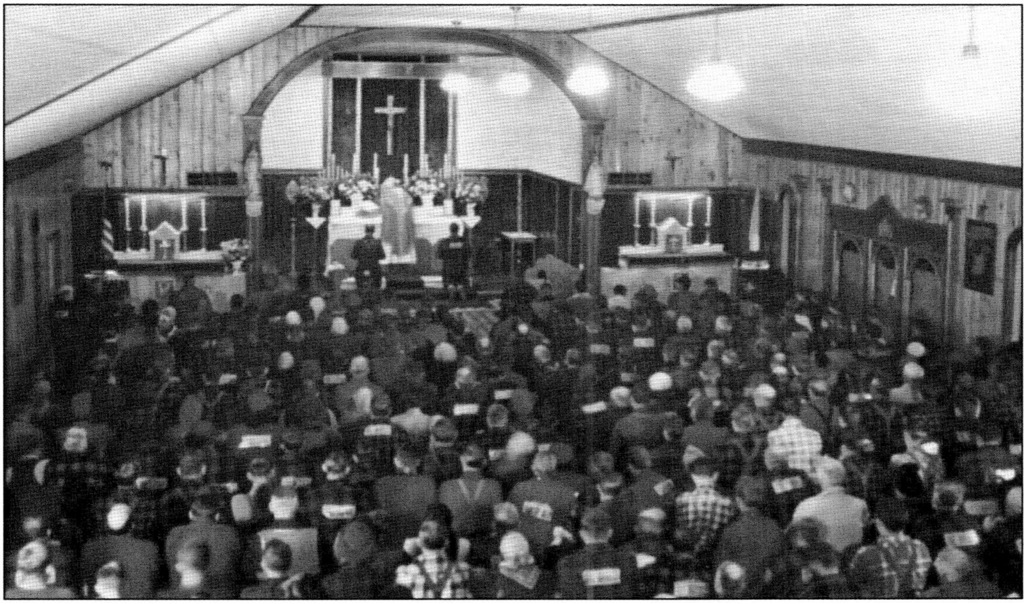

Father Izzo said mass at 5:30 every morning during deer season, from November 15 to November 30. These masses attracted a full crowd, as shown here. Hunters in their red-and-black clothes even stood in the isle to hear mass. A couple of hunters would be altar servers for this mass. Father Izzo would then follow the regular schedule of mass at 9:00 a.m. and 11:00 a.m. The regular altar boys would serve these masses. (Courtesy of Judy and Casey Kronner.)

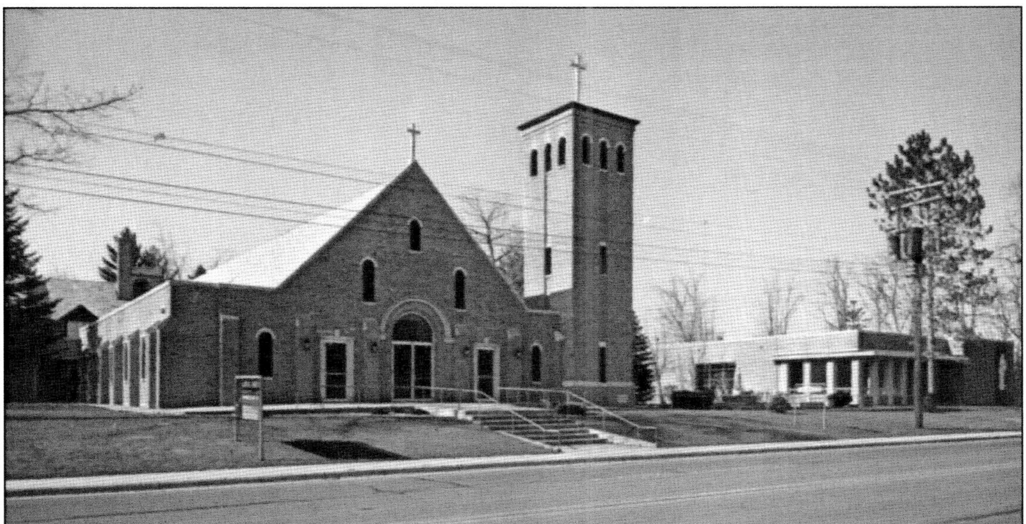

In the late 1950s, the church was enlarged to seat 800 people. A new vestibule with two temperature-controlled cry rooms was added. This remodel included stained-glass windows on the west wall of the church, depicting the mysteries of the rosary. The school was enlarged in 1966. Three additional classrooms and a new office were added. Father Izzo passed away in April 1968. He was replaced by Rev. Father Joseph Ritz. The church and school remained unchanged until 1986, when they were completely remodeled. The stained-glass windows were moved to the entrance of the church. The building was rededicated in 1987.

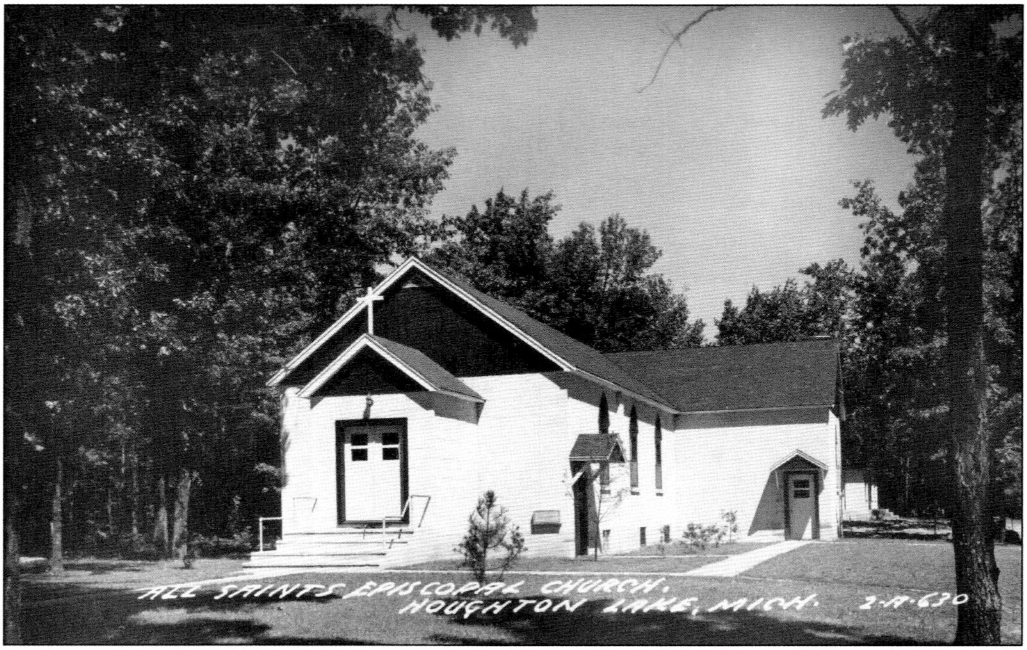

All Saints Episcopal Church of Prudenville was built in 1951. It served the Anglican community in Houghton Lake through the 1960s. After it was closed, the building was eventually sold. It is now a flower and gift shop.

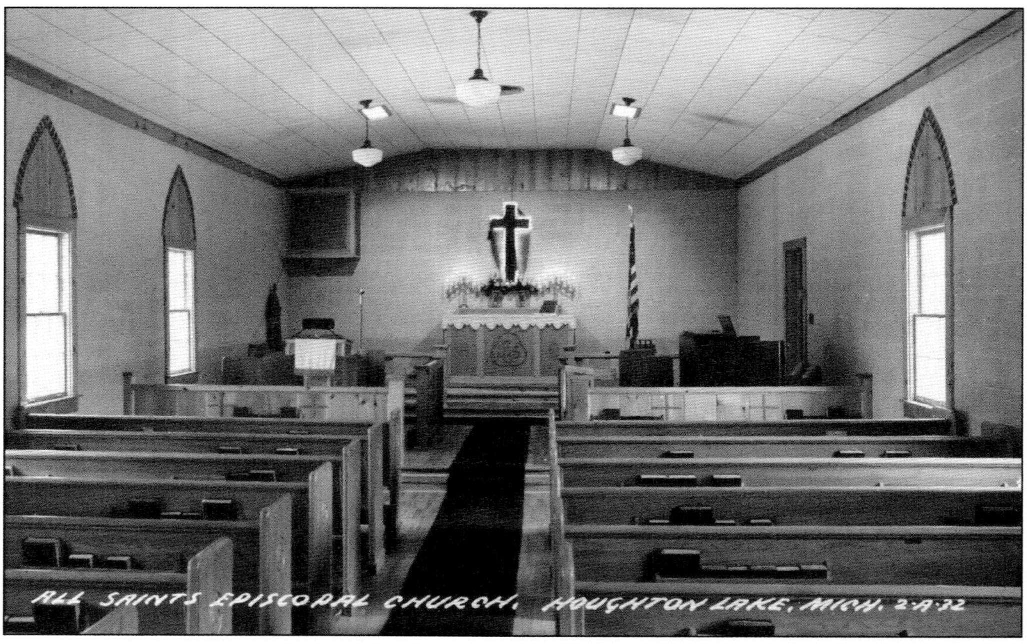

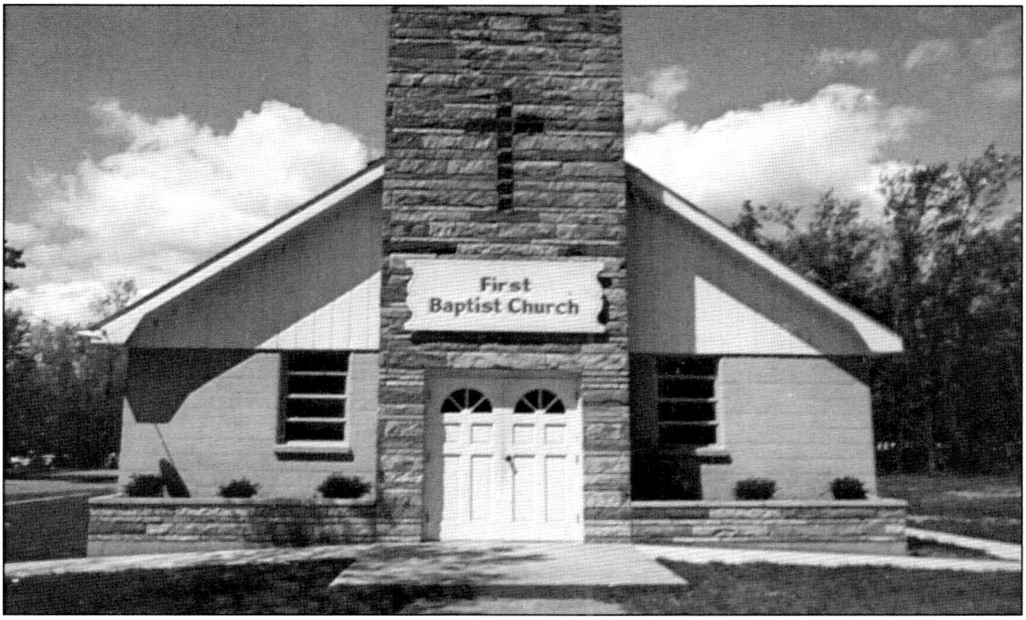

The First Baptist Church of Prudenville started out in a basement on Main Street in 1949. The current building was erected in 1956, and the pastor was Rev. Robert Ingersoll. Rev. John Pruden served the community for 40 years. In 1984, the original building was expanded, and a kitchen, restrooms, and a nursery were added. The First Baptist Church of Prudenville is part of the General Association of Regular Baptist Churches, Central Michigan Association.

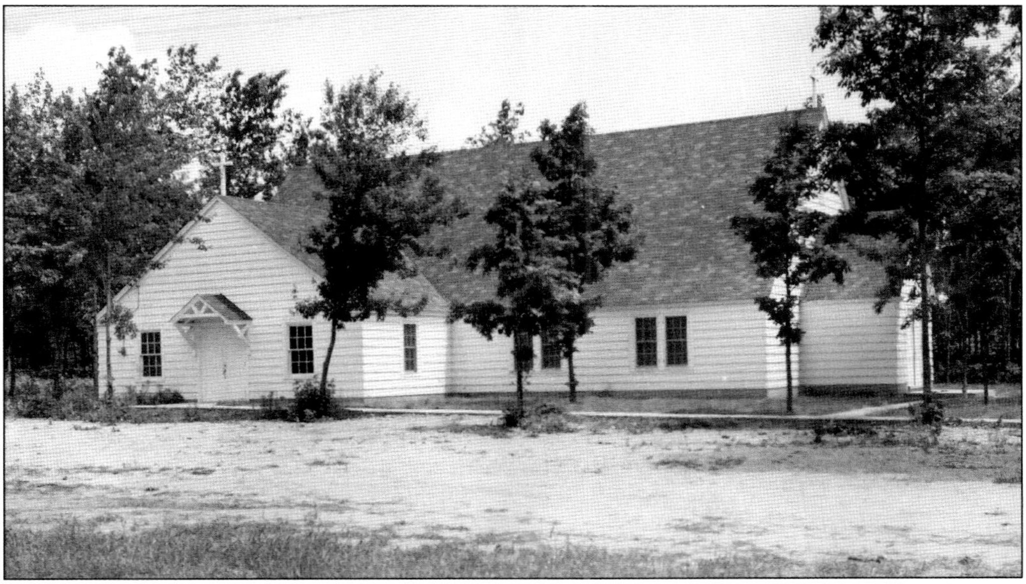

St. Johns Lutheran Church was built in 1940. In its first year, it was a mission church from Mount Hope Lutheran Church in Grayling, Michigan. The first pastor was Rev. Gordon Light. In 1965, a kitchen and a parish hall were added. More room was needed, so, in 1977, an overflow area was built. New parish offices were added in 1999. Rev. William Winters, the longest-serving pastor, currently serves the community.

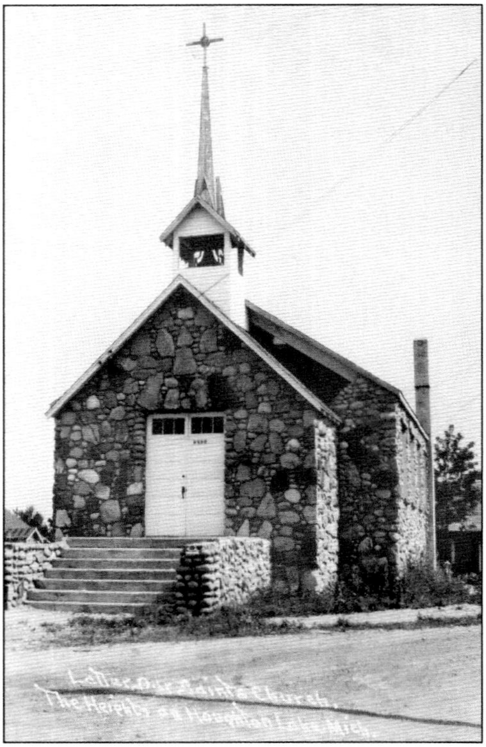

The Reorganized Church of Jesus Christ of Latter-day Saints began in 1913 in the Houghton Lake Heights area. It is the second-oldest church in the area (Markey Baptist is the oldest.) It was started by Elder Samuel Pendleton of Beaverton, Michigan. The church community purchased an old schoolhouse, which they remodeled for their use. It was the only church in the Heights until 1939, when plans were started for a nondenominational church. The community outgrew this small church and moved to School Road, where it still holds worship services today.

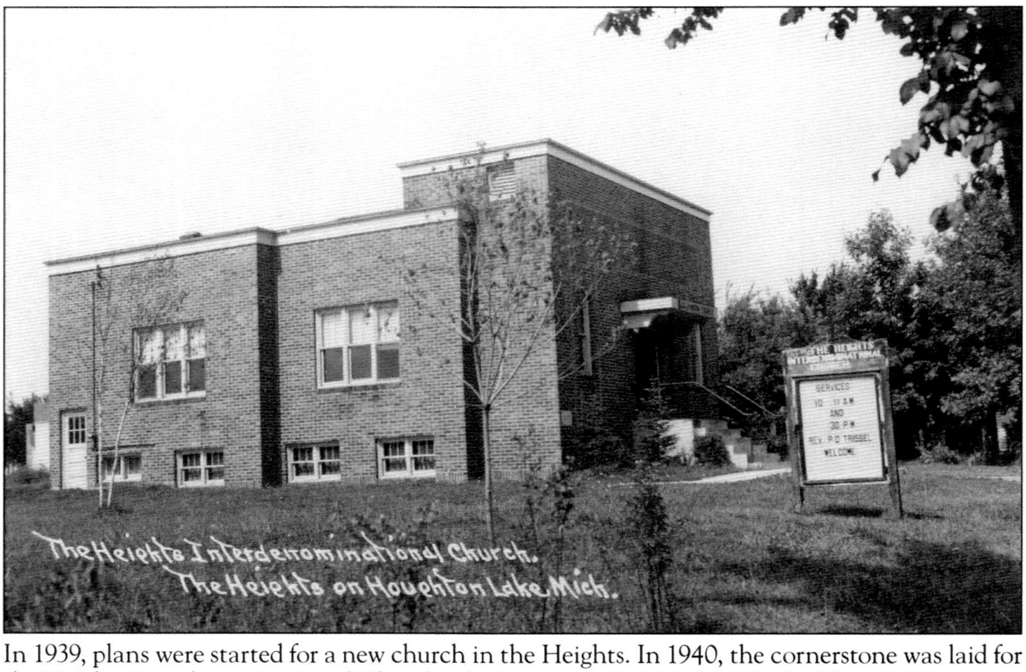

In 1939, plans were started for a new church in the Heights. In 1940, the cornerstone was laid for the Heights Interdenominational Church, also known as the Heights Pilgrim Church. The pastor was P.D. Trissel. In the 1970s, it became a Nazarene church. It was also used as a Methodist church before it became a private residence. It still stands today, but it has a frame front addition.

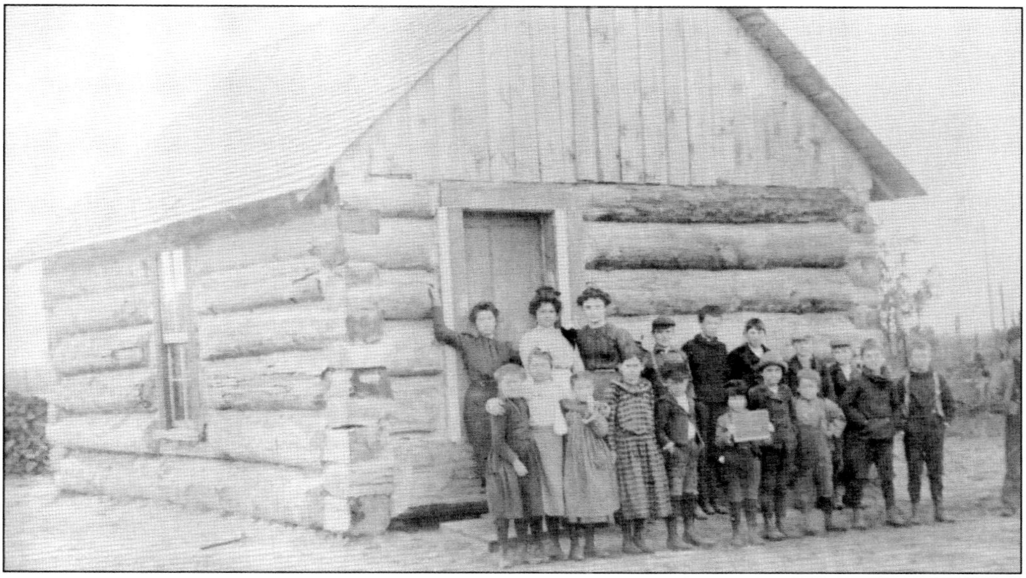

Markey Township originally had two schools: Markey District One, on Doyle Trail, and Markey District Two (shown here), on County Road 100. In the late 19th century and early 20th century, each township operated its own schools. Travel was difficult, so it was necessary to educate children where they lived. (Courtesy of Markey Township.)

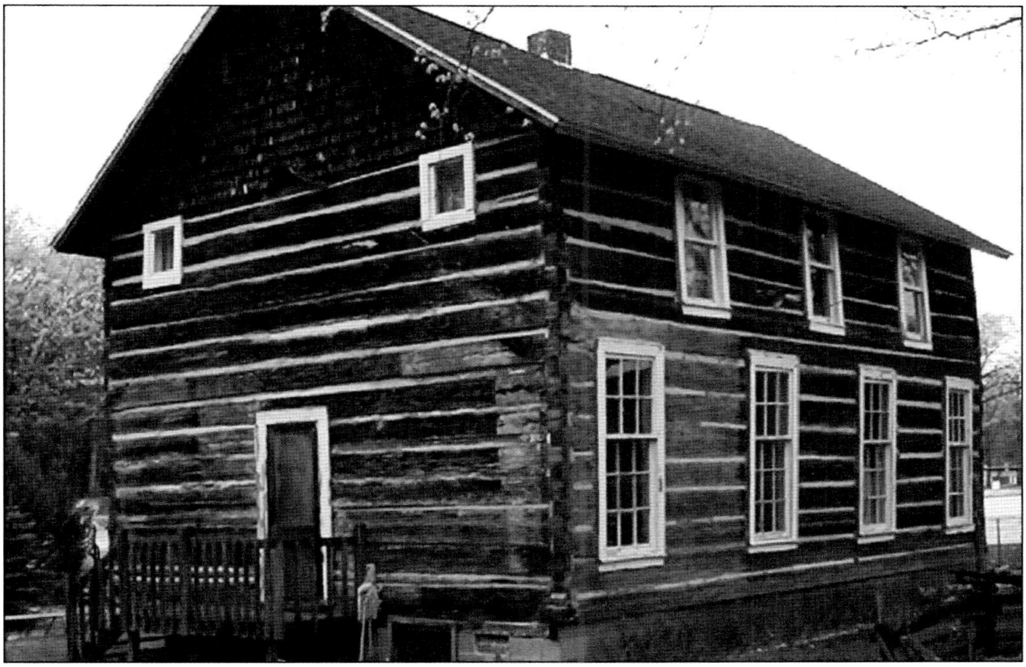

Denton Township had three school districts. They were located in Kirkland, near Denton Creek; in Edna, which is now Prudenville; and in Owens. In 1911, this school building was moved just north of M-55, near the water, and became the Procunier Hotel. In 1972, Kronner Drugs donated it to the Houghton Lake Area Historical Society, and it now stands in the historical village. The other two schools no longer exist.

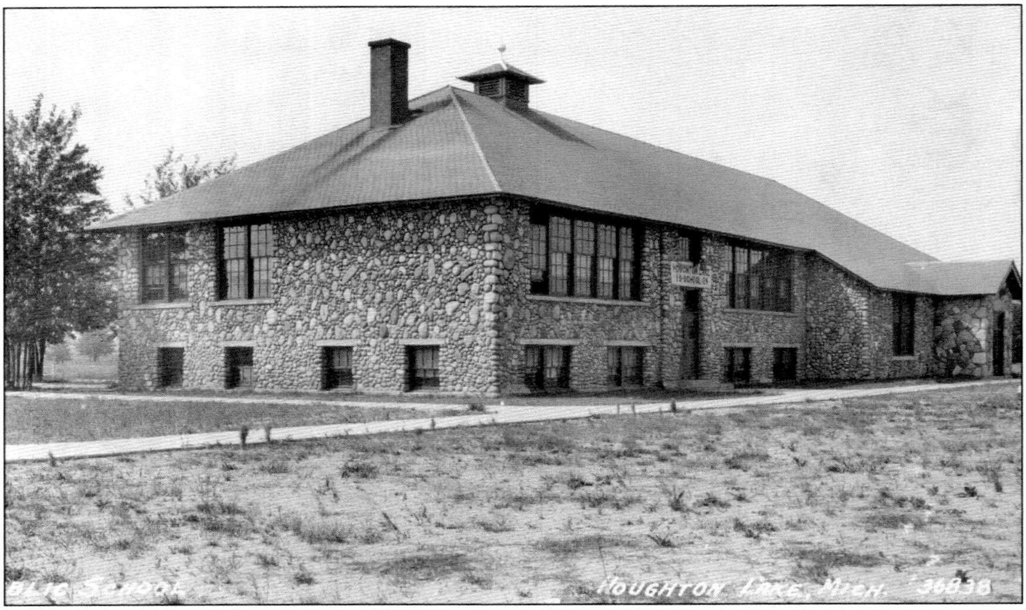

Roscommon Township consolidated its schools in 1924, when the stone school shown here was built. During the first two years, the school served students from kindergarten through the 10th grade. The 11th and 12th grades were added two years later. This school served the community until 1950, when the high school was built. In the late 1940s, other space had to be found, and town halls were used for classrooms while a new school was built.

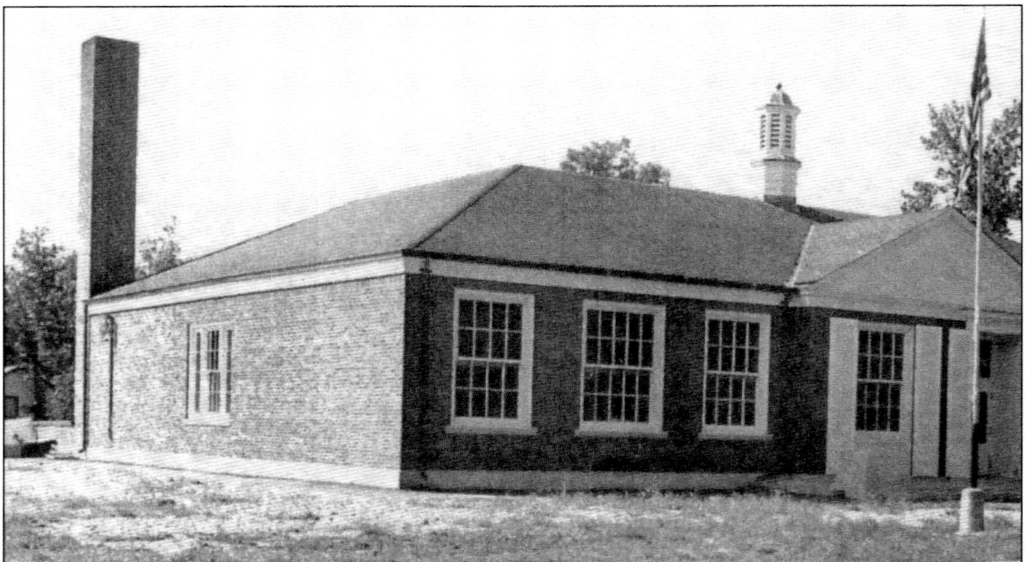

In 1937, the Prudenville School was built when the district consolidated. This school replaced the three district schools, and taught children from kindergarten through 12th grade. Later, when all of the township schools consolidated into the Houghton Lake School District, this school was used as an elementary school. In 1967, it was used as a junior high school, serving the area's seventh and eighth grades. In the 1990s, it was used for the fourth and fifth grades. It is now closed and privately owned.

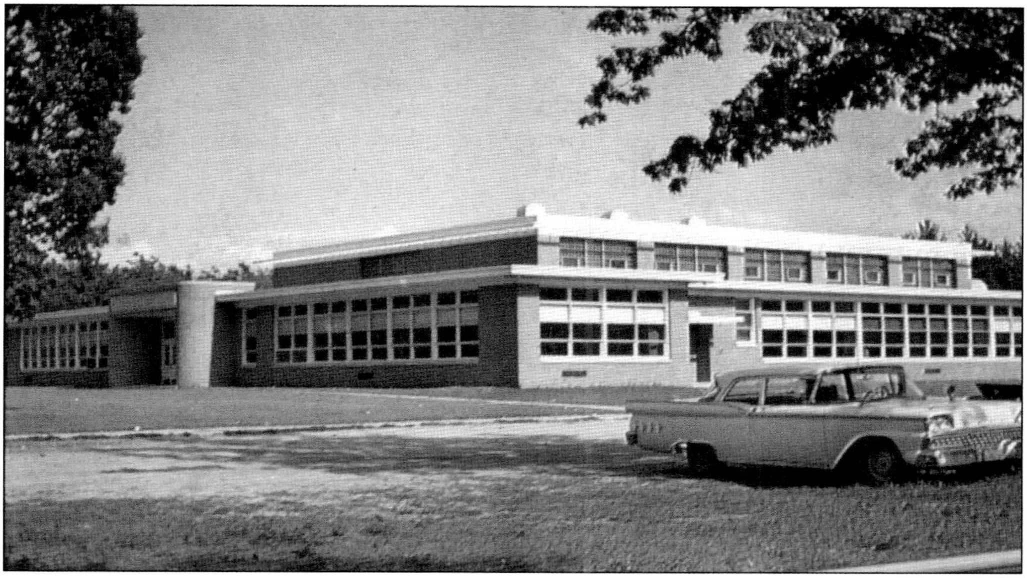

Houghton Lake High School was completed in 1950, and all the school districts around the lake became consolidated into the Houghton Lake Area School District, including North Shore Elementary School. That school is no longer used. A new elementary school, next to the high school, was completed in 1957 and named Collins Elementary, after Jim Collins, the school board president at the time. In 1969, Merritt schools consolidated with Houghton Lake. This school is now a middle school; a new high school was opened in the fall of 1978.

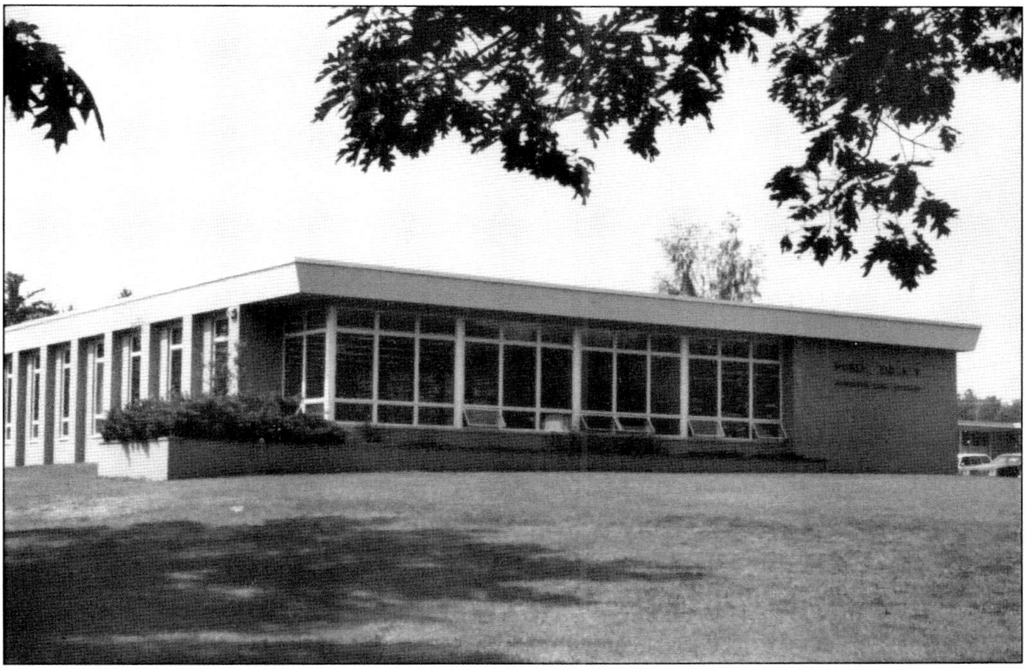

The Houghton Lake community voted to separate the library from the school library system in 1964. In 1969, the new Houghton Lake Public Library was opened. Built with grant money, it is on the campus of the Houghton Lake Area Schools. It shares a parking lot with the middle school.